The Biblical Seminar
36

QUMRAN
QUESTIONS

QUMRAN
QUESTIONS

Edited by
James H. Charlesworth

Sheffield Academic Press

Copyright © 1995 Sheffield Academic Press

Published by Sheffield Academic Press Ltd
Mansion House
19 Kingfield Road
Sheffield, S11 9AS
England

Printed on acid-free paper in Great Britain
by Cromwell Press
Melksham, Wiltshire

British Library Cataloguing in Publication Data

A catalogue record for this book is available
from the British Library

ISBN 1-85075-770-4

CONTENTS

Preface   7
Abbreviations   9
List of Contributors   11

JAMES H. CHARLESWORTH
    The Princeton Theological Seminary Dead Sea Scrolls Project   13

ELISHA QIMRON
    Towards a New Edition of the Genesis Apocryphon   20

GERSHON BRIN
    The Laws of the Prophets in the Sect of the Judaean Desert:
    Studies in 4Q375   28

LOREN T. STUCKENBRUCK
    Bibliography on 4QTgLev (4Q156)   61

ELISHA QIMRON
    Some Remarks on the Apocryphal Psalm 155
    (11QPs^a Column 24)   64

ROBERT A.J. GAGNON
    How Did the Rule of the Community Obtain its Final Shape?
    A Review of Scholarly Research   67

CHRIS H. KNIGHTS
    The Rechabites of Jeremiah 35: Forerunners of the Essenes?   86

CRAIG A. EVANS
    Predictions of the Destruction of the Herodian Temple
    in the Pseudepigrapha, Qumran Scrolls, and Related Texts   92

JAMES D. TABOR and MICHAEL O. WISE
    4Q521 'On Resurrection' and the Synoptic Gospel Tradition:
    A Preliminary Study   151

ROBERT C. STALLMAN
    Levi and the Levites in the Dead Sea Scrolls   164

Index of References   191
Index of Authors   208

This collection of studies is a reprint of a special issue on Qumran research originally published as volume 10 of the *Journal for the Study of the Pseudepigrapha and Related Literature* in April 1992. The studies have been reprinted in the present format in order to make their important contribution to the understanding of the Dead Sea Scrolls available to a wider audience.

There are ten studies assembled here: Charlesworth clarifies the purpose and scope of the Princeton Theological Seminary Dead Sea Scrolls Project. Qimron describes the progress made on the new edition of the Genesis Apocryphon, thanks to the improved photographs taken under the direction of the PTS DSS Project by Bruce and Ken Zuckerman. Brin increases knowledge of the laws regarding prophets in Early Judaism. Stuckenbruck, who with D. Noel Freedman prepared the critical text and translation to the Qumran Leviticus Targum, presents a bibliography on this fragment. Qimron, in a second article, improves the philological understanding of Psalm 155. Gagnon reviews published research on the Rule of the Community. Knights reacts to the claim that the Essenes should be understood in light of the Rechabites. Evans examines the predictions of the destruction of the Temple in the Qumran Scrolls and related literatures. Tabor and Wise introduce and present a preliminary study on 4Q521. Finally, Stallman studies Levi and the Levites in the Dead Sea Scrolls.

As mentioned above, these essays originally appeared in the *Journal for the Study of the Pseudepigrapha and Related Literature*. The full title of that periodical was chosen to indicate that work on the so-called Old Testament Pseudepigrapha must not be isolated from major publications on related topics, including Philo, Josephus, and especially the Dead Sea Scrolls, found in the eleven caves west and northwest of Khirbet Qumran. The relation of these writings to the so-called Pseudepigrapha and Apocrypha is well known. It is imperative to avoid separating documents which are clearly, or apparently, related. This attempt to reconstruct the history and theology of Early Judaism seeks to transcend categories that sometimes arrange works according to where they were apparently (or clearly) found, or according to their alleged relation to an open canon, or according to their genre. All of the early Jewish writings are essential reading in the attempt to understand each of these writings and their relation to other roughly contemporaneous documents, as well as to comprehend Early Judaism and the Origins of Christianity. The editorial board of the *Journal for the Study of the Pseudepigrapha and Related Literature* is grateful to the scholars who have contributed to this collection; I wish to express my thanks to James R. Mueller and John Jarick for their help with the preparation of these articles for publication.

JHC
Princeton
September 1995

ABBREVIATIONS

AB	Anchor Bible
ABRL	Anchor Bible Reference Library
AnBib	Analecta biblica
ANRW	*Aufstieg und Niedergang der römischen Welt*
BAR	Biblical Archaeologist Reader
BARev	*Biblical Archaeology Review*
BDB	F. Brown, S.R. Driver and C.A. Briggs, *Hebrew and English Lexicon of the Old Testament*
BibOr	Biblica et orientalia
BJRL	*Bulletin of the John Rylands University Library of Manchester*
BJS	Brown Judaic Studies
CB	*Cultura bíblica*
CBQ	*Catholic Biblical Quarterly*
CRINT	Compendia rerum iudaicarum ad Novum Testamentum
DJD	Discoveries in the Judaean Desert
EKKNT	Evangelisch-Katholischer Kommentar zum Neuen Testament
EstBíb	*Estudios bíblicos*
GKC	*Gesenius' Hebrew Grammar*, ed. E. Kautzsch, trans. A.E. Cowley
HeyJ	*Heythrop Journal*
HNT	Handbuch zum Neuen Testament
HSS	Harvard Semitic Studies
HTKNT	Herders theologischer Kommentar zum Neuen Testament
HTR	*Harvard Theological Review*
IDBSup	*IDB*, Supplementary Volume
JAOS	*Journal of the American Oriental Society*
JBL	*Journal of Biblical Literature*
JETS	*Journal of the Evangelical Theological Society*
JJS	*Journal of Jewish Studies*
JNES	*Journal of Near Eastern Studies*
JQR	*Jewish Quarterly Review*
JRS	*Journal of Roman Studies*
JSJ	*Journal for the Study of Judaism*
JSOT	*Journal for the Study of the Old Testament*
JSOTSup	*Journal for the Study of the Old Testament*, Supplement Series
JSPSup	*Journal for the Study of the Pseudepigrapha*, Supplement Series
JSS	*Journal of Semitic Studies*
JTS	*Journal of Theological Studies*

LCL	Loeb Classical Library
MGWJ	*Monatsschrift für Geschichte und Wissenschaft des Judentums*
NCB	New Century Bible
NIGTC	The New International Greek Testament Commentary
NovT	*Novum Testamentum*
NovTSup	*Novum Testamentum* Supplements
NTD	Das Neue Testament Deutsch
NTS	*New Testament Studies*
PG	J. Migne (ed.), *Patrologia graeca*
RB	*Revue biblique*
RevQ	*Revue de Qumran*
SBL	Society of Biblical Literature
SBLMS	SBL Monograph Series
SBLSP	SBL Seminar Papers
SBT	Studies in Biblical Theology
SNTSMS	Society for New Testament Studies Monograph Series
SPB	Studia postbiblica
TBl	*Theologische Blätter*
TDOT	G.J. Botterweck and H. Ringgren (eds.), *Theological Dictionary of the Old Testament*
TZ	*Theologische Zeitschrift*
WBC	Word Biblical Commentary

LIST OF CONTRIBUTORS

Gershon Brin, Tel Aviv University, Israel

James H. Charlesworth, Princeton Theological Seminary, Princeton, NJ

Craig A. Evans, Trinity Western University, Langley, BC, Canada

Robert A.J. Gagnon, Framingham, MA

Chris H. Knights, Ashington, Northumberland, England

Elisha Qimron, Ben Gurion University of the Negev, Beer-Sheva, Israel

Robert C. Stallman, Central Bible College, Springfield, MD

Loren T. Stuckenbruck, Institut für Neutestamentliche Wissenschaft und Judaistik, Neue Universität, Kiel, Germany

James D. Tabor, University of North Carolina at Charlotte, NC

Michael O. Wise, University of Chicago, IL

THE PRINCETON THEOLOGICAL SEMINARY
DEAD SEA SCROLLS PROJECT

James H. Charlesworth

The Need

The major Dead Sea Scrolls—for example from Cave 1, 1QS, 1QSa, 1QSb, 1QM, 1QH, 1QpHab, and 1QapGen—are readily available with other documents in modern languages, especially English, French, German, Italian, and Spanish.[1] These selections of the Dead Sea Scrolls are handy; but they may yield false impressions concerning the extent and nature of the creative thoughts contained in the Scrolls.

Hundreds of fragmentary scrolls were found in eleven caves near Khirbet Qumran. Without examining all the published evidence, and being cognizant of what has been published recently or will soon be made available,[2] it is easy to distort a reconstruction of Early Judaism.

---

1. The most complete collection in English is by G. Vermes, *The Dead Sea Scrolls in English* (London: Penguin; Sheffield: Sheffield Academic Press, 4th edn, 1995). The most extensive and up-to-date French selection is by A. Dupont-Sommer and M. Philonenko, *La Bible: Ecrits intertestamentaires* (Bibliothèque de la Pléiade; Paris: Gallimard, 1987). A popular collection, because it contains a pointed Hebrew text, is E. Lohse, *Die Texte aus Qumran: Hebräisch und Deutsch, mit masoretischer Punktation, Übersetzung, Einführung und Anmerkungen* (Munich: Kösel; Darmstadt: Wissenschaftliche Buchgesellschaft, 3rd edn, 1981). A nearly complete collection is by L. Moraldi, *I manoscritti di Qumrān* (Classici delle religioni; Turin: Unione Tipografico/Editrice Torinese, 1971). The most extensive collection now available is by F. García Martínez, *The Dead Seas Scrolls Translated: The Qumran Texts in English* (Leiden: Brill, 1994 [trans. from the Spanish]). Other modern collections, which are widely used, are far less inclusive.

2. See the succinct and helpful survey by H. Lichtenberger, 'Dokumentation über Neuveröffentlichungen aus den Qumranfunden', *Zeitschrift für Althebraistik* 4 (1991), pp. 210-12. Also, see the recent issues of *Revue de Qumran* in which are presented facsimiles and transcriptions of previously unpublished texts. Already out of date, but still helpful, are several articles in *Estudios Biblicos* and *Henoch*:

Scholars and others, including pastors and rabbis, are forced to work from sometimes misleading translations (with no justifying notes). Often the desired documents are not included in a selection. A scroll is frequently published separately in expensive editions, placing it beyond the reach of the lay person and the scholar; the Hebrew and English editions of the Temple Scroll, for example, sell for over $200.

There is a need today for a comprehensive and critical edition of all the non-biblical Dead Sea Scrolls. No collection in any modern language contains many—let alone all—of the documents that would be included in a comprehensive edition. The extent and variety of data collected into such a reference work would surprise those who think that the Dead Sea Scrolls encompass only seven, or at the most twenty, documents.

In order to compile such a collection it would be necessary to bring order to the disparate and unrelated publications of texts. Specifically, a standard system for editing the texts (which follow different guidelines [even in DJD]) needs to be established, the relation between the documents needs to be clarified, some of them renamed,[3] and there should be consistency in the abbreviations defined in *Qumran Cave I* (DJD 1, 1955). The new edition should also be based on better photographs, produced by more advanced techniques and equipment.

The collection must be complete, including apparently meaningless fragments that preserve only one or two words, since these words may be significant in terms of an assessment of the vocabulary of the Scrolls.

F. García Martínez, 'Estudios Qumranicos 1975–1985: Panorama Critico (I)', *EstBib* 45 (1987), pp. 125-205; F. García Martínez, 'Estudios Qumranicos 1975–1985', *EstBib* 45 (1987), pp. 361-402; F. García Martínez, 'Lista de MSS procedentes de Qumran', *Henoch* 11 (1989), pp. 149-232; L. Rosso Ubigli, 'Indice Italiano-Inglese dei Testi di Qumran (Italian-English Index of Qumran Texts)', *Henoch* 11 (1989), pp. 233-70. S.A. Reed's *Dead Sea Scroll Inventory Project: List of Documents, Photographs and Museum Plates*, 2 fascicles (Ancient Biblical Manuscript Center, 1991) is helpful. Two fascicles have appeared, the first on Qumran Cave I and the other on Qumran Minor Caves. Mention must be made of two other publications: R.H. Eisenman and J.M. Robinson (eds.), *A Facsimile Edition of the Dead Sea Scrolls* (2 vols.; Washington: Biblical Archaeology Society, 1991) and B. Zion Wacholder and M. Abegg (eds.), *A Preliminary Edition of the Unpublished Dead Sea Scrolls* (Washington: Biblical Archaeology Society, 1991). These are focused on previously unpublished data. Recently four volumes of primarily biblical scrolls have appeared in DJD.

3. For example, the so-called Wiles of the Wicked Woman should be renamed 'Dame Folly and Lady Wisdom'.

The need for a comprehensive and critical edition of the Qumran Scrolls is evident in numerous publications, which range from philological notes to monographs on Qumran theology.[4] Experts, like Elisha Qimron, have expressed the need for a collection of corrected texts and translations to the already published Scrolls.[5]

These improved texts and translations should be compiled by the leading experts, and where possible and wise by the former editors themselves, who may update and improve their previous publications. Terms and phrases must be *translated consistently*, so that parallels to other writings (especially the New Testament documents) can be meaningful, and an English concordance to the collection useful. The translations must not be loosely idiomatic so as to confuse the reader about the content of a scroll. They should be as literal as meaningful English will allow, and published opposite the Hebrew, Aramaic, or Greek text.

Another need would be met by such an edition. The charges and scandals allegedly related to the lack of available publications have continued unabated for decades, and have exploded into the media since September 1991.[6] A truncated version would scarcely dampen the fire fueled by the repeated charges, highlighted by Edmund Wilson's article (*The New Yorker*, 1955), that the scrolls show that 'the rise of Christianity should, at last, be generally understood as simply an episode

4.   See in particular the articles in this present collection by E. Qimron.

5.   E. Qimron, 'The Need for a Comprehensive Critical Edition of the Dead Sea Scrolls', in *Archaeology and History in the Dead Sea Scrolls* (ed. L.H. Schiffman; JSPS, 8; JSOT/ASOR Monographs, 2; Sheffield: JSOT Press, 1990), pp. 121-31. See also J.H. Charlesworth, 'Concerning the New Comprehensive Edition of Previously Published Qumran Documents', on pp. 132-33.

6.   I began this essay in the spring and summer of 1991. Since then the media has featured the Dead Sea Scrolls, because of the Cincinnati group's attempt to reconstruct texts according to a privately circulated concordance of the unpublished fragments from Cave IV, and because of Dr Moffett's announcement to let qualified scholars study the Qumran photographs in the Huntington Library. Among the most important news features, see the following (in chronological order): J. Noble Wilford, 'Monopoly Over Dead Sea Scrolls is Ended', *The New York Times* (September 22, 1991), front page and p. 20; R. Chandler, 'Library Lifts the Veil from Dead Sea Scrolls', *Los Angeles Times* (September 22, 1991), front page and p. 30; A.I. Goldman, 'Lessons Learned from Unscrolling Two Religions' Turbulent Pasts', *The New York Times* (September 29, 1991), p. 5; D.E. Wood, 'Dead Sea Scrolls Stir Lively Debate', *The Christian Science Monitor* (October 8, 1991), pp. 12, 13.

of human history rather than propagated as divine dogma and divine revelation'. Issues of *Biblical Archaeology Review* have stirred up the controversy surrounding the unpublished scrolls.[7] The only way to expose the resulting polemics as misguided and sometimes simply absurd is to make all the documents available in an attractive and reliable form.

The Genesis of the PTS DSS Project

The Princeton Theological Seminary Dead Sea Scrolls Project was launched in 1985 in order to meet this need for a comprehensive edition of the Dead Sea Scrolls. It has a long history. Over fifteen years ago James A. Sanders, now President of the Ancient Biblical Manuscript Center in Claremont, and I envisioned an English version of Eduard Lohse's German book (*Die Texte aus Qumran*). It was evident that some of the readings published by him were imperfect, that the text should not be pointed with medieval vowel markings, and that far more texts would have to be included. Although we received permission to publish Lohse's Hebrew text, and although Oxford in New York showed interest in publishing this English version, we were forced to revise the entire project.

Recognizing that an edition of corrected texts was needed, those in the PTS DSS Project began to obtain improved photographs. Over ten trips to Israel proved fruitful and the Project now has an extensive collection of photographs that are much clearer than the ones previously published.

I visited Paris and studied the Qumran fragments preserved there. Later, the Project received from the Bibliothèque Nationale infra-red photographs that are often more helpful than the conventional ones. A visit to Cambridge resulted in new photographs of the medieval manuscripts of the Cairo Damascus Document which are outstanding and have helped D.R. Schwartz and J.M. Baumgarten to improve the

---

7. In particular, see H. Shanks, 'Is the Vatican Suppressing the Dead Sea Scrolls?', *BARev* 17 (1991), pp. 66-71. Also see H. Shanks (ed.), *Understanding the Dead Sea Scrolls: A Reader from the Biblical Archaeology Review* (New York: Random House, 1992). A concise and reliable answer to the charges that the Vatican has been hiding the scrolls is found in O. Betz and R. Riesner, *Jesus, Qumran, and the Vatican: Clarifications* (New York: Crossroad, 1994). Finally, see Charlesworth, *Jesus and the Dead Sea Scrolls* (Anchor Bible Reference Library; New York: Doubleday, 1992, 1995).

text of CD. The Project sponsored a major photographic expedition to Jerusalem, and two years later to Amman; Bruce and Ken Zuckerman were able to obtain, using new photographic techniques, some readings that had not been visible for 2,000 years. Permission was received in Tokyo to publish the photographs taken by Kodansha. The Israeli curators and experts (especially M. Broshi) have been most helpful; as has the Director General of the Antiquities of Jordan (then Dr Bisheh).

Working closely with Qimron (who visited Princeton several times), an improved method for recording letters which are difficult to read was developed. Frank Moore Cross, James A. Sanders, and David Noel Freedman helped significantly in this process. Richard Whitaker created sophisticated software for the IBYCUS SC Computer so that exotic forms and marginal strokes could be represented in the computer printout.

A concordance of 223 published texts and 3,500 fragments has been published: *Graphic Concordance to the Dead Sea Scrolls* (Tübingen: Mohr [Paul Siebeck]; Louisville: Westminster/John Knox Press, 1991). This reference work is proving to be a valuable aid to the team of translators (sub-editors). This team of international experts, men and women, Jews, Catholics, and Protestants, have been serving as sub-editors for nearly a decade. They have met, refined the proper methodology, and developed Guidelines.

The Scope of the PTS DSS Project

This new edition of the non-biblical Dead Sea Scrolls features revised texts (often with an *apparatus criticus*), translations (with introductions and notes), and computer produced concordances to the Hebrew, Aramaic, Greek, and English. The volumes, edited by Charlesworth, are entitled *The Dead Sea Scrolls: Hebrew, Aramaic, and Greek Texts with English Translations*. The work is intended to be the comprehensive and critical edition of all the non-biblical Dead Sea Scrolls.

Future volumes in the PTS DSS series will include the texts and translations of the presently unpublished fragments (clearer photographs of some unpublished material have already been supplied to Strugnell and Qimron). The later inclusion of presently unpublished, or only partially published, documents is closely coordinated with Cross, Freedman, Sanders, Talmon, and Qimron, all of whom work closely with the PTS DSS Project.

A one-volume English edition of the translations will be published by Westminster/John Knox Press in Louisville. This idiomatic translation will be separated into paragraphs with heading and subheadings (but it will retain the notations for columns and lines), and poetry will be indented. A general introduction will introduce the interested reader to the history and theologies of the Dead Sea Scrolls, and each section and document will have a short introduction.

Ten volumes are planned: The *Rule of the Community and Related Documents*; *Damascus Document, War Scroll, and Related Documents*; *Damascus Document Fragments, More Precepts of the Torah, and Related Documents*; *Angelic Liturgy, Prayers and Psalms*; *Thanksgiving Hymns and Related Documents*; *Targum on Job, Pesharim, and Related Documents*; *Temple Scroll and Related Documents*; *Genesis Aporcryphon, New Jerusalem, and Related Documents*; *Copper Scroll, Greek Fragments, and Miscellanea*; and *Biblical Apocrypha and Pseudepigrapha*. A parsed concordance of all texts and translations will be published after these volumes are completed.

The first two volumes of texts and translations have been published. The first one appeared in 1994 and contains contributions by Charlesworth, Cross, J. Milgrom, E. Qimron, L.H. Schiffman, and L.T. Stuckenbruck. It is focused on the *Rule of the Community* (1QS, 4Q255-264 [= 4QS MSS A-J]) and documents related to it (5Q11, 1QSa, 1QSb, 5Q13, 4Q159, 4Q513, and 4Q514). The second volume appeared in 1995 and presents texts and translations by Charlesworth, J.M. Baumgarten, M.T. Davis, J. Duhaime, Y. Ofer, H.W.L. Rietz, J.J.M. Roberts, D. Schwartz, and B.A. Strawn. It is dedicated to the *Damascus Document* (CD, 4QD, 5QD, 6QD), the *War Scroll* (1QM, 1Q33, 4QM1-6 with 4Q497), and Related Documents (4Q180-181, 1Q51, 2Q25, 2Q28). Each volume closes with a list of Dead Sea Scrolls organized first by Numbers and then Names.

Conclusion

In conclusion, the new comprehensive edition of the Dead Sea Scrolls will:

1. be the critical and comprehensive edition in the field;
2. contain new readings, and corrections of earlier editions (often provided by the previous editors themselves);
3. contain documents not presently available in any other collection;

4. publish texts according to a system refined in conjunction with Cross, Freedman, Qimron, Sanders, and Strugnell;

5. present English translations that are neither woodenly literal nor misrepresentatively idiomatic;

6. provide introductions so that the reader can be informed of the dates, historical settings, and theological importance of the documents;

7. include philological notes so that difficult readings and translations are clarified;

8. order the corpus of published Dead Sea Scrolls, and correct nomenclature so that there is a coherent system;

9. publish the first complete concordances to the Hebrew, Aramaic, and Greek texts, and to the English translations.

The project will put in the public domain a major reference work for the Dead Sea Scrolls. Finally, people will be able to read, in meaningful English, all the Dead Sea Scrolls that are not simply a copy of one book in the Hebrew Bible (Old Testament).

TOWARDS A NEW EDITION OF THE GENESIS APOCRYPHON

Elisha Qimron

1. *The Text of the Genesis Apocryphon*

The Genesis Apocryphon is one of the seven scrolls discovered in Cave 1 at Qumran. It was written in Aramaic and is of major significance for many aspects of Jewish studies. Numerous studies of this scroll have been made,[1] some by leading scholars, and the scroll has been cited in many books and articles. The scroll was found in a poor state of preservation and its columns were stuck together.[2] After it had been unrolled, it became clear to the editors (Avigad and Yadin) that there were parts on which more work would have to be done before the task of deciphering could begin.[3] They therefore decided to publish only those columns that had been fairly well preserved, namely columns 2 and 19-22. Even these five columns are damaged at the bottom. Columns 2 and 19 are also damaged at the top and at one side.

Of the remaining columns of the scroll, only the readily legible passages were published by Avigad and Yadin. They postponed the publication of those columns needing further physical treatment and, as is well known, no work has yet been done on them.

In 1988 J.C. Greenfield and I were entrusted with the publication of the unpublished columns. It soon became clear that no physical treatment could help in deciphering the scroll. The damage it had suffered over the last forty years has been so extensive that only a small part of what cannot be seen on the photographs is visible in the original. Physical treatment is of no help and the advanced techniques of photography can

---

1. See e.g. J. Fitzmyer, *The Genesis Apocryphon of Qumran Cave One* (Rome: Biblical Institute Press, 1971 2nd edn), pp. 42-46.

2. A detailed description of the physical state of the scroll can be found in the *editio princeps*: N. Avigad and Y. Yadin, *A Genesis Apocryphon, A Scroll from the Wilderness of Judaea* (Jerusalem: Magnes Press, 1956), pp. 12-15.

3. Avigad and Yadin, *A Genesis Apocryphon*, p. 13.

help very little. B. Zuckerman, director of the West Semitic Research Project, produced new photographs of the scroll. On these may be read several words which are not visible from the early photographs. Up to now some nine hundred words from the unpublished seventeen columns have been deciphered.

The task of publishing an edition of the whole scroll is not easy, and will take several years. Difficulties in reading exist not only in the unpublished part, but also in the published part. One has to only compare the existing editions to see how much they differ from one another. The text of the Genesis Apocryphon has been studied and improved by some of the best paleographers, philologists and linguists. Only in a small number of cases have I succeeded in suggesting a reading which has not been proposed previously. What is needed is a comprehensive edition. This would note all the readings that have been suggested and decide in each case which is preferable, which should be given in the transcriptions, and which should be placed in the apparatus. The decision on which of the readings is to be preferred and which rejected is not easy. Therefore the work of editing should not be carried out by one person, however expert, but by a team of experts in various fields.

The following comments offer a brief description of the existing editions of the Genesis Apocryphon, followed by a discussion of eighteen readings which have been suggested in no more than one of the editions. I believe that in these cases the correct reading can be established on paleographical, linguistic and other grounds. The readings will be given according to the order of the scroll.[4]

2. *The Editions*

The first edition, that of Avigad and Yadin, is fairly accurate, although the editors did not succeed in deciphering a number of words which were later read by others. Surprisingly, this is the most reliable edition since it marks damaged letters diacritically and distinguishes between those damaged letters which have highly probable readings and those which have uncertain readings. Beyer, in his edition, used only one diacritical sign, which he applied to letters which are very uncertain. The other editors used no diacritical signs at all.

The Aramaic text in Fitzmyer's edition is somewhat longer than that

---

4.   I thank M. Broshi, the curator of the Shrine of the Book, for providing me with good photographs.

of Avigad and Yadin, since Fitzmyer included a number of new readings suggested by scholars after the publication of the first edition. He also included several fragments which were found in Cave 1 (1Q20). Fitzmyer was severely criticized for not using diacritical signs in his edition. In many places in his edition tenuous readings appear as if they were certain. He ignored this criticism in two further editions, making none of his editions reliable. In order to avoid mistakes, one should consult the photographs of Avigad and Yadin's edition. Another edition of the Genesis Apocryphon was produced at Groningen University by Jongeling, Labuschagne and Van der Woude (see note 5). The text is similar to Fitzmyer's, but there are several new readings, some of them certain. This edition also lacks diacritical signs and is not reliable.

The last edition, that of Beyer (see note 6), differs markedly from the others. Beyer includes many new readings, especially in places where only unclear traces survive. His contribution to the text is significant, his suggestions ingenious (sometimes a little too ingenious). Several suggestions are supported by both the traces and by the context or language, while some which are not should be given as restorations rather than as part of the surviving text. Some others which do not fit either the traces or the context should be rejected entirely.

3. *The Readings*

1.   In column 2, line 1, there is a word which means 'pregnancy'. The reading of this word is doubtful. Avigad-Yadin read הריאהא, Jongeling *et al.* read הריאתא, and this is supported by Puech.[5] Fitzmyer (following Kutscher) reads הריאנתא, and Beyer reads הרי{א}ונא.[6] The word reoccurs in line 15 in a passage referring to line 1. Here all the editors read הריונא. It has been suggested, however, that one should read הריתא which would conform with the reading of Avigad-Yadin in line 1.[7] Yet the use of the masculine demonstrative pronoun דן in line 15 disproves this

---

5.   B. Jongeling, C.J. Labuschagne, A.S. van der Woude, *Aramaic Texts from Qumran, I* (Leiden: Brill, 1976); E. Puech (Review of the edition of Jongeling *et al.*), *RevQ*, 9 (1978), p. 590.

6.   K. Beyer, *Die aramäischen Texte vom Toten Meer* (Göttingen: Vandenhoeck & Ruprecht, 1984), p.

7.   Sokoloff, *The Targum to Job from Qumran Cave II* (Ramat-Gan: Bar Ilan University, 1974), p. 112 (taking it as the determinate form of the f. sg. part. of הרי).

suggestion. Paleographically, the penultimate letter in הריאתא can also be read נ. The *alef* which proceeds the *waw* is not a scribal error, as Beyer believes, but a marker of the glide which evolved in this word: *heryon* (pronounced *heriyon*) → *herion* (the *yod* became quiescent between the two vowels—cf. הֵרוֹנֵךְ Gen. 3.16). The suggested reading is confirmed by the reading in line 15, and is to be preferred over הריאתא on linguistic grounds.

2.   In column 2, line 1, there is a word which Avigad-Yadin read ה[..]א, Fitzmyer reads ה[']א, Jongeling-Labuschagne-Woude read הריה 'pregnancy', Milik reads העדיא,[8] and Beyer reads רוא. None of these suggestions is correct. I think what is really written here is זרעא 'seed, descendent' (the *ayin* was divided by the tear). This suggested reading is confirmed by a comparison of line 1 with line 15:

(1) די מן עירין הריאונא ומן קדישין זרעא

(15) די מנך זרעא דן ומנך הריונא דן

3.   In column 2, line 25, there is an adverb read by all editors except Beyer as להכא 'here'.[9] Beyer's reading לתנא, is materially preferable. Furthermore this adverb is found in Old Aramaic, in Official Aramaic and elsewhere in Qumran Aramaic,[10] whereas the adverb הכא occurs only in later Aramaic dialects.[11]

4.   In column 19, line 15, there is an infinitive form read by all editors except Beyer as ולמשבוק.[12] Beyer reads ולמשבק, which is favored by the traces seen on the photograph. This is confirmed by the width of the word which is exactly the same as that of the word למשבק in line 19. The misreading ולמשבוק has been cited in several studies as a feature of significance for establishing the date of the scroll, since this pattern is typical of late western Aramaic.[13] As far as I know this feature does not

---

8.   J.T. Milik, *The Book of Enoch, Aramaic Fragments of Qumrân Cave 4* (Oxford: Clarendon Press, 1976), p. 55.

9.   Avigad-Yadin: להכא.

10.   A. Tal, *The Language of the Targum of the Former Prophets and its Position within the Aramaic Dialects* (Tel-Aviv: Tel Aviv University, 1975), p. 43 [Hebrew]; Sokoloff, *The Targum to Job from Qumran Cave 11*, p. 148.

11.   Tal, *Language*, p. 56; Sokoloff, *Targum*, p. 149.

12.   Avigad-Yadin: ולמשבוק.

13.   E.Y. Kutscher, *Hebrew and Aramaic Studies* (Jerusalem: Magnes Press,

appear in Qumran Aramaic. It occurs first (once; למפרוע) in the Aramaic documents from Naḥal Ḥever (alongside the regular form למקטל).[14]

5. In column 19, at the beginning of line 17, there is a word whose last three letters are very faint and can hardly be read. Avigad-Yadin read [ ] ולא, Fitzmyer and Jongeling-Labuschagne-Woude read ולא [אתקץ], Beyer reads ולא [קצי׳]. I seem to read ולאתקץ 'and it was not cut down'. Faint traces of the last three letters are seen on the photograph. The spelling -ל instead of לא is known from other Aramaic and Hebrew sources.[15] In this case there is one *alef* instead of two consecutive ones.

6. In column 19, line 19, there is a little hole which damages two letters of a short word whose last letter is a final *mem*. Avigad-Yadin read ו[ב]ס, but this does not fit the context: די יבעון למקטלני ולכי למשבק [בי]ום דא כול טבותא [די תעבדין עמי]. For this reason Fitzmyer did not accept this restoration and read ו[ ]. It was Jongeling-Labuschagne-Woude who suggested the correct reading here [ב]רם 'but'. In fact, there are clear traces of a *beth* and one can rather read ברם. Thus the passage is similar to its biblical source (Gen. 20.13). Surprisingly, Beyer ignored this reading and suggested the strange reading מצרם (in Egypt). This becomes more surprising given that he was aware of Puech's article in which he states that the reading [ב]רם is certain.[16]

7. In column 19, line 23, all the editors read ולבתר חמש שניא אלן. None of the letters of this word were damaged and no editor indicates any doubt in the reading. But what is really written on the scroll is not ולבתר, but ולסוף. The photographs leave little

1977), pp. 10-11; Fitzmyer, p. 29; A. Tal, 'The Form of the Infinitive in Jewish Palestinian Aramaic', in *Hebrew Language Studies Presented to Professor Zeev Ben-Ḥayyim* (Jerusalem: Magnes Press, 1983), pp. 201-202 and n. 3 [Hebrew].

14. See J.C. Greenfield, 'The Infinitive Form in the Aramaic Deed from Murabbaʿat and Nahal Hever', in *Studies on Hebrew and Other Semitic Languages Presented to Professor Chaim Rabin on the Occasion of his Seventy-Fifth Birthday* (ed. M. Goshen-Gottstein, S. Morag and S. Kogut; Jerusalem: Academon Press, 1990), p. 80 [Hebrew].

15. See for example R. Weis, *Biblical Studies: Textual and Linguistic Aspects* (Jerusalem: Magnes Press, 1989), pp. 33-38 [Hebrew].

16. See Puech, review *RevQ*, p. 590.

doubt about this new reading and what doubt there is disappears once the original scroll is checked. The form לסוף occurs in column 20, line 18, in a similar context. This example is instructive, since it proves that the reading of the first editor has a special authority. The other editors do not read the photographs or the original independently but rather check the transcription of the first editor (or that of another editor). Had they checked the sources independently they would not have made the same mistake. The first editor should, therefore, be aware of the consequences of any mistakes. It also demonstrates that even letters that are not marked as doubtful are to be suspected.

8.   At the end of line 25 of column 19, Avigad-Yadin read ל[ ] מלי [ ]אך, Fitzmyer and Jongeling *et al.* read ל[כתב] מלי חנוך, Beyer reads לٰ°° מלי אנٰין. The traces exclude the restoration [כתב]. I therefore suggest reading לٰסٰפٰٰ מלי חٰנٰוך 'the book of the words of Enoch', which suits the traces better.

9.   In column 20, line 7, all editors except Beyer read שפרה.[17] Beyer's reading שפרת 'she is beautiful' is preferable due to paleographical considerations—the upper horizontal line of the last letter is as fine as that of a *taw* and not as thick as that of a *he*.

10.   In column 20, line 26, Avigad-Yadin read וקרא לי אלוֹ. This reading was adopted in the Fitzmyer editions. It was Jongeling *et al.* who suggested that [מ]ל[כא] be read instead of אלוֹ. They based this suggestion on linguistic grounds claiming that אלוֹ is Hebrew and therefore untenable. I would not remark on this reading had Beyer not adopted it, reading וקרא מלכא לי (instead of וקרא לי אלוֹ). As far as I can see on the photograph, Avigad-Yadin's reading is the correct one. The form can easily be explained as a phonetic spelling representing the actual form of the suffix -והי at Qumran: this suffix was pronounced there as *ō*.[18]

---

17. Avigad-Yadin: שֿפֿרֿהֿ.

18. See E. Qimron, *The Hebrew of the Dead Sea Scrolls* (HSS, 29; Atlanta: Scholars Press, 1986), p. 61. Note that אחו in column 21, line 14, may also be read אחוי. The Qumran pronunciation *ō* of this suffix can be represented by four different spellings: -והי, -וי, -י and -ו (-והי in Aramaic, -י in Hebrew are, of course, the standard spellings).

11. In column 20, line 26, Beyer reads מא עבדתה לי בדיל
     [מא] הוית אמר לי די אחתי היא 'what have you done to me? Why
     have you been saying to me she is my sister?'.[19] The other
     editors read מא עבדתה לי בדיל [שר]י ותאמר לי די אחתי היא. Beyer's
     reading fits the traces and is linguistically and contextually
     preferable: this being simply a paraphrase of Gen. 12.19 (למה
     אמרת אחתי היא). The form וְתֵאמַר of the other editions is a
     conversive imperfect. As far as I know, clear cut examples of
     conversive imperfects do not exist elsewhere in Qumran
     Aramaic. It should, however, be admitted that, materially, the
     prevailing reading is also possible.

12. In column 20, line 32, Beyer suggests the reading ואשלמהא 'and
     he handed her over'. This reading is to be preferred to that of
     the other editions וא[ש]למה. Traces of the final *alef* are seen on
     the photographs. The form -*aha* rather than -*ah* in this suffix is
     typical of this scroll.

13. In column 21, line 1, the prevailing reading is והוית שרי [ב]כל
     אתר משריאתי. It was Beyer who suggested the reading עֲל instead
     of [ב]כל. It is hard to tell whether the damaged letter is *ayin* or
     kaf, but obviously there is no space for another letter before it.
     Furthermore, the reading [ב]כל is inconsistent with the
     orthography of the scroll, since the word is generally spelled כול
     (except in 20.6).

14. In column 21, lines 2-3, Avigad-Yadin, Fitzmyer and Jongeling
     et al. read וברכת [א]להא, Beyer reads וברכת אלהא. The right
     margin is torn exactly at the beginning of the line. At the
     beginning of line 3, traces of the flag of a *lamed* can be seen
     on the left part of the tear. But no traces of a *lamed* can be
     seen on the right part of the tear. Yet, the space between להא
     and the right margin is large enough for two letters. Therefore
     I read וברכת לֽאֳלהא (rather than וברכת אֳלהא). This expression has
     a parallel in column 12, line 17 (yet unpublished): והוהית מברך
     למרה שמיא לאל עליון לקדישא רבא.[20]

15. In the middle of column 21, line 30, there is a little lacuna and
     the words on both sides of it are damaged. Nevertheless, Beyer
     succeeded in reading there לעין דינא [ולאנש] די. The words
     אל עין משפט fit לעין דינא in the biblical source (Gen. 14.7; but the

---

19. On the conjunction בדיל מא, see Tal, *Language*, p. 61.
20. Cf. ibid. 11:12, 4QEnᵃ1I1; and Dan. 4.31.

Hebrew text reads ויבאו אל עין משפט and not ויכו את עין משפט, as suggested by Beyer's reading). I was not able to see the words דינא and די, but the reading לעין is quite possible—the fragment containing the lower parts of the letters of this word is misaligned and should be moved to the left.

16. In column 21, line 34, most editors read ושבו לוט בר אחוי די אברם 'and they [the kings] captured Lot the son of Abram's brother'. Beyer reads ושבי instead of ושבו—ושבי is internal passive of *qal* (the subject is לוט). It is confirmed by the parallel: די שבי לוט בר אחוהי (cf. 22.3). The reading ושבו (third person plural of *qal*) is less plausible not only because of the parallel, but also because it forces us to surmise that the subject of ושבו is not מלך עילם (mentioned in line 33) which is singular. The reading ושבו however conforms with ויקחו in the biblical source (Gen. 14.12).

17. In column 22, lines 30-31, all editors read וכען אל תדחל אנה עמך ואהוה לך סעד ותקף. The last letter of ואהוה, however, looks like a *waw*-shaped letter crossed by a diagonal line. The third letter is not a *he*. There is no suggestion of an alternative reading.

18. In column 22, line 34, most editors read]לד רתני [; Beyer reads הוא בעה למֹרתני. None of these readings is accurate. I suggest הוא ילד.. למֹרתני. The reading of the last word is almost certain, but the *lamed* and the *mem* were affected by the tear in the scroll and parts of them disappeared. The form לְמֵרַת is the regular Aramaic infinitive *qal* of פ״י verbs (see for example Onkelos on Lev. 20.24).

THE LAWS OF THE PROPHETS IN THE SECT OF THE JUDAEAN DESERT: STUDIES IN 4Q375

Gershon Brin

The Hebrew Bible contains several laws concerning prophets. The literature from Qumran has a clear attitude regarding the issues of prophecy. It is obvious that among the Sect's members there was an expectation of the reappearance of prophecy, after its disappearance sometime during the Second Temple period. Hence the inclusion of the laws regarding prophets in their writings.[1]

In 4Q375, published by Strugnell, there appears some very important material for this issue.[2] I quote here the text of this document according to Strugnell's reading and translation.

Fragment 1 i

1. את כול אשר[ ]יצוה אלוהיכה אליכה מפי הנביא ושמרתה
2. את כול החו[קים האלה ושבתה עד ה' אלוהיכה בכול
3. לבבה ובכו[ל נפשכה ושב אלוהיכה מחרון אפו הגדול
4. להושיע[כ]ה ממצוקותיכה והנביא אשר יקום ודבר בכה
5. סרה לחש[י]בבה מאחרי אלוהיכה יומת [ ]וכיא יקום השבט
6. אשר[ ]הואה ממנו ואמר לוא יומת כיא צדיק הואה נביא
7. נ[אמן הואה ובאתה עם השבט ההוא זקניכה ושופטיכה
8. א[ל המקום אשר יבחר אלוהיכה באחד שבטיכה לפני
9. ה[כוהן המשיח אשר יוצק על ר[ו]אשו שמן המשיחה

---

1. Regarding the issue of prophecy see Brin, 'Biblical Prophecy in the Qumran Scrolls', in *'Sha'arei Talmon': Studies in the Bible, Qumran, and the Ancient Near East Presented to Shemaryahu Talmon* (ed. M. Fishbane and E. Tov; Winona Lake: Eisenbrauns, 1992), pp. 101*-112* [Hebrew].

2. J. Strugnell, 'Moses-Pseudepigrapha at Qumran: 4Q375, 4Q376, and Similar Works', *Archaeology and History in the Dead Sea Scrolls* (ed. L.H. Schiffman; JSPS, 8; Sheffield: JSOT Press, 1990), pp. 221-56. The space in the copied text is as in the original. In the continuation I will suggest some modifications in his reconstructions.

Fragment 1 ii

.1

.2

3. ולקח [פר בן בקר ואיל אחד   והזה

4. באצב[עו על פני הכפורת   [   ]

5. בשר האי[ל   [ושעיר עז]ים האחד אשר

6. לחטאת יק[ח ושחט אותו וכ]פר בעד כול העדה ואה[רון יזה מן הדם

7. לפני פרוכת [המסך ונגש ע]ד לארון העדות ודרש את [כול מצוות

8. ה' לכול [   ] הנסת]רות ממכה ו[י]צא לפני כ[ול ראשי אבות

9. העדה וזה [   ] ל[ל]

Fragment 1 i

[(1) ...thou shalt perform all that] thy God will command thee by the mouth of the prophet, and thou shalt keep [(2) all these sta]tutes, and thou shalt return unto Yahweh thy God with all (3) [thy heart and with al]l thy soul and (or: then) thy God will turn from the fury of His great anger [(4) so as to save th]ee from [all] thy distress.

But the prophet who rises up and preaches among thee [(5) apostasy so as to make thee] turn away from thy God, he shall be put to death. But, if there stands up the tribe [(6) which] he comes from, and says 'Let him not be put to death, for he is righteous (or: truthful), a [(7) fai]thful prophet is he', then thou shalt come, with that tribe and thy elders and thy judges, [(8) t]o the place which thy God shall choose among one of thy tribes, into the presence of [(9) the] anointed priest, upon whose head poured the oil of anointing.

Fragment 1 ii

(1-2) [...] (3) and he shall take [one bullock, a son of the herd, and one ram...and he shall sprinkle] (4) with his fin[ger on the surface of the Kapporet...]...[...] (5) the flesh of the ra[m...] one go[at which is] (6) for a sin offering shall he ta[ke and he shall slaughter it and he shall] make atonement on behalf of all the assembly. And Aa[ron (or: afterwards he) shall sprinkle part of the blood] (7) before the veil of [screen and shall draw ne]ar to the Ark of the Testimony, and shall study a[ll the laws of] Yahweh for all [cases of prophecy...those laws that have been con]cealed from thee. And he shall come forth before a[ll the leaders of] (9) the assembly. And this [...

The first fragment consists of three sections concerning prophecy, while the second fragment consists of a ritual of atonement being conducted in the Temple. According to the present state of the document, Strugnell's opinion, that there is a connection between these two fragments, must be accepted. This means that the ritual is to be performed following the appearance of the people 'in the place which the Lord your God will choose' in order to clarify the fate of the prophet, whether he was to be executed or allowed to live.

The issues of prophecy in the first fragment are:

1.   One must obey God's commandments, which will be announced 'by the mouth of the prophet' (lines 1-4).

2.   A prophet who tries to persuade the people to leave God's commandments and ways will be put to death. These two laws which deal with the two sides of prophecy have parallels in the Bible.

3.   Following the second law comes a third paragraph, which does not have an explicit parallel in biblical material and especially not in any judicial text. I refer to lines 4–9 concerning the tribe that opposes the decision to execute its prophet [אשר] הואה ממנו, by demanding that he be rescued.

So, despite the severe accusation against the prophet that he persuaded the people to leave God's ways, it was thought sufficient to point to his past deeds (ll. 6-7 נבי]א אמן הואה) as an important excuse for his delivery. This is strange, because the opposition to the execution of that prophet contradicts the biblical laws of Deuteronomy 13. It is even stranger that this opposition is based not on the denial of the accusation, but on the good elements in the prophet's biography.

In Deut. 13.2-6 the law concerning the seducer prophet reads:

> If a prophet arises among you or a dreamer of dreams, and gives you a sign or a wonder, and the sign or wonder which he tells you comes to pass, and if he says: 'Let us go after other gods, which you have not known, and let us serve them'. You shall not listen to the words of that prophet or that dreamer of dreams, for the Lord your God is testing you to know whether you love the Lord with all your heart and with all your soul. You shall walk after the Lord your God and fear him, and keep his commandments and obey his voice and you shall serve him and cleave to him. But that prophet or that dreamer shall be put to death, because he has taught rebellion against the Lord your God, who brought you out of the land of Egypt and redeemed you out of the house of bondage, to make you leave the way in which the Lord your God commanded you to walk. So you shall purge evil from the midst of you.

In 11QTem 54. 8-18, the same law is used with slight textual variations. Some of these variations are typical of the Temple Scroll, such as the use of first-person speech referring to God, but the fact that the author of 4Q375 did not use these changes shows that his elaboration of the biblical text did not depend on the Temple Scroll. On the other hand, as demonstrated below, in some issues, textual and others, he was close to the Temple Scroll.

With the aid of the text of Deuteronomy 13 it is clear that the version in 1. 4-5, despite its wording in a formula of a *beginning*, is actually based on the *final* part of the law of the prophet of Deuteronomy 13. However, as its wording is, 'But the prophet who rises up' (1. 4), a beginning formula, not as written in the Bible, 'But *that* prophet or *that* dreamer shall be put to death' (Deut. 13.6), it is clear that the author built his composition by combining two pieces of texts: the beginning of the [biblical] text together with its middle. Thus he established his words on the basis of v. 2, 'If a prophet arises among you', together with v. 6, 'But *that* prophet', etc. However, as the main structure of the words is based on v. 6 he changed the inner-part of the verse, which originally referred backwards, in such a way that it could stand independently.

Verse 6 does not contain an accusation of that prophet, because one has already been made at the beginning of the section: 'Let us go after other gods, which you have not known, and let us serve them' (v. 3). Therefore the author decided to use *the causal clause*, which in the Bible immediately follows the order to execute that prophet, by transferring it in a form which may be used as part of the prophet's definition, '...who rises up and preaches among thee [(5) apostasy so as to make thee] turn away from thy God'.

In the Bible: 'יומת כי דבר סרה על ה' אלהיכם...'. In 4Q375: 'ודבר בכה סרה להש[יבכה מאחרי אלוהיכה יומת'. The changing of these components caused another change. Instead of accusing the prophet of uttering words of apostasy *against God*, the text accuses him of uttering words of apostasy *to the people*, persuading them to leave God's ordinances. This changing of accusation has parallels in other compositions (the Temple Scroll for example). The outcome of this change is that the author could not use the other part of the biblical verse, which describes God as the one 'who brought you out of the land of Egypt and redeemed you out of the house of bondage' (v. 6).

In the Bible there are accusations against a prophet in Jer. 28.16, in a prophecy against Hananiah ben Azur: 'This very year you shall die, because you have uttered rebellion (*sara*) against the Lord', and in Jer. 29.32 against Sh'ma'aiah: 'for he has spoken rebellion (*sara*) against the Lord'. In both cases the applications of the laws of Deuteronomy 13 combined with Deuteronomy 18 may be seen. In 4Q375 the detailed accusation which derives from the speech of apostasy (*sara*) is slightly different from the biblical text. Instead of, 'to make you leave the way in which the Lord your God commanded you to walk' (Deut. 13.6), it says, '[as to make thee] turn away from thy God' (1.5). Such an accusation is found in CD 6.1-2: 'and because they prophesied falsehood so as to turn Israel away from God'. Even here this wicked behavior is ascribed to prophets as in 4Q375. Conversely, the positive way is described in terms of negation: 'all those...shall enter into the Covenant before God to obey all His Commandments so that they may *not abandon...*' (1QS1.16-17).[3] The biblical description finishes here, while in 4Q375 there is an additional element, without a parallel in the Bible: the appeal of the prophet's tribe against his execution.

The Sources and the Idea of 1 i

4Q375 starts with the words, '[(1)...thou shalt perform all that] thy God will command thee by the mouth of the prophet, and thou shalt keep [(2) all these sta]tutes, and thou shalt return unto Yahweh thy God will all (3) [thy heart and with al]l thy soul and (or then) thy God will turn from the fury of His great anger [(4) so as to save th]ee from [all] thy distress'. The beginning of the document, then, deals with the demand that the people obey God's instruction, which is transmitted to them by the true prophet.[4] Such a demand does not appear in the text of Deuteronomy 13, but such a demand (which the people refused to obey) is found in 4QpHos=4Q 166 2.3-5: 'but they forgot God who...They cast His Commandments behind them which He had sent [in the mouth

---

3. According to Strugnell (p. 229) the phrase, (1. 5) ['to make thee] turn away from thy God' is a non-biblical elaboration of Deut. 13.6, 'to make you leave the way'. However, I have already explained that the author has difficulties in using the biblical wording of accusation against the prophet of Deut. 13.6. Moreover, the use of להשיבכה (1. 5) aims to suit with the key-word of the document: ושבתה (1. 2); ושב (1.3); [להשי]בכה (1. 5). The author uses this word as an influence of 2 Kgs 23.25-26.

4. A counterpart phrase comes in 1QH 4. 15-18, 'and they set before them the stumbling block of their sin. They come to inquire of Thee from the mouth of lying prophets deceived by error who speak [with strange] lips to Thy people, and alien tongue...For [they hearken] not [to] Thy [voice], nor do they give ear to Thy word'.

of] His servants the prophets, and they listened to those who led them astray, They revered them'.[5] Following this, in 1. 4-5, comes the issue of the seducer prophet according to Deuteronomy 13, elaborated by the method described above: 'But the prophet who rises up and preaches among thee [apostasy so as to make thee] turn away from thy God' (1. 4-5).

In my opinion the origin of 1. 1-3 is also Deuteronomy 13. Deut. 13.1 is an ending formula of the last section of chapter 12: 'Everything that I command you you shall be careful to do, you shall not add to it or take from it'. However, in this document it appears as the beginning of the first subject—the true prophet—which precedes the law regarding the seducer prophet. It should be noted that the Temple Scroll (54. 5-7) also cites Deut. 13.1 *before* the law of the seducer prophet. Another common factor of 4Q375 and the Temple Scroll is that Deut. 12.29-31, of which 13.1 is the ending formula, is not used.[6] Instead, 13.1 is used without the section which is its immediate context. However, in the Temple Scroll, Deut. 13.1 is still used as an *ending formula* for the law of vows. Thus the author of the Temple Scroll replaced the original ending of that law (Num. 30.17) with Deut. 13.1. The wording of this section in 4Q375 is: 1. 1-4 [(1)...thou shalt perform all that] thy God will command thee by the mouth of the prophet, and thou shalt keep [(2) all these sta]tutes, and thou shalt return unto Yahweh thy God with all (3) [thy heart and with al]l thy soul and (or then) thy God will turn from the fury of His great anger [(4) so as to save th]ee from [all] thy distress'.

Closer examination of the beginning of this section shows that Deut. 13.1 was elaborated on here: 'Everything that I command you you shall

5. See J.M. Allegro, *Discoveries in the Judaean Desert of Jordan* (Oxford: Clarendon Press, 1968), V, p. 31, 4Q166 col. ii 1.3-5. This text deals with the issue of the disobedience to the true prophet and the following of the false prophets. Regarding these subjects see Brin, 'Biblical Prophecy'.

6. V. 13.1 closes the previous section, but despite this it comes at the beginning of a chapter in contradiction to the ancient Jewish division into *Parashot*, according to which the borderline comes after 13.1. So the mistake of Langton, while dividing the Bible into chapters, has ancient roots as it is repeated in 4Q375. Both this author and Langton see in 13.1 the beginning of a unit, instead of the end. In modern Bibles (English, German, etc.) chapter 13 starts in v. 2 of the MT, which is correct from the exegetical point of view. However, there are some commentators who see here (13.1) a beginning, but in a very complicated process, see, for example, S.R. Driver, *Deuteronomy* (ICC; Edinburgh: T. & T. Clark, 3rd edn, 1902), *ad loc.*

be careful to do, you shall not add to it or take from it'. Moreover, if the various versions of parallel sources, ancient translations, etc. are taken into account, it resembles 13.1 even more. For example, according to the Samaritan Pentateuch, LXX (most manuscripts) the Peshitta and the Vulgate, the text starts in the singular: God orders 'thee' (singular), instead of 'ye' (plural). Our document follows this version.

By comparing these texts it may be seen that this is the same text as Deut. 13.1 with the following differences. The first-person speaker of Deuteronomy is transferred into third-person. This is opposite from the usual way of elaboration of the Temple Scroll, which transfers third-person speech into first-person speech by God. It may be that the author was influenced by other texts from Deuteronomy which deal with the law of following the directions of the (true) prophet, which is mentioned, for example, in Deut. 18.18: 'and he shall speak to them all that I command him'. The word 'everything' (Hebrew singular) in, 'Everything that I command you, you shall be careful to do' (Deut. 13.1), comes in our document in the plural: (1)...and thou shalt keep [(2) all these sta]tutes'. The same applies to 11QTem 54. 5-7: *kol had*ᵉ*barim...'othamah...'alehemah...mehemah* ('...all the things that... concerning them...to them...from them').

The final part of 13.1: 'you shall not add to it or take from it', is not used in the document because it is an ending formula while the author had used that verse as a beginning formula, as shown above. The author added the phrase: 'by the mouth of the prophet'.(1.1). He also changes Moses' first-person speech of Deut. 13.1 into a third-person speech by God: [thou shalt perform all that] thy God will command thee by the mouth of the prophet' (1.1), in order to describe God as the lawgiver. There follows an explanation of how God's orders have come to the knowledge of the people. By doing this he differentiated between the true prophet and the prophet who speaks apostasy (*sara*) to the nation in order to dissuade them from obeying God's orders.

The author planned to provide a full range of laws regarding prophecy, stating that the true prophets are God's agents who are assigned the task of notifying the people of his instructions. This is a complementary task to that found in the Torah.[7] In addition, the author described in legalistic style the deeds of the seducer prophet. He used the related section in Deuteronomy 13 with minor changes, which are due to his

---

7.   Regarding the proofs for such role of the prophets see Brin, 'Biblical Prophecy'.

method of elaboration. In ll. 2b-3, which are a continuation of ll. 1-2a, he wrote: '...and thou shalt return unto Yahweh thy God with all (3) [thy heart and with al]l thy soul'. This is an elaboration of Deut. 13.4-5: 'for the Lord your God is testing you to know whether you love the Lord with all your heart and with all your soul. You shall walk after the Lord your God and fear him, and keep his commandments and obey his voice and you shall serve him and cleave to him'. However, while in the Bible the text speaks about the hypothetical outcome of the seducer prophet's work, and the demands of the law that the people should not listen to him but reject his ideas and fulfil God's orders, in 4Q375 the author transferred this section so that it becomes the aim of true prophecy, announced 'by the mouth of the prophet' (1.1).[8]

The section of ll. 3b-4: 'and (or then) thy God will turn from the fury of His great anger [(4) so as to save th]ee from [all] thy distress', shows the difficulty faced by the author in arranging the material. In the framework of the positive section he spoke about God's decision to cancel his planned punishments (which shows the position of these mixed sections). The author used Deut. 13.18: 'that the Lord may turn from the fierceness of his anger' by changing God's name from Yahweh to Elohim. The author then dealt with the issue of the seducer prophet which has been described earlier.

In ll. 5ff. the author focused attention on the appeal which the prophet's tribe raised against his execution: (5) 'But, if there stands up the tribe [(6) which] he comes from, and says "Let him not be put to death, for he is righteous (or: truthful), a [(7) fai]thful prophet is he"'. The form, 'if there stands up the tribe' is based on the beginning of the law of the seducer prophet: 'If a prophet arises among you' (Deut. 13.2), and on such passages as '$w^e qam$ $shebet$ $b^e yisr'ael$' (Num. 24.17), which also appeared in Qumranic writings (1QM 11.6; CD 7.19-20).

The idea of associating the prophet with a certain tribe is not a biblical one. Therefore its origin must be investigated. Even this may be based on Deuteronomy 13, using an exegesis which represents the author's own understanding rather than the plain meaning of the original. Deut. 13.2 read: 'If a prophet arises among you'. This wording caused our author to explain that the text deals with a prophet, who stems among

8.   I cannot accept Strugnell's references. A proof which supports my reference can be found in the fact that the source of the next section is also in Deuteronomy 13, (see further). Moreover, from the usage of God's names in 4Q375, which is dealt with later, there is additional proof for the identification of the reference.

'you' (*miqirbᵉka*), that is, from a certain circle of people. One of the biblical phrases for describing such 'circles' is 'tribe'. See also the usage in 1.8, 'among one of thy tribes'.

Despite the fact that the Bible does not include any connection between prophets and tribes, there are some passages which show a *local* flavor to prophecy. In 2 Kings 2 'sons of prophets' from Jericho (vv. 5 and 15) and others that dwell at Beth El' (v. 3) are mentioned. In 1 Kgs 13.11, 'an old prophet in Beth El' is mentioned (cp. v. 25: 'told it in the town where the old prophet dwells'). Beside him another 'man of God...who came from Judah' (2 Kgs 23.17) is mentioned. Regarding Jonah Ben Amitai it was said: 'the prophet who was from Gat-Hepher' (2 Kgs 14.25). Hananiah Ben Azur, Jeremiah's rival, was defined as 'the prophet from Giveon' (Jer. 28.1). The dispute concerning Amos' prophecy also has a local flavor. The authorities tried to drive him to Judah, 'O Seer, go flee away to the land of Judah, and eat bread there, and prophesy there' (Amos 7.12). In all these texts there is a local connotation, with an implicit connection to the tribe. Therefore the idea in 4Q375 that the tribe felt that it wanted to protect its prophet is logical. Connections between prophets and their tribes can also be found in the Talmudic literature. Compare B. Suk. 27.2: 'There was not even one tribe in Israel which did not produce (שלא יצאו ממנו) prophets'; Tos. Suk. 1.9: 'You do not have a single tribe in Israel which did not raise up (שלא העמידו) a prophet'. This idea is found in the Pseudepigrapha. In Liv. Proph. 5.1 Hosea is identified as stemming from the tribe of Issachar; in 6.1: Micah from Ephraim; in 8.1: Joel from Reuben; in 11.1: Nahum from Simeon; and in 13.1: Zephaniah from Simeon.

The appeal of the tribe is worded, 'Let him not be put to death', which contradicts the wording of the very law, 'he shall be put to death'. This resembles the episode in Jeremiah's trial where the accusers demand: 'This man deserves the sentence of death' (Jer. 26.11),[9] while Jeremiah's defenders state: 'This man does not deserve the sentence of death' (v. 16). If it were not for the usage of *mawet* as a noun, the wording would have been the same as in our document. See also in Deut. 17.6, 'a person shall not be put to death on the evidence of one witness'; Deut. 24.16: 'Fathers shall not be put to death for the children, nor shall children be put to death'; Lev. 19.20: 'They shall not be put to death'. These passages are important for their judicial contexts. Two of

---

9. Regarding the situation of Jeremiah 26 see Brin, *The Prophet in His Struggles* (Tel Aviv: Mifalim Universitaim, 1983), pp. 33-55 [in Hebrew].

them have the same construction as the line in 4Q375: *l' yumat...ki...* (Lev. 19; Deut. 24). It is worth noting that most of these parallel texts are from Deuteronomy, which is the source for most of the phrases of this document.[10]

In the Bible there is one case of opposition to the execution of a death penalty. During the battle against the Philistines Saul demanded that the people should not eat until the victory against the Philistines was achieved. Jonathan violates that oath without knowing about it. By using the Urim and the Thumim the identity of the violator was revealed and he was to have been executed according to Saul's vow to execute anyone who violated the oath. The people intervened in order to save him, 'Shall Jonathan die who has wrought this great victory in Israel? Far from it. As the Lord lives, not one hair of his head shall fall to the ground...So the people ransomed Jonathan that he did not die' (1 Sam. 14.45). Despite this case of intervention by the people to avoid an execution, the two incidents are not identical, or even similar. In Jonathan's case there was no violation of a law of the Torah, but an unintentional violation of an oath of the ruler. The intervention of the people brought about the cancellation of the execution, but it could be defined as an attempt to act against an explicit law. (For other parallel cases, see the end of this article.)

The argument which was brought by the tribe is worded: (6) 'for[11] he is righteous (or truthful), a [(7) fai]thful prophet is he'. The statement about his being a righteous (person) had no special connections with his prophetic career, and it may have meant that the accusation against him was not true. On the other hand the phrase, 'a [fai]thful prophet is he', applied to his profession as a prophet. There are many sources in the Bible for such a usage as the first phrase (cp. 'he is righteous', Ezek. 18.9).[12] On the other hand the second phrase had no parallel in the

10. The tribe's phrase, 'Let him not be put to death' contradicts the explicit law, 'But the prophet who rises up and preaches among thee (5) apostasy so as to make thee] turn away from thy God, *he shall be put to death*'. This resembles the serpent's saying, 'You will not die' = (לא מות תמתון) which contradicts God's order, 'you shall not eat of the fruit of the garden...lest you die' לא תאכלו...פן תמתון (Gen. 3.3-4).

11. There is a space between the two words.

12. Strugnell (p. 229) compares it with Isa. 41.26, 'Who declared it from the beginning, that we might know, and beforetime, that we might say, "He is righteous"'. However, it is not certain that it is about the prophet or about God Himself. Moreover, 'righteous' is not a typical term to define a prophet, and this verse in Isaiah does not prove to be ascribed to a prophet.

Bible, but there are others which resemble it. Samuel was described thus, 'for Samuel is faithful (*ne'eman*) to be a prophet of the Lord' (1 Sam. 3.20). Connections between God, prophets and faithfulness are found, *inter alia* in 1 Chron. 20.20: 'Believe in the Lord and you will be established (*w°te'amenu*), believe his prophets and you will succeed'.

The argument of the tribe can also be compared with God's statement about Moses: 'If there is a prophet among you...Not so with my servant Moses, he is entrusted (*ne'eman* = faithful) with all my house' (Num. 12.6-7). This definition refers to Moses' prophecy, which can be seen from the continuation, 'With him I speak mouth to mouth clearly, and not in dark speech, and he beholds the form of God' (v. 8). The use of the term 'faithful' in such a central text regarding prophecy and its definition can inform about an important factor in the direction of the thinking of the author of 4Q375. In the LXX to Num 12.7 *ne'eman* is translated πιστός. This may be added to Strugnell's remark concerning the phrase προφήτην πιστόν in 1 Macc. 14.41, referring to the future prophet.[13] Another interesting passage is Isa. 1.26: 'afterward you shall be called the city of righteousness the faithful city'. The two components of the prophet used in 6-7 appear.

Hab. 2.4 also has such usage, 'but the righteous shall live by his faith'. It is interesting that when dealing with this passage, 1QpHab. 8.1-3 reads, 'This concerns all those who observe the law in the house of Judah, whom God will deliver from the house of Judgment because of their suffering and because of their faith in the Teacher of righteousness'. This is an amazing parallel with 4Q375 regarding the three components: righteousness, faithfulness and the house of Judgment. In 4Q375 the court is the supreme court in 'the place which thy God shall choose'. Psalm 19.10 includes the two components, and there are other biblical texts like these, e.g. Isa. 1.21; Ps. 15.2; 85.11.

In general it must be stated that the distribution of the components *'emet* and *zedeq* or *'emet* and *z°daqah* in the Bible is sparser than in the smaller corpus of the Qumranic writings. In the sectarian literature there appear many phrases about faithfulness, truth and righteousness, e.g. CD 9.22-23: 'two faithful witnesses'; 9.21-22: 'if they are faithful'; 3.19: 'and He built them a sure (literally faithful) house'. Compare also in a liturgical text 'a faithful shepherd' (1Q 34^b 3 21. 8).[14] In 11QTem 56. 3-4, while dealing with Deut. 17.10-11, the version is modified by adding

13. See Strugnell, p. 229.
14. *DJD*, 1, pp. 152-54.

the word *'emet*, 'and declare to you truly', which the author of the Temple Scroll inserts in the law of the supreme court. In the Songs of the Sabbath Sacrifice there appears such a usage: *'emet (w^e)zedeq* (4Q404 5.6); *ruḥei da'at 'emet w^{e}zedeq* (4Q405 19.4); *'emet w^{e}zedeq 'olame*...(4Q405 20, ii 21-22.5).[15] In 1QM 4.6 is the form: *'emet 'el...zedeq 'el*.

The use of 'faithfulness' is typical of the literature of the Second Commonwealth, some texts making specific reference to *prophecy* (!): B. Sir. 46.13-15, 'Sanctified by Yahweh in the prophetical office Samuel acted as judge and priest...Because of (his) truthfulness they sought the Prophet (חזה) and the seer (רואה),[16] and was found reliable by his words'. Thus, Samuel is described using the terms prophecy, seer, and faithful.[17] In 36.20-21 the prophets are generally referred to: 'Give testimony to the first of Thy work and establish the vision spoken in Thy name. Give reward to them that await for Thee that Thy prophets may be proved trustworthy'. The verb 'be trusted' (from the root *'mn*) means that they will be acknowledged as faithful, because their predictions are fulfilled. The term 'faithful' also refers to Abraham (44.20 who has a title of 'prophet', Gen. 20.7); and Job is named 'prophet' (49.9): 'He also made mention of Job among the prophets who maintained all the ways of righteousness'.[18] Here there appears only *zedeq* (= righteousness) without 'faithful'. In 34.2 there appears the phrase 'a faithful friend'.

It is worth pointing to the Haftarah Blessings which use these phrases, 'God...who has chosen good prophets and wants their words which were said truly (*b^e'emet*)...who chooses the Torah...and the prophets of truth and righteousness' (*'emet wazedeq*).[19] These prayers stem from

15. C. Newsom, *Songs of the Sabbath Sacrifice: A Critical Edition* (Atlanta GA: Scholars Press, 1985).

16. In Charles's edition of Ben Sira *ro'eh* (= shepherd) is seen as a mistake of *ro'eh* (= seer).

17. In The Academy of the Hebrew Language edition of Ben Sira (Jerusalem, 1973), it is recorded that the root *'mn* comes 24 times in the various passages, 11 of which are from the same conjugation (= *nif'al*), as the usage which we are dealing with.

18. Regarding Job's 'prophecy' see Seder Olam Rabbah, ch. 21.

19. In the following section there are phrases referring to God which are close to those which are said about the prophets, 'faithful God...whose all words are of truth and righteousness. You are faithful, O God...and Your words of truth are faithful... for You are a faithful king...God who is faithful in all His words'. These phrases of righteousness, truth and faithfulness bring the definition of the prophet in the tribe's

the Second Commonwealth period.[20] The blessings refer to the prophets using terms such as faithfulness, truth and righteousness, which resemble those of our 4Q375.[21]

After mentioning the issue of the appeal of the tribe (ll. 5-7) the procedure in 4Q375 continues with the demand: (7) 'then thou shalt come, with that tribe and thy elders and thy judges, [(8) t]o the place which thy God shall choose among one of thy tribes,[22] into the presence of [(9) the] anointed priest, upon whose head poured the oil of anointing'. It must be asked, to whom does the text speak? Until this point the addressee was Israel, who hears the laws. However, now the lawgiver calls the addressee to come with the appealing tribe 'and thy elders and thy judges'. So, the local elders and judges are also referred to in the second-person speech. It may be that the text refers to Israel here. According to law, the people must come ['t]o the place which thy God shall choose' including their leaders and judges. All of these should

argument closer to those relating to God. I have cited phrases of righteousness and truth relating to God from the Scrolls, and there are many more, see, for example, 1QH 1.31, 'in all Thy works of truth and [in all thy] righteous [judgements]'; 4.40, 'for You are (the) truth and all Thy deeds are in righteousness'; 1QM 13.3, "Blessed be all those who [serve] Him in righteousness and who know Him by faith'.

20. See J. Heinemann, *Prayer in the Talmud* (Studia Judaica 9; Berlin-New York: Walter de Gruyter, 1977), pp. 228-29, regarding the early date of these Blessings. Heinemann states that they precede the Seven Benedictions on Sabbaths. See p. 227 about their history as derived from the High Priest's Benedictions. He explains (p. 34) that they were composed in opposition to the false prophets of that period, for example, against the visions which are included in the Apocrypha. See also D. Flusser, 'Sanctus und Gloria', in *Abraham unser Vater* (ed. O. Betz *et al.*; Leiden: Brill, 1963), pp. 142-52.

21. Phrases of truth and righteousness relating to the biblical prophets are found in Josephus' writings. In *Contra Apionem* 1.37-39, he defines the differences that exist between the Jewish Canon and the Greek writings. Among the advantages of the Bible he mentions the existence of an uninterrupted line of prophets, and that all the biblical literature is written with righteousness. He states that these two factors are missing from the Greek writings. He also adds that the lack of an uninterrupted line of prophets after the Bible has caused the post-biblical compositions to be valued lower. In *Ant.* 10.35 Josephus defines Isaiah as a truthful prophet who knew that during all his mission he did not utter any lie, therefore he wrote down his prophecies in order that their truth will be revealed in the future. Josephus says that the same applies to the other prophets.

22. Regarding the space in the text, see supra, note 2.

accompany the appealing tribe. This wording shows that the process would be done on a general and national level. It has to be done in that way because the issue was sensitive: a prophet had spoken against God and, despite this, his tribe supported him. Another sign for the general and public procedure is found in the second fragment (1 ii), in which the high priest has to conduct a certain ritual which resembles that of the Day of Atonement. At the end of this, and after studying the hidden laws, it is said, 'And he shall come forth before a[ll the leaders of] (9) the assembly. And this [...' (ll. 8-9). Therefore, as these two fragments are in one sequence, it is logical that the phrase, 'then thou shalt come' does indeed refer to the whole nation.

If this interpretation is not accepted, the 'thou' may refer to all those who would attend the appearance of the prophet and who would listen to the protest of his tribe. Refuting this are the words, 'and thy elders and thy judges' which cannot be connected with a single individual or random group. It suits better the first interpretation regarding a national (or at least a tribal) atmosphere. Reference to the elders and judges is still appropriate to a national affair. For example, in Josh. 23.2: 'Joshua summoned all Israel, their elders and heads, their judges and officers'. A similar and impressive picture comes also in Deut. 29.9 (Heb., Eng. 10): 'You stand this day all of you...the heads of your tribes, your elders, and your officers'. In the ceremony of blessing and cursing in Josh. 8.33 it is said: 'And all Israel...with their elders and officers and their judges'.

Thus the author of 4Q375 used such phrases in order to achieve the special impression necessary for such an event. Moreover, if until now the basic biblical text has been Deuteronomy 13, which the author used as a source for the two kinds of prophets (ll. 1-5), from l. 7 onwards the basic text is Deuteronomy 17, the law of the supreme court. This states that if one does not know the law of a difficult case, 'you shall arise and go up to the place...and come to the levitical priests' (vv. 8-9). The word is *uba'ta* (you shall *come*) which is also used at the beginning of the new stage in 4Q375. In Deut. 17.9 it refers to a local judge who has a difficulty in deciding a difficult case, but it may also apply to one of the sides in the judicial dispute whose case cannot be solved by the local judges. Thus, as the author uses the biblical text in a different way such phrases that are missing in the original must be added. By doing this his own later style is revealed.[23]

---

23. Regarding this consideration see Brin, 'The Bible as Reflected in the Temple Scroll', *Shnaton* 4 (1980), p. 212 [Hebrew].

In ll. 8-9 it is written, '[(8) t]o the place which thy God shall choose among one of thy tribes, into the presence of [(9) the] anointed priest'. While using the wording of Deuteronomy 17 the author inserts two changes: (1) 'the place which thy God shall choose' is given instead of 'the place which the Lord your God will choose' (Deut. 17.8); and (2) the location of the phrase regarding 'the place' is different. The second change is a result of the author's adoption of a *principal* law, which has a different starting formula dealing with difficult cases, into a usage for an appeal regarding a *specific* case, the law of the seducer prophet. This caused him to abandon the starting formula and to compose a suitable substitute. This in turn caused the location of 'the place' to be different from Deut. 17.8, which forces the author to find a new location for it while using v. 9.

As for the first change, in which 'the place which thy God shall choose' is used, the phrase does not appear in any biblical text. In Deut. 17.8 it is written, 'the place which the Lord your God will choose'. The phrase, 'among one of thy tribes' is a result of the influence of Deut. 12.14, which is the only text of the Bible which uses it. The change of God's name from יךהלא 'ה (Deut. 17.8) into אלוהיכה (1.8) is a clear result of the author's policy regarding God's names.

1.1	יצוה אלוהיכה
1.2	תשבתה עד ה' אלוהיכה
1.3	תשב אלוהיכה
1.5	להשיבכה מאחרי אלוהיכה
1.8	יבחר אלוהיכה

First, it may be noted that there is an overall majority of the usage of *Elohim* (5 times) against the usage of *Yahweh* (once only and this instance—1.2—is of the double name *Yahweh Elohim*). Moreover, in all the texts which the author composed rather than copied, when referring to God as the actor of some deeds, the author used *Elohim*: in l. 1 God's first-person speech is changed: 'that I command you' (Deut. 13.1), into third-person speech, 'thy God will command thee' (l. 1). The line 'then thy God will turn from the fury of His great anger' (l. 3), is an elaboration of Deut. 13.18: 'that the Lord may turn from the fierceness of his anger'. The author changed the status of this sentence (as described above) as well as God's name from *Yahweh* to *Elohim*. Line 8, 't]o the place which thy God shall choose' is, as stated above, a change of either Deut. 17.8: 'the place which the Lord your God will choose' or 17.10: 'from that place which the Lord will choose'. In both the name Yahweh is omitted, according to the author's general tendency.

The only usage of Yahweh (in its dual form: Yahweh Elohim) comes in ll. 2-3: 'and thou shalt return unto Yahweh thy God with all (3) [thy heart and with al]l thy soul'. This is an elaboration of Deut. 13.4-5: 'with all your heart and with all your soul. You shall walk after the Lord your God and fear him'. So this is not the author's usage but a repetition of the biblical source, which remains unchanged. In fragment 1 ii there appears the phrase: (7) 'a[ll the laws of] (8) Yahweh'. As in the last example (1 i ll. 2-3) the author felt that such a phrase which spoke about studying God's (hidden) laws was to have reference to Yahweh.

In 1.7 there is a phrase which has not yet been discussed: 'then thou shalt come, with that tribe and thy elders'. The usual phrase in biblical Hebrew for describing going in a company is: *uba'ta ('ata)...wᵉ* ...(see, for example, Gen. 6.18; Exod. 3.18; Ezek. 38.15). Here is a different construction: *uba'ta 'im...wᵉ*.... The form *bo' 'im* meaning to come with is used only rarely in the Bible (Gen. 29.6; Ps. 26.4; Esth. 5.14), or in post-biblical texts. *Bo' 'im* can also be used for describing a quarrel, a dispute, or a trial. 'The Lord enters (literally comes) into judgment with the elders and princes of his people' (Isa. 3.14); or 'Is it for your fear of him that he reproves you, and enters (literally comes) into judgment with you?' (Job 22.4). The author may have chosen such a construction to describe those who go *together*, the whole nation, *uba'ta...wᵉ*, on the one hand; and on the other hand, the one who appeals, *uba'ta 'im*. The first side is described according to the usual biblical method (*uba'ta...wᵉ*), while the other form (*uba'ta 'im*) is used for those who oppose the execution of the prophet. Using different forms enables the author to define the status of each group.[24]

Another combination of verb and preposition comes in the same context, (7) 'then thou shalt *come*, with that tribe...(8)...*before* [(9) the] anointed priest'. The form 'to come before' appears in the Bible very rarely, and only in certain contexts, which do not have any connections with the usage in the case of 4Q375. All have the meaning of priority in time or in space. In 2 Sam. 20.8, 'and Ama'sa came before them' (a literal translation), the text describes the location of Amasa in comparison with Joab and his men. The same applies to 2 Sam. 19.9 (Hebrew, 8 in English), 'and all the people came before the king'. Their coming before

24. I have found one text with *bo' 'im*, 4Q 402 1, 2, 'as they came with the God' (see Newsom, *Songs*).

him does not have any connection with the king's status: it is just a sign for their gathering around him after the events following Absalom's death. This description contradicts the previous one regarding their behavior beforehand, 'and the people stole into the city that day as people steal in who are ashamed when they flee in battle' (v. 4 Hebrew, 3 in English). Their gathering around the king came after Joab's condemnation of him.[25]

The other usage of the phrase 'to come before' is for cult purposes, and describes Moses' (or Aaron's and others) coming before God. Thus in Exod. 34.34, 'but whenever Moses came in before the Lord to speak with him'; 28.30, 'and they shall be upon Aaron's heart when he comes before the Lord'; 1 Chron. 16.29, 'bring an offering and come before him'; in the parallel text, Ps. 96.8 it is, 'bring an offering and come into his courts' (compare also LXX to 1 Chron. 16.29); Ps. 100.2, 'come before him with singing'; Ezek. 46.9, 'When the people of the land come before the Lord'.

Another usage of this form in reference to God has the meaning of approaching, or being accepted. Thus, in Ps. 79.11, 'Let the groans of the prisoners come before thee'; 88.3 (English 2), 'Let my prayer come before thee'. Some of these texts using this phrase when referring to God have the meaning of bringing a case before His judgment, 'This will be my salvation, that a godless man shall not come before him' (Job 13.16).

Only in the Scroll of Esther is there the locution: coming before (*a person*) (8.1), but in context even this phrase has the meaning of being allowed to get closer to the king, rather than of a case being brought under the authorities' (kings; judges) decisions. As for 9.25: *ub^ebo'a lipne hammelek*, it should be stated that this is a difficult text. Usually scholars find in it a reference to Esther approaching the king and asking him to cancel Haman's orders. (This follows some ancient translations. The LXX, however, ascribes this action to Haman). Others understand it to mean that Haman's order has come under the review of the king (consult the commentaries for this passage). Therefore, this text may actually mean 'to bring a case for the authority's decision'. If so, then this is the only evidence for such a usage in the Bible.[26] On the other

---

25. The *compound* phrase of *come* (and) *go out before* which have a different meaning are irrelevant here, therefore not included.

26. Esther 1.19 reads, 'If it please the king, let a royal order go forth...that Vashti is to come no more before king Ahashe'rus'. In this case the phrase intends to

hand there is a rich body of usage of this locution in the Rabbis' writings, meaning to come before an authority, teacher and the like, the same usage as in 4Q375. Thus, 'As they came before the court' (m. Rosh Hash. 1.5); 'As the case came before R. Aqiba' (m. Yeba. 12.5); 'He then came before the court' (m. Baba Batra 10.6); and others. This is a common usage in the Talmudic compositions.[27]

In the Bible other phrases occur demonstrating the same idea, and especially *'md lipne*, 'standing before someone'. Thus, Num. 27.22, 'he took Joshua and caused him to stand before El'azar the priest'; 27.2, 'And they stood before Moses and before El'azar the priest'; Gen. 41.46, 'And Joseph was thirty years old when he stood before Pharaoh'; and elsewhere.[28]

The research into the usage of the phrase 'to come before' which is used in 1.7 is important because, although the author uses the law of the supreme court of Deuteronomy 17, it has to be changed to suit the different manner in which it is used. The gap is filled by the author's own composition, worded in a new style. Therefore while the Bible states, 'You will come...to...and to...', the 4Q375 author writes, (7)

describe her approach to the king and the issue of her marriage to him, as the following passage says, 'and let the king give her royal position to another that is better than she'. Compare also v. 11, 'to bring Queen Vashti before the King'. See also vv. 2, 12, 13, 14, 15.

27. It seems that the changing of the prepositions in which *before* replaces others is typical of the late literature of the Bible and post-biblical literature. See 1 Chron. 16.37, 'to serve always *before* the Ark'. See also 11QTem 56.9, in the context of the law of the supreme court there appears the phrase, 'to serve *before* Me' instead of 'to serve there' (in the chosen place) in Deuteronomy.

28. Three passages from 1 Kings show a different picture. They contain the phrase, to *come before* the king. However, a simple reading in these passages reveals that the discussed (later) meaning is not used in them. Verse 23 reads, 'and he (the prophet Nathan) came in before the king'. However, at the beginning of the passage it says, 'and Nathan the prophet came in. And they told the king: Here is Nathan the prophet. And then he came in before the king'. So, the text describes in stages Nathan's approach to the king. The particular phrase describes the moment at which he reaches the king. In v. 28 a similar phrase occurs: 'Then King David answered: Call Bath-She'ba to me. So she came in before the king'. As in the previous passage the phrase is used to mean the approach to the king, especially here as this approach was a result of the king's initiative. The same idea is reached with a parallel phrase, 'and she stood before the king'. So the text describes David's meeting with Bath-She'ba in two ways. The same applies to the third passage v. 32, 'And David said, Call to me Zadok...and Nathan...So they came before the king'.

'then thou shalt come...before [(9) the] anointed priest', the more usual way of expression in his own days. In this context I would like to point to an important finding from the Temple Scroll. In 11QTem 58.18-19 it is written, 'And he [the king] shall not go out [to a war] until he comes before the high priest, who shall inquire for him by the judgment of the Urim and the Thummim'. This is an additional contribution to the evidence for the late language of the Temple Scroll, which has not been mentioned in research so far.

There is no doubt that ll.8-9 refer to the high priest.[29] This should be added to the signs indicating the *national* significance of the issue, that all Israel has to be present in the special appeal of the tribe regarding the fate of its prophet. The author changed the basic text of Deuteronomy 17 when referring to the procedure of the supreme court which demands that the high priest *himself* should be in charge of that case. This shows that the author evaluated it as very important.[30] The Bible states: 'and coming to the Levitical priests and to the judge who is in office in those days, you shall consult them and they shall declare to you the decision' (Deut. 17.9). The text is worded in general terms without any dramatization. The authorities in the supreme court are depicted in the plural and are described as belonging to two groups: (1) the Levitical priests; and (2) the judge who is in office in those days. This suits the daily matters which the law speaks about (Deut. 17.8), while in 4Q375 the procedure surrounds a unique and terrible case of an appeal against the fulfilment of the demand of a holy law.

29. As is well known, only Aaron was anointed by pouring the oil on his head during the ceremony of his inauguration (Exod. 29.7; Lev. 8.12). The general statement which resembles the phrase in 4Q375 comes in Lev. 21.10, 'The priest who is chief among his brethren, upon whose head the anointing oil is poured'. All the components of 4Q375 are found here, except that he is defined as, 'chief among his brethren' while in 4Q375 he is called 'the anointed priest'. The word משחה comes in 4Q375 in a different construction מ‏ח‏יחה. Compare also 1QM 9.8, 'and they shall not profane the anointing (משיחת) of their priesthood with the blood of nations of vanity'. This construction is not found in the Bible, but in Talmudic literature it is used, which shows its late date, compare *m. Men.* 6.3; *m. Hor.* 3.1; 3.2.

30. The wording of the law of Deut. 17.8-13 was known in Qumran as it is used in 11QTem 56.1-11. The text is repeated with all its details but with differences of style and content to suit the method of its writer. None of these changes is identical with those in 4Q375. Regarding this law in the Temple Scroll see Brin, 'Bible as Reflected', pp. 184-85.

Fragment 1 ii

The second fragment depicts a ceremony which resembles the ritual of the Day of Atonement (see below). This is another sign of the extraordinary event which is dealt with in 4Q375. The text of the fragment reads:

> (1-2) [...] (3) and he shall take [one bullock, a son of the herd, and one ram...and he shall sprinkle] (4) with his fin[ger on the surface of the Kapporet...]...[...] (5) the flesh of the ra[m...] one go[at which is] (6) for a sin offering shall he ta[ke and he shall slaughter it and he shall] make atonement on behalf of all the assembly. And Aa[ron (or afterwards he) shall sprinkle part of the blood] (7) before the veil of [screen and shall draw ne]ar to the Ark of the Testimony, and shall study a[ll the laws of] (8) Yahweh for all [cases of prophecy...those laws that have been con]cealed from thee. And he shall come forth before a[ll the leaders of] (9) the assembly. And this [...

The ceremony which the anointed priest arranges has several aspects: sacrifices, sprinkling blood and inquiring about God's ordinances.

First I will deal with the issue of the sacrifices. In the surviving parts of this fragment appear a ram and a goat, but in the missing parts there is space for other components of sacrifices. There is also mention of an act of sprinkling blood. In the ceremony of the Day of Atonement in Leviticus 16 a bull for a sin offering and a ram for a holocaust offering are mentioned as the sacrifice of Aaron, and two goats for a sin offering and a ram for a holocaust offering for Israel. The wording of ll. 5-6, 'one go[at which is] for a sin offering' shows that there may be more than one goat, and as it mentions in 1.6 , 'and he shall] make atonement on behalf of all the assembly', the conclusion is that ll. 5-6 speak about one of the two(?) goats of Israel's sacrifices. Thus, it may be concluded that ll.1-3 could have mentioned the sacrifices of the anointed priest. The act of sacrificing the people's goat is mentioned as the *last* one before the priest approaches the ark and before he enquires about all the laws of Yahweh. In the ceremony of Leviticus 16 the sacrifice of the holocaust offering is mentioned as the last act. In 1.5, 'the flesh of the ra[m'[31] is mentioned, which means that the priest does something with the ram as either his holocaust offering or the people's. This act comes before the sacrifices of the sin offerings, while in the Bible the holocaust offerings

---

31. The term 'the flesh of the ram' comes in the Bible only once, in the inauguration of Aaron, Exod. 29.32.

are sacrificed *after* finishing the actions of the sin offerings and after sending the second goat of the people to the desert.[32]

In 1.6 it is said, '[and he shall] make atonement on behalf of all the assembly'. Such an idiom is found several times in Leviticus 16 (vv. 6, 11, 17), 'and he shall make atonement for himself and for his house'; 'and make atonement for himself and for the people' (v. 24). Even from this point of view the text follows certain phrases from the Book of Leviticus, especially in the text regarding the Day of Atonement.

After the slaughtering the goat of the people the document mentions the sprinkling of its blood, '(7) before the veil of [*holiness*]'. This completion of the text seems preferable to Strugnell's 'before the veil of [*screen*]' for two reasons. First the usage of *haqodesh* (holiness) as *nomen rectum* is typical of the Sect's writings. Secondly, the phrase *paroket haqodesh* (the veil of holiness) is used in Lev. 4.6 (this also applies to v. 17 according to one Hebrew manuscript, the Samaritan Pentateuch and the LXX). These two verses contain phrases which are followed closely by the document, v. 6, 'and the [anointed- (see v. 5)] priest shall dip his finger in the blood 'and sprinkle part of the blood seven times before the Lord in front of the veil of the sanctuary (or holiness)'; v. 17, 'and the [anointed- (see v. 16)] priest shall dip his finger in the blood and sprinkle part of the blood seven times before the Lord in front of the veil [of the holiness]' (see above). Compare this to 4Q375, (6) 'And Aa[ron (or: afterwards he) shall sprinkle part of the blood] (7) before the veil of [the holiness] and shall draw near to the Ark of the Testimony'.

From the mentioning of the sacrifices, the veil and the Ark of the Testimony I believe that Strugnell's reconstructions are correct, with the exception of 'screen', for which I prefer 'holiness', and A[aron etc.], for which I prefer Strugnell's second suggestion: [*afterwards* (ואחר) he shall sprinkle]. It is worth noting that in the ceremony of the Day of Atonement in Leviticus 16 this kind of blood sprinkling is not mentioned. In v. 15 sprinklings on and before the *kapporet* are mentioned,[33] and vv. 18-19 mention acts of sprinkling on the altar. On the

---

32. Strugnell (p. 230) has a mistake in his statement that Leviticus 16 does not describe the sacrifice of the ram. See the description in v. 24.

33. Strugnell's completion in ll. 3-4, ['and he shall sprinkle] (4) with his fin[ger on the surface of the Kapporet' is reasonable because there is an agreement with the description of the various kinds of sacrifices of the Day of Atonement and also for the blood sprinkling which is described there in vv. 14-15.

other hand, blood sprinklings before the veil are mentioned in Lev. 4.6-17. This text deals with the sin offering which is brought because of a mistake made by the high priest (Lev. 4.3ff.), while the second section in this chapter deals with a sin offering being brought for the people's sin, 'If the whole congregation of Israel commits a sin' (vv. 13ff.). The conductor of the two ceremonies is the *anointed priest* as in 4Q375. Perhaps the author uses the same wording of sprinkling because it was thought that the type of sin here resembles the sin of the nation (and of the anointed priest) as in Leviticus.

In the ceremony of the Day of Atonement in 11QTem 26.3-13 the two goats of the people are mentioned and the fate of the goat is compared with that of the bull (ll.7-9). In column 27 the continuation of the ritual is given, where, after the sacrifice of the goat and the sending of the second live goat to the desert, 'Then he shall offer the bull and the [ra]m and the [male lambs, according to] their ord[inance,] on the altar of burnt offering' (ll.3-4). This may be seen as a continuation of 25.12-16 regarding the sacrifice of the Day: 'You shall make a burnt offering thereon to the Lord, one bull, one ram, seven male lambs a year old {...} one male goat for a sin offering, besides the sin of atonement' (ll.12-14). In ll.15-16 it is said: 'And for the sin offering of atonement you shall offer two rams for burnt offering, one shall be offered by the high priest for himself and his father's house'. So, the system of the Temple Scroll follows that of Num. 29.8. This passage says: 'besides the sin offering of atonement' (v. 11), probably referring to the sin offering of Leviticus 16. All this shows that the system of 4Q375 differs from the Bible as well as from the Temple Scroll, which bears a close resemblance to the Bible in many details.

After the sprinkling of the blood of the goat, 'before the veil of [holiness]' (1.7) the priest approaches 'the ark of the testimony and shall study a[ll the laws of] (8) Yahweh for all [cases of prophecy...those laws that have been con]cealed from thee. And he shall come forth before a[ll the leaders of] (9) the assembly. And this [...'. The act of studying the scriptures, therefore, will be done before the ark of the testimony. The fact that no one may enter such a holy place shows that the studying of 'the concealed' *nistarot* will be done between God and the high priest in the Holy of Holy without the cooperation of others. Only afterwards does the high priest goes out (8) 'before a[ll the leaders of] (9) the assembly'. As the high priest has to interpret the scriptures to find out the decision which he must reach for that case, he himself does not know what the law is. So the phrase '[that have been con]cealed *from thee*' may be understood to refer not only to the people; these are 'concealed laws' from everyone, including the high priest. It may be deduced from this that there are two stages of *nistarot*:

1.   Those which are for the people, but which the *doresh hatorah* and the other leaders of the Sect do know how to solve; and

2.   Those that neither the ordinary people nor the leaders know how to solve. The document demonstrates that in the second cases only the high priest, not a regular *doresh hatorah* as in 1QS 6.6, has a procedure to reveal these *nistarot* and give God's answer.

If the completion of Strugnell, '[that have been *con*]*cealed* from thee', is correct, then there are parallel texts which contain such phrases: 1QS 8.11-12, 'and the *interpreter* shall not conceal from them, out of the fear of the spirit of apostasy, any of *those things hidden from Israel* which have been discovered by him'. Against the wicked people it is said, 'They have neither inquired nor sought after Him concerning His laws that they might know the hidden things in which they sinfully erred' (v. 11). Regarding God, who knows all the 'hidden things' it is said in Deut. 29.28 (English 29), 'The secret things belong to the Lord our God'. It seems that the same idea is expressed in the words of the prayer 'You know the *nistarot* and the *nigl[ot]*' (4Q 508, 2).

This shows that the application to the anointed priest is a sign of the great severity of the issue being considered. Moreover, the special ceremony which resembles the Day of Atonement has a double function: on the one hand it is an indication of the unique and difficult incident. On the other, the mention of the Ark of the Testimony and the studying of the hidden laws together is one of the reasons for the ceremony. As the Book of the Torah is found in its neighborhood (see Deut. 31.6, 29 and CD 5.2-3, 'but David had not read in the sealed Book of the Law which was inside the Ark of the Covenant'), the ceremony is arranged to enable the priest to read by approaching the Book of the Law.[34]

The word for the priest's study of (7) 'a[ll the laws of] (8) Yahweh' is *drš*, as is usually the case in the Sect's literature. This verb is used for

---

34. Regarding the connection between the unique ceremony and the studying of the Law see Strugnell (pp. 232, 246). About the text of CD see also J. VanderKam, 'Zadok and the *SPR HTWRA HHTUM*', *RQ* 11 (1982–1984), p. 565.

the study of scriptures, appearing only in late biblical books (Ezra and Chronicles).[35] In the Sect there was a special office of *Doresh Hatorah* (see 1QS 6.6). In CD 6.7 there comes one of the 'identifications' of the *Doresh Hatorah*, which reads, 'and the Staff is the Searcher of the Law'. A different 'identification' appears in 7.18, 'and the Star is the Searcher of the Law';[36] and in 4Q Flor 1.11, 'He is the Branch of David who shall arise with the Searcher of the Law'. However in 1QS 5.8 there is an important passage which shows that the (ordinary) priests have the task of searching the scriptures as a procedure in the Sect's life. In 1Q 29 5-7,2 this phrase is used regarding the priest, 'הכוהן לכל רצונו ידרוש' 'and the priest will study according to his desire' (regarding the connections between 4Q375 and 1Q 29 see below). Such a task is dealt with in 1QS 5.7-10 which begins, 'Whoever approaches the council of the community shall enter the covenant...to return with all his heart and soul to every commandment of the Laws of Moses in accordance with all that has been revealed of it to the sons of Zadok, the keepers of the covenant and seekers (*dorshei*) of His will'. Against this there is a description of the wicked people, 'men of falsehood who walk in the way of wickedness...They have neither inquired nor sought after Him concerning His laws that they might know the hidden things in which they have sinfully erred. And matters revealed they have treated with insolence' (ll.11-12).[37] So it is clear that the study of the Law, including the *nistarot* and the *niglot*, is the basis for the behavior of the members of the Sect, making them different from the wicked people. However, there is no reference to the function of the high priest in special ceremonies such as the one in 4Q375. It seems that under extraordinary circumstances the high priest has the task of studying the scriptures.

In literature from that period such as Ben Sira there is mention of *nistarot* connected with the figure of Isaiah: 'and saved them by the hand of Isaiah. Unto eternity he declared things that should be and hidden things before they come to pass' (Sir. 48.20-25). God is defined in 42.19, 'He declares what is past and what is future and reveals the profoundest secrets'. In the two verses *nistarot* and *niglot* come in a

35. A. Hurvitz, *The Transition Period in Biblical Hebrew* (Jerusalem: Mosad Bialik, 1972), p. 134 [Hebrew].

36. This 'identification' in these passages is for the purpose of the *pesher*, and is not a significant idea in the Sect's philosophy.

37. Regarding the *niglot* and *nistarot* see L. Schiffman, *The Halakhah at Qumran* (Leiden: Brill, 1975), pp. 75-76.

parallel which shows that *nistarot* means future events. Compare also
v. 18, 'For Yahweh possesses all knowledge and sees what comes unto
eternity, and all their secrets he surveys'. In another passage Ben Sira
reads, 'Meditate upon that which thou must grasp and be not occupied
with what is hidden'. The idea here is that ordinary human beings are
excluded from dealing with some issues and subjects; which should be
left to God and those who are 'appointed' (3.22).

The outcome of the appeal of the tribe against the explicit law
regarding the seducer prophet would be established by the findings of
the priest (or the revelations to him) after his study of the hidden laws
(1. 8). This resembles the case of the wood gatherer in the Bible where
the case is defined, 'They put him in custody, because it had not been
made plain what should be done to him' (Num. 15.34). This differs from
the case in 4Q375 which deals with an explicit law about the seducer
prophet, and the penalty of death (Deut. 13.2-6); such law is mentioned
even in 4Q375. Moreover, with the wood gatherer there may have been
a question about whether the type of labor was to be defined as a
defilement of the Sabbath, or a question about the form of the death
penalty, which was not stated explicitly in the law, and therefore meant
that they should keep him until they had God's instructions. These do
not apply to the case of 4Q375. On the other hand in the incident
regarding the curser (Lev. 24.10-16) the form is repeated, 'And they put
him in custody till the will of the Lord should be declared to them'
(v. 12). However, it may be that they did not have a law which suited
that particular case. Proof for this is that, as well as the decision regarding
that individual, a general law was announced, as in similar cases such as
the law of inheritance of daughters which is connected with the story of
the daughters of Zelophehad. Again this case is different.

Ll.8-9, 'And he shall come forth before a[ll the leaders of] (9) the
assembly', deals with the rule of the priest after he finishes studying the
scripture in front of the ark of the testimony. The phrase 'come ‖ go
out' appears in the Bible in a military context, 'Fear not... tomorrow go
out against them' (2 Chron. 20.17); or to indicate the action of the
leader who leads the people, 'and that our king may...go out before us'
(1 Sam. 8.20). However, there is a third type of usage with a *cultic
meaning*. It seems that the author intends to give that connotation.
Exod. 28.35 reads, 'And it shall be upon Aaron when he ministers...
when he goes into the holy place before the Lord, and when he comes
out'. This description is of the entrance of the high priest into the holy

quarter and his departure from it. Compare this to Lev. 16.17-24, which describes the movements (both in and out) of the high priest during the ceremony dealt with in 4Q375, 'There shall be no man in the tent of meeting when he enters to make atonement in the holy place until he comes out...Then he shall go out to the altar which is before the Lord...and come forth and offer his burnt offering'. Compare also Ezek. 46.9-10, 'When the people of the land come before the Lord at the appointed feasts...he...shall go out by the south gate...he...shall return by the north gate...the prince...when they go out he shall go out'.

It may be that the author preferred to finish the high priest section with parallel wording to the section which describes the appearance of the tribe and all the people before him. Therefore, as it says at the beginning, 1i (7) 'then thou shalt come...before [(9) the] anointed priest', it concludes, 1ii (8) 'And he shall come forth before a[ll the leaders of] (9) the assembly'. The last line contains only one word beyond the description of the approach of the priest to the people, w^eze (1. 9). Strugnell suggests that the priest's announcement regarding the fate of the prophet starts here, with the beginning of a formula like Deut. 15.2, 'And this is the manner (of the release)'.

The Intervention of the Tribe in Favor of the Prophet

A feature of 4Q375 is the intervention of the tribe in favor of its prophet, '(6) Let him not be put to death, for he is righteous (or truthful), a [(7) fai]thful prophet is he'. Strugnell's interpretation that the text deals with a discussion about a true or false prophet does not seem satisfactory.[38] It may be seen from the contents of 4Q375 as well as the tribe's words of defense that that argument is not correct. These words are directed to the prophet's *biography*, (6) 'for he is righteous (or truthful), a [(7) fai]thful prophet is he'. Even this is based on Deuteronomy 13 which introduces the prophet on the basis of his past, 'If a prophet arises among you or a dreamer of dreams, and gives you a sign or a wonder, and the sign or wonder which he tells you comes to pass' (vv. 2-3), despite this the lawgiver demands that the people should not follow the prophet's advice, stating, 'But that prophet or that dreamer shall be put to death' (v. 6). This shows that the appeal of that tribe challenges an explicit law of the Bible. Moreover, if Strugnell's

38. Strugnell, p. 246.

theory regarding the situation were right, then the author would have based the description on Deuteronomy 18, which suits the issue of true or false prophet and not on Deuteronomy 13, which deals with the seducer prophet.

It is noteworthy that, contemporaneous with the authorship of 4Q375, Philo writes about a prophet or other public leader who acts sinfully against God, saying that the authorities have to execute him *without bringing him to trial* (On The Special Laws 1.55). There is no doubt that he refers to Deuteronomy 13 regarding the seducer prophet.[39] By stressing the lack of trial, does Philo oppose the idea as described in 4Q375?

Laws of Prophets in the Bible

In the Pentateuch there are two laws of prophets: Deuteronomy 13 and 18, as well as some other texts which provide additional data. Numbers 12 compares the prophecy of Moses to that of other prophets, 'If there is a prophet among you I the Lord make myself known to him in a vision, I speak with him in a dream. Not so with my servant Moses, he is entrusted with all my house, With him I speak mouth to mouth, clearly, and not in dark speech' (vv. 6-8). The question here is about the level of the prophets and their comparison to Moses, who is in closest contact with God.

In the Books of the Prophets the study of the issue of prophecy is found in two texts: Jeremiah 28 and Ezekiel 14. In Jeremiah 28, during the debate of Jeremiah and Hananiah, Jeremiah says, 'The prophets who preceded you and me from ancient times prophesied war, famine and pestilence against many countries and great kingdoms. As for the prophet who prophesies peace, when the word of that prophet comes to pass then it will be known that God has truly sent the prophet' (vv. 8-9). The definition in Jeremiah's words contains a detailed interpretation of the law of the prophets of Deuteronomy 18. It does not belong to the issues which are dealt with in 4Q375.[40]

In Ezek. 14.1-11 there is a statement equating the status of a prophet who prophesies with that of a wicked person who has worshiped idols, 'and I will stretch out my hand against him, and will destroy him from the midst of my people Israel and they shall bear their punishment. The

39. See the edition of F.H. Colson (LCL; London: Heinemann), *ad loc.*
40. See Brin, *The Prophet*, pp. 94-104.

punishment of the prophet and the punishment of the inquirer shall be alike' (vv. 9-10). So it is about the death penalty of a prophet who does not fulfill his task according to his status. According to the contents and wording it is not a judicial punishment, but a punishment by God.[41]

The common denominator of Ezekiel 14 and 4Q375 is the behavior of the prophet toward God when related to his mission. In both cases the prophets die as a punishment for neglecting their tasks. The difference between the two texts is that Ezekiel does not address the issue from a judicial angle, and the sin is different. In 4Q375 the prophet is accused of an attempt to cause apostasy by the worship of idols. However, in Ezekiel 14 the prophet is not involved in worshiping the idols, his people are. The prophet's sin is defined by his willingness to prophesy to such sinners.

The Relation between 1Q29, 1Q22, 4Q376 and 4Q375

Strugnell points to the connections between the document discussed here and three other texts, two from cave 1 and one from cave 4. However, the text named 'The sayings of Moses' (1Q 22) has only one connection with the point which relates to the ritual of the Day of Atonement. However, this is the *ordinary* ritual of the Day of Atonement which is to be conducted on time. This is not the case in 4Q375, where the ritual resembles that ordinary one, but is actually a special ceremony conducted to decide the fate of the prophet.

In 4Q376 the anointed priest (or his deputy, as Strugnell suggests) is mentioned. Some sacrifices are also mentioned (1 i). In 1 ii the priest appears, the text reading, 'until the priest finishes speaking' (l.2). Another common denominator comes in 1. 3, 'and thou shalt keep and perform all that he (the priest) shall tell thee', which resembles the beginning of 4Q375, (1) ['thou shalt perform all that] thy God will command thee by the mouth of the prophet, and thou shalt keep [(2) all these sta]tutes'. In both texts the people are asked to keep the laws or orders and to obey them. In 4Q375 the laws are given by the mediation of the prophet (l. 2), while in 4Q376 the priest takes his place, 'until the priest finishes speaking...and after [the cloud or the light] has been removed from' (ll. 2-3). Only afterwards comes the order, 'and thou shalt keep and perform all that he (the priest) shall tell thee' (l. 3). Therefore I

---

41. Brin, *Studies in the Book of Ezekiel* (Tel Aviv: Hakibbutz Hamenhad, 1975), pp. 64-70 [Hebrew].

ascribe to the priest the giving of God's orders.

The priest is described as speaking, 'before the eyes of all the assembly' ('until the priest finishes speaking') (l. 2). However, I disagree with Strugnell's proposal that after this the fate of the prophet of 4Q375 was mentioned. Even if it is correct to read in 1Q29 והנביא (and the prophet) instead of והנגע[י and המדבר סרה (who utters rebellion) and instead of המדבר שבה (?), the further attempt to 'insert' these words into 4Q376 cannot be proved, even if these texts have words and subjects in common. In the next section of 4Q376 there is a change of subject, with reference to the prince being in a military camp and another section referring to his going to besiege a city. All this shows that the document covers different subjects, and gives no proof that it is a continuation of 4Q375. As for 1Q29, it contains several idioms which resemble the text of 4Q375, but there are also connections between it and 4Q376, so I do not accept it as a text which can solve the problems of 4Q375.

The Date of 4Q375 and its Situation

According to this examination 4Q375 is a text dated to around the Hasmonean Period. This date is reached by the paleographical (which gives a *terminus ad quem*) as well as by the linguistic and ideological examinations.[42] It may be concluded that the author of 4Q375 based his composition in fragment 1 i on Deuteronomy 13 and 17, and in fragment 1 ii on Leviticus 16. The gaps are filled with his independent writing. Such a method can reveal the time of composition. The phrases which give indications about the author, the date and the society are:

'השבט [אשר] הואה ממנו'

1i (5) 'the tribe [(6) which] he comes from'

'ובאתה...לפני [ה]כהן המשיח'

1i (7) 'then thou shalt come...before [(9) the] anointed priest'

'שמן המשיחה'

1i (9) 'the oil of anointing'

'ודרש את [כול מצוות] ה'

1ii (7) 'and shall study a[ll the laws of] (8) Yahweh'

'ודרש...[הנסת]רות ממכה'

1ii (7) 'and shall study...those laws that have been con]cealed from thee'

---

42. See Strugnell's proofs in his article, pp. 224-26.

These linguistic proofs, together with the ideological ones (including the author's behaviour regarding the use of divine names), enable a clear conclusion regarding the origin of the document as stemming from the Sect of the Judaean Desert to be reached.

The main innovations in 4Q375 when compared to the biblical sources are: 1. An appeal against an explicit law of the Pentateuch, well known by the Sect because they cite it in the same document; and 2. A demand to arrange a special ceremony which resembles the ritual of the Day of Atonement in order to solve the complicated case. Such an appeal against a law cannot be found in the Bible, the closest incident being about the widow from Theqoa in 2 Samuel 14. That woman tells David about her family's affairs where during a quarrel one of her sons killed his brother, and now the family asks that the murderer be executed, 'Give up the man who struck his brother, that we may kill him for the life of his brother whom he slew and so we[43] would destroy the heir also. Thus they would quench my coal which is left, and leave to my husband neither name nor remnant upon the face of the earth' (v. 7). David states as a judge-king, 'Go to your house, and I will give orders concerning you' (v. 8), and after a second request of the widow, 'and my son be not destroyed' (v. 11), he restates, 'As the Lord lives, not one hair of your son shall fall to the ground'. So, despite the fact that the case calls for the execution of the murderer, David frees the evildoer from any kind of punishment. Even if the case were deemed to fall under the law of unintentional homicide, David's decision does not meet the demands of Exod. 21.13 or the like.

It is impossible to say whether in David's time the laws of homicide did not exist—some of the laws were of early date. One very ancient statement speaks against manslaughter from a religious point of view, 'Whoever sheds the blood of man his blood shall be shed, for God made man in his own image' (Gen. 9.6). Therefore the previous ideas about David's action must be returned to with David acting as an authority who can pardon any convicted person. In 4Q375 such authority is given to the high priest who comes to his decision only after conducting a unique ritual. His authority is limited and dependent on the Highest Authority.

Another case which is worth mentioning is the affair of Gib'ah. An inhabitant of that town tortured to death the concubine of the guest of

---

43. See Brin, 'Working Methods of Biblical Translators and their Relevance in Establishing the Text', *Tarbiz* 57 (1988), pp. 445-49 [in Hebrew].

one of the inhabitants of the town. The entire nation asked the inhabitants of Gib'ah to surrender the evildoers in order to punish them (Judg. 20.13). However, the Benjaminites refused and therefore Israel declared war against that tribe.

In that case as in 4Q375 the tribe defends a person (or persons) who are condemned to die in accordance with the law that specifies a death penalty for this crime. However, in 4Q375 the nation is asked to bring the case, '[(8) t]o the place which thy God shall choose' in order to solve the problem using an extraordinary ceremony to request God's help for this terrible event. On the other hand, in Judges 20 the people ask the high priest (Pinchas son of El'azar) to give God's decision. In the continuation Pinchas provides God's announcement regarding their success against the rebellious tribe. So in spite of some resemblance the matters are different.

The Reasons for the Introducing the Case in 4Q375

It may be unclear why the author dealt with this case in 4Q375. As I have shown elsewhere, the Sect dealt with the issue of prophecy intensively.[44] There is no doubt that they waited for the reappearance of prophets. See, for example, 1QS 9.11, 'until there shall come the prophet and the messiahs of Aaron and Israel'. Additional proof comes from the fact that they studied the law of prophecy of Deuteronomy 18 in two documents from cave 4 (4Q175 1.5-8. For another version, see 4Q158, VI l. 6-10).

This text introduces the issue of the seducer prophet on the basis of Deuteronomy 13 with an innovation regarding the option of an appeal given to the tribe, whose prophet stands at the center of the crisis. The tribe's excuse refers to his being a true prophet, (6) 'for he is righteous (or truthful), a [(7) fai]thful prophet is he'. As I have said, they do not deny the particular accusation against him, but they do say that his being right in the past defends his present deeds. Thus for such as he, even present deeds may be explained by saying that what he has done was part of his mission which will be proved in the future, as his deeds in the past have been proved. By opposing his execution they come out against the law.

Moreover, by relying on his righteousness in the past the law of Deuteronomy 13 is opposed. The law says, 'If a prophet arises among

44. See Brin, 'Biblical Prophecy'.

you or a dreamer of dreams, *and gives you a sign or a wonder, and the sign or wonder which he tells you comes to pass*' (vv. 1-2; Heb. 2-3). This biblical law speaks clearly about a *faithful* prophet, one whose former predictions have been found to be fulfilled, but even so, the lawgiver warns the nation, 'You shall not listen to the words of that prophet' (v. 3; Hebrew 4). It is interesting that such signs which contribute to the definition of that incident are used by the author of 4Q375 as an excuse for the protection of the prophet. The polemic against the law is found to be explicit and systematic.

As shown above, the author changes the beginning of the law regarding the prophet intentionally. He does not describe the prophet's past which had been included in the biblical law, 'and gives you a sign or a wonder, and the sign or wonder which he tells you comes to pass' (vv. 1-2; Hebrew 2-3). Even this change is significant, because he needs this feature for the *defense* of the prophet, spoken out by the tribe. This kind of defense would have been avoided if he had copied the law as it is in the Bible.[45]

Why does the author protect that seducer prophet through the 'tribe'? Added to this is the fact that the phrases justifying the prophet, (6) 'for he is righteous (or truthful), a [(7) fai]thful prophet is he' suit the language of the late period of the Second Commonwealth. Thus using this justification shows the author's positive attitude toward that prophet. The fact that the document is incomplete does not give an opportunity to know the priest's decision regarding the prophet precisely. However, it may be that as a result of the high priest's ceremony the incident ends with the official announcement of the prophet's innocence. If this is so then the historical background of this 'law' means that the prophet may represent one of the leaders of the Sect, perhaps this a polemical issue against Jerusalem's leaders.

It is known that Jerusalem did not recognize the Sect's leaders (see 4Qp Hos and 1Qp Hab). So the document represents a polemic against such a spiritual leader, defined by Jerusalem as a seducer prophet, but whom the Sect evaluated positively. That polemic has been defined in a judicial style. By doing this the author has no hesitation about composing two wordings against an explicit biblical law: 1. In the definition of the prophet the issue of the sign of wonder (vv. 1-2, Heb. 2-3) that the prophet has given in the past is omitted, as it is needed as a

---

45. Regarding other changes in elaborating this law see above.

justification, instead of as a part of the definition; and 2. A new law was invented which says that in such cases there is justification for an appeal by the circle close to the prophet-'tribe' in the language of the author, which may be a term used for the Sect itself, (5) 'the tribe [(6) which] he comes from'. The authority for a final decision was ascribed to the high priest who can come to the godly verdict only after conducting a unique ceremony.

BIBLIOGRAPHY ON 4QTGLEV (4Q156)

Loren T. Stuckenbruck

In 1977 J.T. Milik published two Aramaic fragments (4Q156) identified as belonging either to a targum of the Pentateuch or to a liturgical work that happened to include a targumic translation. The fragments, each of which preserve on parts of 7 lines an Aramaic version of the *Yom Kippurim* ritual in Lev. 16.12-15 and 18-21, have been the subject of considerable discussion ever since.

The extent of this discussion clearly demonstrates that the importance of these fragments is disproportionate to their relatively minute size and poor state of preservation. In addition to the Job Targum materials found at Qumran (11QTgJob, 4QTgJob), 4QTgLev provides, for the first time, clear evidence for the existence of written targums before the common era. Indeed, the fragments offer the earliest textual witness for an Aramaic translation of the Pentateuch. Thus the significance of 4QTgLev for targumic and NT studies may be briefly summarized as follows: In analysis of Jewish traditions from the Second Temple period, the pertinence of targumic traditions can no longer be categorically dismissed. A comparison of the later targums with 4QTgLev reveals, in addition to independent readings, instances of exclusive correspondence to either Onkelos or Neofiti I. Though until now the existing targumic materials (Onkelos, Jonathan, Neofiti 1, Samaritan Targum) can, on linguistic grounds, be dated to the Amoraic period at the earliest, now one must reckon with the existence of an even earlier translation tradition that either developed into or was independent from the later ones. A full discussion and comparison of 4QTgLev and corresponding targumic passages is forthcoming *ad loc* in the Princeton Theological Seminary Dead Sea Scrolls.

For the sake of convenience, the bibliography below is divided into five main groups: (1) the *editio princeps*; (2) notices previous to the publication of 4QTgLev; (3) reviews of the *editio princeps*; (4) recent references to the fragments; and (5) major recent treatments.

1. *Editio Princeps*

Milik, J.T. *Qumran Grotte II 4: Tefillin, Mezuzot et Targums (4Q128-157)* (Discoveries in the Judaean Desert, 6; Oxford: Clarendon Press, 1977), pp. 86-89 and Plate XXVIII.

2. *Notices Previous to Publication*

Diez Macho, A., 'La lengua hablada por Jesucristo', *Oriens antiquus* 2 (1963), pp. 96-132 (107).
—'Targum', in *Enciclopedia de la Biblia* (6 vols.; Barcelona: Ediciones Garriga, 1965), VI, pp. 865-81 (867).
—(ed.) *Neophyti I: Targum Palestinense MS de la Biblioteca Vaticana* (vols. 1-6; Madrid-Barcelona: Consejo Superior de Investigaciones Cientificas, 1968–1979), I, p. 77*; 3, p. 32*.
Fitzmyer, J.A., 'Some Observations on the Targum of Job from Qumran Cave 11', *CBQ* 36 (1974), pp. 503-24 (510-11, n.'s 29, 30).
Le Déaut, R., *Introduction à la litterature targumique: Premiere partie* (Rome: Pontifical Biblical Institute, 1966), pp. 64-65.
McNamara, M.J., *Targum and Testament* (Shannon: Irish University Press, 1968), p. 66.
—'Targums', in *IDBSup* (Nashville: Abingdon Press, 1976), pp. 856-61, esp. p. 857.
Milik, J.T., *Ten Years of Discovery in the Wilderness of Judaea* (trans. J. Strugnell; SBT, 26; Naperville, IL: Allenson, 1959), p. 31.
Muñoz Leon, D., *Dios-Palabra. Memra en los Targumim del Pentateuco* (Institucion San Jeronimo, 4; Granada: Santa Rita–Monachil, 1974), pp. 576-77.

3. *Reviews*

Ben-Hayyim, Z., 'יִשִׁיַּס נֹס חֲדָשִׁים מִן צְפוּנֵי מִדְבַּר יְהוּדָה', *Leshonenu* 42 (1978), pp. 278-93.
Fitzmyer, J.A., Review of *Qumran Grotte 4 II: Tefillin, Mezuzot et Targums (4Q128-4Q157)*, ed. R. de Vaux and J.T. Milik. *TS* 39 (1978), pp. 158-60.
Licht, J., Review of *Qumran Grotte 4 II: Tefillin, Mezuzot et Targums (4Q128-4Q157)*, ed. R. de Vaux and J.T. Milik. *Israel Exploration Quarterly* 28 (1978), pp. 134-36.
Martinez, F.G., 'Estudios Qumránicos 1975–1985: Panorama Critico (II)'. *EstBib* 45 (1987), pp. 361-402, esp. pp. 399-401.
Puech, E., Review of *Qumran Grotte 4 II: Tefillin, Mezuzot et Targums (4Q128-4Q157)*, ed. R. de Vaux and J.T. Milik, *RB* 86 (1979), pp. 275-77.
Schiffman, L.H., Review of *Qumran Grotte 4 II: Tefillin, Mezuzot et Targums (4Q128-4Q157)*, ed. R. de Vaux and J.T. Milik, *JAOS* 100 (1980), pp. 170-72.
Vermes, G., Review of *Qumran Grotte 4 II: Tefillin, Mezuzot et Targums (4Q128-4Q157)*, ed. R. de Vaux and J.T. Milik, *JJS* 29 (1978), pp. 193-94.

4. *Recent References*

Fitzmyer, J.A., 'The Languages of Palestine in the First Century A.D.', in *A Wandering Aramean: Collected Aramaic Essays* (SBL Monograph Series, 25; Chico, California: Scholars Press, 1979), pp. 29-56 (42).

Forestell, J.T., *Targumic Traditions and the New Testament* (SBL Aramaic Studies, 4; Chico, California: Scholars Press, 1979), p. 1.

Hayward, R., *Divine Name and Presence: The Memra* (Oxford Centre for Postgraduate Hebrew Studies; Totowa, New Jersey: Allanheld, Osmun, 1981), p. 140 n. 7.

McNamara, M., *Intertestamental Literature* (Wilmington, DE: Michael Glazier, 1983), p. 268.

— *Palestinian Judaism and the New Testament* (Good News Studies, 4; Michael Glazier, 1983), p. 206.

E. Schürer, *The History of the Jewish People in the Age of Jesus Christ (175 BC-AD 135)* (rev. and ed. G. Vermes, F. Millar and M. Black; 3 vols.; Edinburgh: T. & T. Clark, 1973–1987), I, p. 105; III, p. 380 n.

5. *Major Treatments*

Angerstorfer, A., 'Ist 4QTgLev des Menetekel der neueren Targumforschung?', *Biblische Notizen* 15 (1981), pp. 55-75.

Beyer, K., *Die Aramäischen Texte vom Toten Meer* (Göttingen: Vandenhoeck & Ruprecht, 1984), pp. 278-80.

Fitzmyer, J.A., 'The Targum of Leviticus from Qumran Cave 4', *Maarav* 1/1 (1978), pp. 5-23.

Kasher, M.M., 'Appendix', in *Qumran Grotte 4 II* (ed. R. de Vaux and J.T. Milik; Discoveries in the Judaean Desert, 6; Oxford: Clarendon Press, 1977), pp. 92-93.

[May, 1990]

SOME REMARKS ON THE APOCRYPHAL PSALM 155
(11QPsª COLUMN 24)

Elisha Qimron

The Hebrew original of the Apocryphal (Syriac) Psalm 155 has been found in the Psalms scroll from Qumran cave eleven.[1] The editor of this scroll has done an excellent job of reading and interpreting this psalm and other scholars have also made contributions to its interpretation.[2] The following remarks attempt to give a new interpretation of several words (or passages) which, in my opinion, have been misunderstood.

In line 6, the editor reads גמולי הרע ישיב ממני דין האמת taking ישיב as a causitive jussive verb whose subject is דין האמת. It has, however, been claimed that the words דין האמת do not belong to this sentence but to the following one; they then begin a new strophe initiating with the letter *daleth* (the fourth strophe of the acrosticon).[3] The verb ישיב seemingly can still be taken as causitive jussive verb with God as its subject. This, however, is not correct for two reasons: (1) in requests directed to God, when He is the subject, the second person imperative rather than the third person jussive is used.[4] This is the case in this psalm in particular and in biblical Hebrew in general; (2) the *hifil* jussive in Qumran Hebrew and in biblical Hebrew is ישב (= דשֵׁב) rather than ישיב.[5] One therefore

1. J.A. Sanders, *The Psalms Scroll of Qumran Cave 11 (11QPsª)* (DJD 4; Oxford, Oxford University Press, 1965), p. 70 (col. 24).

2. For an extensive bibliography see J. Magne, 'Recherches sur les psaumes 151, 154 et 155', *RevQ* 8 (1972–75), pp. 503-507; *idem*, 'Le psaume 155', *RevQ* 9 (1977–78), pp. 103-11; and P. Auffret, 'Structure littéraire et interprétation du psaume 155 de la grotte 11 de Qumran', *RevQ* 9 (1977–78), pp. 323-56. See also H.F. Van Rooy, 'Psalm 155', *RevQ* 16 (1993), pp. 109-22.

3. A. Hurviz, 'Observations on the Language of the Third Apocryphal Psalm from Qumran', *RevQ* 5 (1964–65), p. 227 n. 6.

4. Auffret, 'Structure', p. 333 suggests reading הָשֵׁב.

5. See for example: אל ימש 1QS 6.3,6; אל חשב 1QH 16.18 and cf. תהי, תחי (but תעזה) in our scroll (Sanders, *Psalms Scroll*, p. 35), תהייא (Sanders, p. 26), יהי (Sanders, p. 24).

should read ישוב ממני (= דשב), the subject being גמולי הרע 'let the rewards of wickedness be removed from me'. The *waw* is also preferable materially, judging from its length.

In line 13, we find כבוד אתה יהוה. Sanders took כבוד as the noun כָּבוֹד 'honor', but the context requires an adjective instead, as also suggested by the Syriac translation כביר. I therefore suggest that the word be read as a passive participle of *qal* כָּבוּד 'mighty'.[6] The word כָּבוּד occurs several times in the Dead Sea Scrolls and apparently existed also in biblical Hebrew. Here is the evidence which I have found:

1. I have already suggested to read in the Songs of the Sabbath Sacrifice כְּבוּדֵי instead of the editor's (עם בינות דעת כבודי אלוהים) כְּבוּדֵי '...those honored by God'; 4Q400 1 I 6,[7] and have mentioned other places where the word occurs (e.g. Ezek. 23.41);[8]

2. כָּבוּד meaning 'mighty' apparently occurs in 1QIs[a] 16.14 for כביר in the MT. Kutscher has explained that the scribe of the scroll substituted a more common word for the original כביר, which was a rare word in Hebrew.[9] But the word כביר was known to the Jews of the period from Aramaic, and is the Syriac translation of כבוד in our psalm. Why would the scribe have substituted a word which hardly fits the context for a well-known word which fits the context well (assuming with Kutscher that he meant the word כָּבוֹד 'honor')? Possibly כָּבִיר is a graphical substitution of כָּבוּד with a similar meaning. In this case כָּבוּד is the *lectio deficilior*;

3. There are apparently other passages in which the word כָּבוֹד has been wrongly read for כָּבוּד. This may be the case in the phrases בשולחן כבוד (1QM 2.6), עם כבוד (4Q405 20 II 21-22), and מי בכבודי

---

6. For כָּבוֹד = 'might', see for example Ps. 24.7-10, 1QM 12.10, 19.1.

7. E. Qimron, 'A Review Article of Songs of the Sabbath Sacrifice: A Critical Edition by Carol Newsom', *HTR* 79 (1986), pp. 358-59.

8. See commentators. The Tiberian vocalization can be taken as the feminine of the adjective כָּבֵד—see W. Gesenius: Friedrich Christian Wilhelm Vogel, *Neues hebräisch-deutsches Handwörterbuch über das Alte Testament* (Leipzig, 1815), p. 282; F. Brown, S.R. Driver and C.A. Briggs, *A Hebrew and English Lexicon of the Old Testament* (Oxford: Clarendon Press, 1907), p. 458, s.v. I [כָּבוֹד]. For כְּבוּדָה in Medieval Hebrew, see Ben Yehuda, V, p. 2230, s.v. כְּבֻדָּה.

9. E.Y. Kutscher, *The Language and Linguistic Background of the Isaiah Scroll (1QIsa[a])* (Leiden: Brill, 1973), p. 246.

ידמה לי. 'who among my mighty ones is like me' (4Q491 11.15);[10]

4. The word כבוד 'great, mighty' occurs also in a Samaritan *piyut*.[11] Ben Ḥayyim discerned the exact meaning and took the form transmitted in the Samaritan pronunciation *kabod* as representing כָּבוֹד. Yet *kabod* may also represent כָּבוּד (the *ū* being pronounced *o* in a closed syllable);

5. Finally, the word כָּבוּד has been known to the ancient Greek (and Latin) translators.[12] The Septuagint (and the Vulgate) render Ps. 4.3 עד מה לכלמה as עד מה כבודי לב (ἕως πότε βαρυκάρδιοι ἵνα τι; *usquequo gravis corde*). Aquila (and Hieronimus) render (לכלמה) כְּבוּדִי (עד מה) (οἱ ἔνδοξοι μου; *incliti mei*).

The existence of the word כָּבוּד in Hebrew is well established. However, the word has sometimes been read as כָּבוֹד, which is more common.[13]

In line 14 is found שלמה שאלתי 'fulfill my request!'. Most scholars have failed to recognize that שלמה is a lengthened imperative (= שַׁלְּמָה).[14] They took it either as a perfect or as a participle. This however is inconsistent with the rest of the psalm which has requests from God rather than statements. Hurvitz dealt with the combination שאלה + שלם, and supplied parallel expressions, but failed to find this combination elsewhere. I found it once in Aramaic, in the Targum to Ps. 20.6: ישלים ה כולהון שילתך.

10. *DJD*, VII, p. 27.

11. Z. Ben Ḥayyim, *The Literary and Oral Tradition of Hebrew and Aramaic Amongst the Samaritans*, IIIb (Jerusalem: The Academy of the Hebrew Language, 1967), p. 127 [Hebrew].

12. cf. A. Geiger, המקרא ותרגומיו (Jerusalem, 1972), p. 206.

13. The same thing has happened with the word טָהוּר. Thus for example, in the combination טהור בכור (1QM 5.11), טהור was taken by most commentators as טָהוֹר. But a few commentators have interpreted correctly as a passive participle of *qal* (= טָהוּר)—see B. Jongeling, *Le Rouleau de la Guerre des manuscrits de Qumran* (Assen: Van Gorcum, 1962), p. 162). Should קדושי ברית (1QM 10.11) be read קְדוּשֵׁי?

14. The exception is J.H. Charlesworth and J.A. Sanders, in *The Old Testament Pseudepigrapha* (ed. J.H. Charlesworth; New York: Doubleday, 1985), II, p. 622.

HOW DID THE RULE OF THE COMMUNITY OBTAIN ITS FINAL SHAPE? A REVIEW OF SCHOLARLY RESEARCH

Robert A.J. Gagnon

In reviewing the state of research on the question of the literary development of the Rule of the Community, primary attention will be given to the proposals of Guilbert and Murphy-O'Connor since the work of each has constituted the primary starting-point (or at least foil!) for two fundamentally different approaches to the literary history of the Rule. Attention will also be given to the views of other scholars (primarily Leaney, Dupont-Sommer, Knibb, Dimant, Puech, and Milik), particularly at points where valid criticisms of the work of Guilbert and Murphy-O'Connor can be made. In the interests of presenting the state of research, my own analysis will be primarily parenthetical in nature. The incompleteness of the data presently available (cf. below on 4QS), combined with the fact that scholarly research on the subject is still in its early stages, will permit few judgments to be inscribed in stone. Yet it is hoped that these discussions will at least make clear the areas still in dispute and thereby in need of further investigation.

The Rule of the Community (סרך היחד, cf. the 4QS[a] fragment which fills in the lacuna of the first line of 1QS)[1] is largely extant in a manuscript from Cave 1 (1QS). As is well known, Cross characterizes its script as 'Hasmonean semi-formal' and dates the manuscript to 100–75 BCE.[2] Milik gives it a date of 125–100 BCE.[3] Given the occasional

---

1. Note also the title of the work written on the outside of 1QS by a later hand: [ ] סר]ך היחד ומן].

2. F.M. Cross, 'Introduction', in *Scrolls from Qumrân Cave I* (Jerusalem: Albright Institute of Archaeological Research and the Shrine of the Book, 1974), p. 4. Cf. also Cross, 'The Development of the Jewish Scripts', in *The Bible and the Ancient Near East: Essays in Honor of W.F. Albright* (ed. G.E. Wright; New York: Doubleday, 1961), pp. 133-202.

3. J.T. Milik, 'Milki-Sedeq et Milki-Resha dans les anciens écrits juifs et chrétiens', *JJS* 23 (1972), p. 135.

blanks, copyist's mistakes, and extensive corrections in 1QS (especially in cols. 7–8), it is probable that the scribe was working from an earlier, damaged manuscript.[4] In addition to 1QS, Milik has published two late fragments from a cave 5 manuscript (5Q11) which overlap with a part of 1QS 2.4-7, 12-14.[5] More important is Milik's report on a sequence of fragmentary manuscripts from cave 4 which he designates 4QS[a-j] and characterizes as having 'a purer text than that of 1QS'.[6] According to Milik, the text in 1QS 5 is antedated by a 'shorter and more intelligible' form in 4QS[b, d, g].[7] 4QS[e], 'the oldest manuscript' of the Rule,[8] not only lacks the extensive superlinear texts of 1QS 8.10-13 but also follows 'by the hand of Moses' in 1QS 8.15a with 'These are the precepts...' in 1QS 9.12 (thereby omitting everything in 8.15b–9.11, including the reference to 'the Messiahs of Aaron and Israel' in 9.11).[9] Paleography and textual criticism (not to mention literary criticism, cf. below) thus provide us with a *terminus ante quem* for the composition of the autograph of no later than 100 BCE 'to permit the textual development and parenetic expansions' found in the texts.[10] It is also clear that one cannot simply identify 1QS with 'the Rule'; it should be regarded rather as a significant witness to an early stage in the Rule's literary history.[11]

As for the literary history of the Rule, two early responses stake out the extreme options. H.E. Del Medico called the Rule 'un amalgame de

---

4. Cross, *Scrolls from Qumrân*, p. 4.

5. M. Baillet, J.T. Milik and R. de Vaux, *Les 'Petites Grottes' de Qumrân* (DJD, 3; Oxford: Clarendon Press, 1962), p. 180. Note also 5Q13 which is related to 1QS 3.4-5.

6. J.T. Milik, *Ten Years of Discovery in the Wilderness of Judaea* (SBT, 26; Naperville, IL: Allenson, 1959), p. 37.

7. J.T. Milik, 'Recension de Wernberg-Møller, *The Manual of Discipline*', *RB* 67 (1960), p. 412. Cf. also 'Le Travail d'édition des manuscrits du Désert de Qumran', *RB* 63 (1956), p. 61, where Milik cites a different opening line in two 4QS fragments corresponding to 1QS 5.1: instead of 'and this is the rule for the men of the community who freely devote themselves...', the 4QS fragments read 'exposition [מדרש] for the *maskîl* regarding the men of the Torah who freely devote themselves...'.

8. Milik, *Ten Years*, p. 123.

9. Milik, 'Recension', p. 413. Moreover, 1QS 8.13-14, 25-27 are abbreviated in other 4QS fragments. For other variants from the 4QS mss., see 'Recension', pp. 412-15.

10. F.M. Cross, *The Ancient Library of Qumran and Modern Biblical Studies* (rev. edn; Grand Rapids: Baker, 1961), p. 121.

11. I am grateful to J.H. Charlesworth for emphasizing this point in oral discussion.

fragments, les plus disparates, que les copistes ne se sont même pas donné la peine de grouper de façon logique'.[12] He postulated five major sources which the compiler of the Rule arbitrarily divided into thirty fragments and scattered haphazardly throughout the work. Fortunately, Del Medico was able to restore for us the original order!

The opposite position was taken by Pierre Guilbert who treated Del Medico's 'patchwork hypothesis' as a last resort which should be adopted only after all attempts to seek out a text's own inner logic had been exhausted.[13] Guilbert sought 'données objectives' from three indices in 1QS:

1. the transparent introductory formulas contained in the text itself, for example, those addressed 'to the *maskîl*' in 1.1 (?); 3.13; 5.1 [in 4QS ms.]; 9.12, 21; those which begin with a demonstrative subject 'this is' or 'these are' as in 4.2; 5.1, 7; 6.8, 24; 8.20; 9.12, 21; and those which begin with the preposition ב followed by an infinitive construct as in 1.18; 8.4, 12; 9.3);

2. paragraph indentations and blank spaces interspersed throughout the text of 1QS by the copyist, sometimes coinciding with the introductory formulas (for example, 3.13; 5.1; 6.24; 9.12), sometimes not (for example, 1.21; 2.4, 11);

3. and signs on the right-hand margins of the texts (usually 'hooks', sometimes more complicated symbols) inserted later as benchmarks for cutting up the text into recognizable units, as in 3.18; 7.25; 11.15.

With regard to the last two criteria, Guilbert is aware that at times the scribal indicators of new pericopes are badly placed (5.13; 6.10; 9.19)[14]

---

12. H.E. Del Medico, *L'énigme des manuscrits de la Mer Morte* (Paris: Plon, 1957), p. 160.

13. P. Guilbert, 'Le plan de la Règle de la Communauté', *RevQ* 1 (1959), pp. 323-44. Cf. also his commentary on the Rule in J. Carmignac *et al.*, *Les Textes de Qumran* (2 vols.; Paris: Letouzey et Ané, 1961, 1963), I, pp. 11-80, especially the introduction on pp. 11-17. 'Les différences [en style] que l'on peut observer ici ou là s'expliquent suffisamment par la variété de genre littéraire, par la diversité des objectifs poursuivis par l'auteur et par la distinction des sujets traités' (pp. 11-12).

14. Often blank spaces are nothing more than the remnants of an erasure (e.g., 11.9) or a sign of a damaged *Vorlage* (frequently in cols. 7-8). In these instances they have nothing to do with markings off pericopes (Guilbert, 'Le plan', p. 325). Cf. Guilbert, 'Deux écritures dans les colonnes VII et VIII de la Règle de la Communauté', *RevQ* 1 (1958), pp. 199-212.

and at best tells us only how later readers divided up the text. Yet he regards them as more 'objective' than present-day reconstructions.

On the basis of these indicators, Guilbert divides the literary structure of the Rule into six sections, with a general introduction opening the document in 1.1-15. The first section deals with 'the entry into the covenant' (1.16–3.12) and divides along the lines of a prolegomena (1.16-18), the ritual of the covenant entry ceremony (1.18–2.18), and rules regarding covenant entrance (2.19–3.12) in terms of the order of precedence in the ceremony (2.19-23) and the sincerity of the converts (2.24–3.12). Scanning the texts and commentaries by Dupont-Sommer, Vermes, Leaney, and Knibb,[15] there seems to be a scholarly consensus about this outline; however, they divide the text not at 2.24 but at 2.25b ('and no one who refuses to enter [into the covenant of Go]d...'). The second major section treats the doctrine of the two spirits (3.13–4.26) and is organized by way of introductory summary (3.13-15a) and descriptions of the two kinds of spirits which divide humanity into two camps under either of two angels (3.15b–4.1), the two 'ways' and 'visitations' of divine recompense which characterize these two spirits (4.2-14), and the eschatological destinies of the two spirits (4.15-26). Again, there is general consensus on the correctness of this outline from a literary point of view.[16]

15. A. Dupont-Sommer, *The Essene Writings from Qumran* (Gloucester: Peter Smith, [1961] repr. 1973); G. Vermes, *The Dead Sea Scrolls in English* (3rd edn; New York: Penguin, 1987); A.R.C. Leaney, *The Rule of Qumran and Its Meaning* (Philadelphia: Westminster, 1966); and Michael A. Knibb, *The Qumran Community* (Cambridge: Cambridge University Press, 1987). Cf. also D. Dimant, 'Qumran Sectarian Literature', *Jewish Writings of the Second Temple Period* (CRINT 2/2; Philadelphia: Fortress, 1984), pp. 483-550, esp. pp. 497-503. Dimant arranges 1.16–2.25 in a chiastic structure (p. 500 n. 84). Surprisingly, the first modern commentary on the Rule, that of P. Wernberg-Møller (*The Manual of Discipline* [Grand Rapids: Eerdmans, 1957]), makes no attempt to outline its literary structure.

16. The parameters of this section are especially clear given the opening formula in 3.13 ('For the *maskîl* to instruct and to teach all the children of light') and the continuous instruction concerning the two spirits until the clear introductory formula in 5.1. Guilbert also points to 4.23b-26 as forming an *inclusio* with 3.15-18; to an extent this is true, although it also recapitulates the discussion in 4.15-18a (cf. Murphy-O'Connor below). For detailed studies of this section, see: J. Licht, 'An Analysis of the Treatise of the Two Spirits in DSD', *Scripta Hierosolymitana* 4 (1958), pp. 88-100; P. Wernberg-Møller, 'A Reconsideration of the Two Spirits in the Rule of the Community 1QSerek III, 13-IV, 26', *RevQ* 3 (1961), pp. 413-41; M. Treves, 'The Two Spirits in the Rule of the Community', *RevQ* 3 (1962), pp. 449-

Guilbert entitles the third major section 'the internal regulation of the community' (5.1–7.25).[17] He distinguishes three subheadings: 'general and personal rules' (5.1–6.8a); 'general rules of the session of the Many' (6.8b–23); and 'the penitential code' (6.24–7.25). The first subsection (5.1–6.8a) is a heterogeneous collection of general rules and, consequently, Guilbert's further subdivisions of 5.1-2a, 2b-7a, 7b-10a, 10a-20a are as credible as others.[18] The second subsection (6.8b-23), which is clearly set off in 1QS by an introductory formula הזה הסרך למושב הרבים), blank space, and marginal hook at 6.8b, neatly divides by content into a discussion of pecking order during formal community sessions (6.8b-13a) and a detailed explanation of the (2-year plus) procedure by which a pledge moves to the status of full membership (6.13b-23). The penal code (6.24–7.25)[19] is a miscellaneous listing of prescribed penalties for community infractions. It should be noted here that while columns 5–7 can be ordered under various headings, this is not the same as asserting an orderly sequence.[20]

The fourth section, which Guilbert defines as 8.1–9.11 and calls

---

62; and Peter von der Osten-Sacken, *Gott und Belial: Traditionsgeschichtliche Untersuchungen zum Dualismus in den Texten aus Qumran* (SUNT, 6; Göttingen: Vandenhoeck & Ruprecht, 1969), pp. 17-27.

17. Cf. other designations for this section: 'the common life' (Knibb), 'purpose and way of life of the community' (Leaney), and 'the life of the community' (Dimant).

18. My own characterization of the loose structure of 5.1-6–6.8a is as follows. 5.1-7a describes the basic obligations of community members (separatism, adherence to the community's authority, a righteous life which preserves a holy remnant in Israel). 5.7b-20a epitomizes the covenant oath as a pledge to: (1) obey the Torah as interpreted by the community; and (2) separate from 'the people of injustice' (Guilbert [cf. Knibb] divides 5.7b-20a at 5.10b, but the division could just as well be made at 5.11b [cf. Vermes, Dupont-Sommer]). 5.20b–6.8a is a random collection of instructions for community interactions: yearly ranking and examination of members (5.20b-24); rules for rebuking other community members (5.25–6.1b); and rules for promoting communal solidarity for groups of 10 or more in matters of property, eating, prayer, and study (6.1c-8a).

19. This section is also clearly set off in 1QS by the formula (ואלה המשפטים אשר ישפטו בם במדרש יחד על פי הדברים), paragraph indentation, and marginal hook at 6.24. Both Leaney and Dimant cordon off the penal code as a separate major section of the Rule.

20. For example, there is no reason why the discussion of stages of membership (6.13b-23) should not be more closely tied to the discussion of the entry oath (5.7b-20).

'Dernier degré d'implantation de la Communauté: La vie au désert',[21] is the most difficult section for Guilbert's theory of the unity of the Rule. In addition to the numerous indices (the threefold repetition of the formula בהיות אלה בישראל [8.4, 12; 9.3];[22] and the frequent blank spaces [8.5, 11; 9.1, 18], indentations [8.20; 9.3], and marginal hooks [8.4, 10, 12, 19; 9.3, 5, 11]), not to mention supralinear texts and divergences from 4QS manuscripts, there are the problems of doublets regarding penitential rules (8.16–9.2),[23] the complete authority given to the priests (9.7; contrast 5.2-3, 9 in which 'the sons of Zadok' share rule with 'the multitude of the men of the community'), and the presence of distinctive terminology (especially the designation 'men of holiness' rather than 'men of the community' used elsewhere in the Rule. Guilbert attempts to account for these differences by postulating 'une réalité différente' for 8.1–9.11: whereas the rest of the Rule refers to Essene life in the villages of Israel, 8.1–9.11 addresses only the founding of the monastic community at Qumran (cf. 8.13-14: 'they will separate from the habitation of the people of injustice in order to go into the desert').

According to Guilbert, the section has two parts: the definition and aims of this restricted community at Qumran which serves as an Israel in microcosm (8.1-16a; further subdivided into lines 1-4a, 4b-8a, 8b-12a, 12b-16a); and the regulations for this desert community (8.16b–9.11; further subdivided into 8.16b-19; 8.20–9.2; 9.3-11). No consensus seems to exist over whether the instructions for the *maskîl* in 9.12-26 should be included in the fourth major section (Leaney, Knibb; cf. Murphy-O'Connor) or seen as a distinct unit of its own (Dimant, Milik) or conjoined with the final hymn (Guilbert). Formulaic introductions indicate clear breaks in the text at 8.1 ('in the council of the community, 12 men and 3 priests'), 4b ('when these are in Israel'), 12a ('when these are in Israel'[24]), 16b ('and everyone from the men of the covenant of

---

21. Cf. 'constitution of the pioneer community' (Leaney); and 'program for a new community' (Knibb, for 8.1–9.26); 'the model community' (Dimant).

22. The phrase can be translated either as 'when these [men of holiness] are [in place] in Israel' (cf. Wernberg-Møller, Leaney, Knibb) or 'when these [things] come to pass in Israel' (Dupont-Sommer, Guilbert).

23. See esp. 8.20: ואלה המשפטים אשר ילכו בם אנשי התמים קודש איש את רעהו ('and these are the rules in which the men of perfect holiness shall walk, one with another'). Cf. the more lengthy and detailed description of specific infractions and punishments in 6.24–7.25, introduced also by the formula…ואלה המשפטים (6.24).

24. 1QS reads ובהיות אלה ליחד בישראל ('and when these become a [part of the?] Community in Israel'), where ליחד is written above the line. Neither 4QS[d] nor 4QS[e]

the community'[25]), 20 ('and these are the rules'); 9.3 ('when these are in Israel'), 12 ('these are the statutes for the *maskîl*'). That each of these constitutes a new subsection is confirmed by the accompanying presence of a paragraph indentation, space, or marginal hook. Guilbert's suggestion of other minor subsections beginning in 8.8b,[26] 9.3, 5b, and 10b is more debatable.

The fifth and final section of the Rule, according to Guilbert, discusses 'rules for the personal training of new members' (9.12–11.22). This in turn consists of two primary units: the *maskîl*'s role as instructor of candidates and community members (9.12-21a, framed by marginal hook, introductory formula, and final paragraph indentation of the Rule in 9.12 and by intervening space after 'from all injustice' in 9.21a); and 'conduite pratique et éléments essentiels de cette instruction' (9.21b–11.22; note the formula in 9.21b, 'And these are the norms of behavior for the *maskîl*'), which Guilbert further breaks down into a description of what the *maskîl* should love and hate (9.21-26), the times of prayer (10.1-8), and the final hymn (10.9–11.22).[27]

The conclusion which Guilbert draws from his analysis

> is the incontestable unity of the *Rule of the Community*: unity in plan, all of whose parts develop according to an order which, though not 'cartesian', nevertheless reveals a certain logic... [There is] unity also in language, vocabulary, syntax, and style, in spite of the occasional use of different terms... [S]ince it is entirely possible to account for the text of the *Rule* in a logical way, by viewing it as a homogeneous and coherent whole, there is no need of resorting to the hypothesis of a compilation of assorted fragments... This does not mean that no borrowing could have been made by the author from pre-existing rules... But these borrowings have then been profoundly assimilated and recast to form a new whole.[28]

have the word. Strangely, 4QS[d] incorporates the word in the same phrase in 9.3 while 1QS does not include it.

25. Reading from 4QS[d] rather than 1QS ('and everyone from the men *of the community*, the covenant of the community').

26. Leaney, Dupont-Sommer, and Knibb would make a minor division not of 8.8b-12a but of 8.10b-12a. 8.10b not only receives a marginal hook in the mss. of 1QS but also seems to mark a shift in content from the idealistic role of the desert community to rules regarding probationary periods and the Interpreter's responsibilities.

27. Leaney and Dimant both begin the final major section of the 'closing hymn' at 10.1.

28. 'Le plan', pp. 343-44.

Guilbert views the whole Rule, not just columns 8–9, as written during an 'embryonic stage' of the Community's existence, before its departure into the desert and probably even before the persecution of the Teacher of Righteousness by the Wicked Priest (which Guilbert, wrongly, connects with the persecution of the Pharisees by Alexander Janneus in about 100 BCE). Guilbert even goes so far as to name the Teacher of Righteousness himself as the likely author of the entire Rule and to identify the Teacher with Judas the Essene. This hypothesis yields a tentative date for the Rule of 110 BCE.[29]

However, Guilbert's hypothesis has not won wide acceptance. Quite apart from the late dating of the Qumran sect[30] is the unlikely notion that in its earliest stages the Essenes would already have developed the kind of detailed penal codes and cultic ceremonies that we find in 1QS 1–3, 6–7. Time and again Guilbert fails to distinguish between discrete literary units in the Rule (even if arranged with some sense) and natural literary unity; the presence of the former does not prove the latter. In fact, the presence of discrete literary units tends to emphasize the fragmentary quality of the docament (not, to be sure, tiny fragments but rather major independent blocks). Moreover, Guilbert's insistence on fundamental literary unity seems to run counter to the evidence culled from the 4QS fragments which already show a different recension for 1QS 5 and the striking omission of 8.15b–9.11.[31]

Despite these problems, considerable attention has been given to Guilbert's position for two reasons. First, it represents the earliest and most significant defense of the unity of the Rule. Secondly (and more importantly), it provides one of the best discussions of the structural

---

29. Guilbert, in *Les Textes*, pp. 14-15.

30. For a summary of scholarly consensus on the subject of the dating of the Qumran community (at least in the time of John Hyrcanus [135–104 BCE], and perhaps as early as Simon [142–134 BCE] or even Jonathan [160–142 BCE]), based on archaeology and (more importantly) likely historical referents in 1QpHab and CD, see J.H. Charlesworth, 'The Origin and Subsequent History of the Authors of the Dead Sea Scrolls: Four Transitional Phases Among the Qumran Essenes', *RevQ* 10 (1980), pp. 213-33.

31. Milik (*Ten Years*, p. 96) also mentions fragments written in Herodian script which mix, in altered form, the statutes at the end of CD with texts drawn from the Rule (1QS 8.1-10; 6.24ff.). Guilbert's own work confirming the additions of a scribe 'B' to the text of 1QS seems to militate against his opposition to literary development ('Deux écritures dans les colonnes vii et viii de la *Règle de la Communauté*', *RevQ* 1 [1958], pp. 199-212).

divisions of the Rule, which any theory about the literary development of the document must take as its starting point.[32]

Although there have been dissenters, in general the trend in scholarship has been towards the kind of source critical work which Murphy-O'Connor pioneered in 1969 with 'La genèse littéraire de la *Règle de la Communauté*'.[33] Murphy-O'Connor does not want to argue that the Rule was compiled by a single person who, at a particular moment, drew together diverse traditional materials haphazardly. Rather, he sees the Rule as a product of literary 'evolution' in which an early nucleus of material was expanded over the course of four stages early in the Qumran community's development—stages which can also be correlated

32. Leaney, for example, bases his structural analysis of the Rule to a large degree on Guilbert's work (*The Rule*, p. 112).

33. Jerome Murphy-O'Connor, 'La genèse littéraire de la *Règle de la Communauté*', *RB* 76 (1969), pp. 528-49. For earlier, but vaguer treatments of the composite character of the Rule, cf. Dupont-Sommer, *Essene Writings*, pp. 69-72 (who simply asserts that the work is 'composite' and suggests, on the basis of the Rule's popularity at Qumran, the probable writing of some portion of the document during the Righteous Teacher's lifetime [cf. the mention of retreat into the desert in 8.12-14; 9.19-20], and the conspicuous absence of any explicit mention of the Teacher, that the Teacher is himself the author of the 'basic recension from which [the present recension] stems'); Johann Maier, *Die Texte vom Toten Meer*, I, (Munich: Reinhardt, 1960), p. 21; J. Becker, *Das Heil Gottes* (Göttingen: Vandenhoeck & Ruprecht, 1964), pp. 39-42; A.-M. Denis, 'Évolution de structures dans la secte de Qumran', in *Aux origines de l'Église* (RechBib, 7; Bruges: Desclée, 1964), esp. pp. 40-44 (arguing that 8.10b-12; 8.16–9.2 were interpolations); and Leaney, *The Rule*, pp. 113-16. E.F. Sutcliffe ('The First Fifteen Members of the Qumran Community: A Note on 1QS 8:1ff.', *JSS* 4 [1959], pp. 134-38) appears to have been the first to suggest that 8.1–9.26 was a distinct literary unit composed (by the Teacher of Righteousness) just before the withdrawal of the Essene community into the desert. Leaney accepts this view in his commentary on the Rule (dating the time of the founding of the Qumran community to c. 130 BCE) and also considers the possibility that 5.1–6.23 ('originally a handbook for instructors of members' at 'the time when the community was being founded', p. 162) and some halakhic material in 6.24–7.25. 'may date from the time before the desert withdrawal' (p. 114, noting also that 5.1-7, 13b-20a; 6.1-7, 13-23; 6.24–7.25. were probably traditional materials). The final hymn was probably composed by the Teacher at a later time (c. 100 BCE to fit Leaney's theory that the Teacher arrived some 20 years after the founding of the community *at Qumran*!). Some later, unknown compiler (c. 100 BCE) added to these materials other sources (notably the ceremony of covenant renewal and different forms of the teaching of the two spirits), together with his own comments (especially the introduction in 1.1-17 and the denunciation of insincere converts in 2.19–3.12).

with the periods of occupation of Qumran known from archaeological research.[34]

According to Murphy-O'Connor, the first stage in the literary development of the Rule comprises 1QS 8.1-16a plus 9.3–10.8a (that is, 8.1–10.8a minus the two sets of adjoining משפטים in 8.16b-19; 8.20–9.2). The repeated refrain 'when these will exist in Israel' (8.4b, 12b; 9.5b) combined with the injunction 'to go to the desert' (8.13) shows that what is presented here is a 'manifesto' (Murphy-O'Connor's word) for the community's expectation of setting apart 15 qualified members to go to Qumran and, by a life of holiness and prayer, to constitute a spiritual temple which could 'atone for the land'. Murphy-O'Connor includes the rules for the *maskîl* (9.12–10.8a) in Stage I because statements there indicate that the *maskîl* was not yet in the desert.[35] The designation אנשי היחד ([8.11];[36] 9.5, 7, 10, 19) is said to refer to the Hasideans out of which the Qumran community probably arose; and 'the first rules' (המשפטים הרשונים, 9.10; cf. CD 20.31) to the regulations which guided the community before the arrival of the Teacher of Righteousness.[37] As for the absence of 8.15b–9.11 from 4QSᵉ, Murphy-O'Connor argues, with only partial success, that it is easier to account for the later deletion of this section than for its subsequent insertion.[38]

34. The pioneering work on archaeology at Qumran was done by Roland de Vaux, for which see: *Archaeology and the Dead Sea Scrolls* (rev. edn; Oxford: Oxford University Press, 1973).

35. In 9.16b–17a the *maskîl* still lives 'in the midst of the men of injustice'. In 9.19b-20 the present is spoken of as a 'time for preparing [to go] to the desert'. Moreover, Murphy-O'Connor contends that at issue in 9.12–10.8a is the training of the men for the mission to Qumran.

36. The mention of the 'men of the community' in 8.11, however, belongs to Stage II in Murphy-O'Connor's revised analysis (cf. below).

37. Like Sutcliffe, Leaney, and others before him, Murphy-O'Connor sees the omission of explicit reference to the Teacher (as well as the apparent 'second-billing' which the Teacher receives vis-à-vis the 'first rules' in CD 20.30-33) as evidence that the Teacher himself is the author of this manifesto.

38. Murphy-O'Connor (p. 532) suggests that the legislation in 8.17–9.2 (Stage II) would have been superseded by the more detailed rules and punishments of cols. 5-7 (Stage III), and that 9.3-11 would have been disqualified by virtue of the sole authority granted to the priests (9.7; contrast 5.2-3). Moreover, the points of contact between 9.3-5 and 8.4b-7 are too strong to discount 'common origin'. In any case, the variants in 4QSᵉ are not always superior to the text of 1QS. Even so, has Murphy-O'Connor taken seriously the generally superior readings of this oldest text of the

Finally, it should be noted that, with the publication of Pouilly's work,[39] Murphy-O'Connor has added 8.10b-12a to the material in cols. 8-9 which belongs to Stage II.[40]

Under Stage II, Murphy-O'Connor includes 8.16b–9.2 and (subsequent to Pouilly's work) 8.10b-12a. For him, this 'piece of penal legislation' has no place in a manifesto which calls for the raising up of 15 'idealists':

Rule? Until the full text is published, judgments can be only tentative. Other questions might be raised: Why should a later editor deliberately omit all of 9.3-11 when the centralization of power solely in priestly hands is mentioned only in one line (9.7)? Was the reference to atoning 'for guilty rebellion and for sins of unfaithfulness' (9.4, Vermes) too generous for a community which by now accepted only atonement for fellow community members (5.6)? Did the expectation of the eschatological Prophet and the two Messiahs (9.11) no longer match the community's messianic hope? Against this is the apparently opposite tendency of the community reflected in 5.2-3 to expand lay power, as well as the popularity of the two-Messiah concept in other Qumran writings (e.g., 1QSa, 4QTest), not to mention the Testaments of the Twelve Patriarchs. In his extensive review of Pouilly's *La règle* (*RevQ* 10 [1979], pp. 103-11) Émile Puech, who sees all of cols. 8-10 as a literary unit without interpolations, prefers 'une explication matérielle, le texte pouvant tenir sur une colonne du manuscrit recopie. Les derniers mots de la colonne recopiée devaient être אשר צוה (VIII, 15), après lesquels le scribe a dû tracer dans la marge gauche une marque d'arrêt. A la reprise de son travail, il a dû commencer deux colonnes plus loin, le signe marginal pouvant tout aussi bien affecter la fin de la colonne suivante, mais dans la marge droite cette fois, comportant בי"ד מושה ... jusqu'à וישראל' (p. 104).

39. Pouilly, *La règle de la Communauté de Qumrân: Son évolution littéraire* (Cahiers de la Revue Biblique, 17; Paris: Gabalda, 1976). In the Foreword to this work (pp. 7-8), Murphy-O'Connor accepts the two corrections which Pouilly makes of his own thesis: (1) that 8.10b-12a belongs not to Stage I but to Stage II; and (2) that the interpolation from Stage IV that begins in 5.13b ends not in 5.15a but in 6.8a.

40. Pouilly's justification for regarding 8.10b-12 as belonging to the second stage of redaction along with the rules of 8.16b–9.2 is as follows (*La règle*, pp. 36-38): (1) The opening phrase in 8.10b (בהכין אלה ביסוד היחד) bears a close structural resemblance to the introductory formula ('when these are in Israel') used elsewhere. Moreover, 8.10b-12a is set off by marginal hooks, a blank space, and a supralinear insertion; and (2) 8.10b-12a fits better as an introduction to 8.16b-19 both because it supplies the introductory formula missing from the latter and because, in terms of content, it shares the same concern for practical regulations regarding membership. A question might be posed about the dichotomy which both Pouilly and Murphy-O'Connor make between idealism and practical rules. The very fact that both scholars include the rules for the *maskîl* (9.12-26) in Stage I seems to speak against such a dichotomy.

> Dans ces conditions, il est impossible que l'auteur puisse, en même temps,
> légiférer sur un manquement grave commis par l'un de ces personnages.
> Une législation telle qu'on la trouve ici requiert une certaine expérience de
> la vie de communauté, donc un *Sitz im Leben* complètement différent de
> celui où la communauté n'est encore qu'en projet.[41]

Furthermore, there is a shift in the terminology used to designate
community members, from 'the men of the community' to the 'men of
holiness' (אנשי הקודש, 8.17, 20, 23).[42] The introductory formula in 8.20
divides the legislation into two parts (8.16b-19; 8.20–9.2). Since the
second part is far less tolerant of deliberate violations and more casuistic
and administrative in its sanctions, Murphy-O'Connor dates it slightly
later than the first part, but still within Stage II.[43] In any case, the

41. 'In these conditions, it is impossible that the author could, at the same time,
legislate on a serious infraction committed by one of these persons [that is, the 15
"idealists"]. Such a piece of legislation as one finds here requires a certain
experience of community life and, consequently, a *Sitz im Leben* completely different
from the one in which the community is still only in the planning stages' ('La
genèse', p. 532). Again, the issue which needs to be addressed is why 9.12-26 has a
place in Stage I, since there the *maskîl* himself is made subject to 'statutes' החוקים,
9.12) and 'standards' (חכוני, 9.21) and is also called upon to evaluate both candidates
and community members 'according to their spirits' (9.14-15; cf. 3.13-15). But 9.12-
26 seems to require some kind of community life already in existence, one in which
some minimal regulations for members already have a place. Puech thinks it absurd to
regard the '15 idealistic founders' of the Qumran community as 'totally without
experience and morally certain of never themselves seriously going astray!' (*RevQ* 10
[1979], p. 105).
42. The strength of this argument is diminished by the fact that: (1) the term
'every person from the men of the community, the covenant of the community'
occurs in 8.16b-17a (allegedly part of Stage II); Murphy-O'Connor contends that
this is already a more stereotyped use of 'the men of the community' than is found in
Stage I (more importantly, 4QS^d does not contain the first היהד but instead reads
'every person from the men of the covenant of the community'); (2) 'the men of the
community' does not occur at all in the first section of the Manifesto as redefined by
Murphy-O'Connor after Pouilly's study (8.1-10a, 12b-16a; 9.3-11); and (3) the term
'the men of the community' remains in (stereotyped?) use at later stages (cf. 5.1-3).
43. Both Dupont-Sommer (*Essene Writings*, p. 92 nn. 3-4) and Leaney (*The
Rule*, p. 224) explain the different degrees of punishment for deliberate infractions in
the two sections by interpreting 'all that is commanded' in the first section to refer not
to the 'Law of Moses' mentioned in the second section, but only to the community's
rules. Yet such a distinction in priority between community regulations and Torah
observance may be difficult to maintain in light of the fact that members (at least
according to 1.16-17; 5.7b-10) return to the Law of Moses *as interpreted by the*

minimal and general nature of the regulations in both sections suggest that they were drawn up close to the Qumran community's beginnings and at a time when membership was limited—in other words, in the archaeological period 1a (pre-100 BCE).[44]

The material from Stage III consists of 1QS 5-7. Murphy-O'Connor detects a marked transition to institutionalization (note the dominant emphasis on authority in the opening lines of col. 5), democratization (members of the community now share authority with the priests, 5.2-3), and heightened self-definition (the absolute use of היחד [x12] and, more importantly, the frequent parochial use of ברית [x16], indicating that 'covenant' can no longer be understood in any other way than in narrow reference to the community).[45] Although 4QS[b, d, g] shows that this section has undergone at least 'partial recensions' in conjunction with the community's developing needs, still 'les colonnes V-VII, dans leur forme actuelle, sont une codification consistante des pratiques en

Council of the Community (cf. 7.16-17 where a member can be expelled and eternally condemned for slandering the congregation). Knibb argues persuasively that, given the new introductory formula in 8.20 and its clear separation in the mss. of 1QS (note paragraph indentation and marginal hook), the two sections probably 'reflect a change of practice over a period of time' (*Qumran Community*, p. 136).

44. As alluded to earlier, the absence of this section from 4QS[e] (although one would have to add 8.15b-16a; 9.3-11 as well) is another indication that these regulations were not originally part of the material in the rest of 1QS 8-9.

45. Murphy-O'Connor also sees further isolation of the community from Israel at large in the references to the atoning value of the community's righteous living: whereas in Stage I the community made atonement 'for the Land' (8.3-4, 6, 10a; 9.4-5), in Stage III the atonement only works for fellow community members (5.6-7). It should be kept in mind, however, that even in Murphy-O'Connor's Stage I the Fifteen are to 'separate from the abode of the men of injustice' (8.13; cf. 5.1b-2a: 'to separate from the congregation of the men of injustice') and as 'witnesses to the truth at the Judgment' are to 'pay to the wicked their reward' (8.6-7, Vermes). The community is already forbidden to merge its property 'with that of the men of falsehood' (9.8). The instructions given to the *maskîl* in 9.12-26 are even more saturated with a sociological dualism ('sons of righteousness' versus 'the men of the Pit'; 'everlasting hatred in a spirit of secrecy for the men of perdition!' [Vermes]). From all this, one can only conclude that the atonement of the Land spoken of in 1QS 8-9 is not an olive branch extended to Jews outside the community, but rather an assurance to the community that God will preserve their inheritance in the land of Israel. Murphy-O'Connor has grossly underestimated the heightened self-definition and narrowing of the community as portrayed in 1QS 8-9.

vigueur à Qumran à une certaine époque'.[46] In the opinion of Murphy-O'Connor, Stage III correlates well with Period 1b (which began no later than early in the reign of Alexander Janneus, 103–76 BCE) when extensive rebuilding took place at Qumran apparently to accomodate a large influx of new members. Such an increase would have necessitated a more detailed regulation of the life of the community. Particularly intriguing is Murphy-O'Connor's suggestion that this influx could be attributed to the persecution of the Pharisees at the end of the reign of John Hyrcanus and throughout that of Alexander Janneus.[47]

As already stated, Murphy-O'Connor thought of Stage III as 'essentially' comprising cols. 5-7. He makes an exception of 5.13b-15a which he considers to be an interpolation from Stage IV. His reasons are convincing: (1) in this portion of text there is an abrupt transition from the third-person plural to the third-person singular; and (2) the subject matter seems to switch from 'the men of injustice' from whom the community ought to keep separate (that is, those who have never joined the community)[48] to insincere members/novices of the community (cf. 2.25b–3.12), indicating a similar *Sitz im Leben* as that of Stage IV (loss of religious fervor in the community, leading to an assimilation of the fate of insincere members with that of outsiders). One might also add the confirmation which comes from the manuscript of 1QS itself, which marks off the beginning of this text with a blank space and marginal hook. Later, Murphy-O'Connor accepted Pouilly's arguments for extending the interpolation to 6.8a: (1) the similar sentence structures of

---

46. 'La genèse', p. 536.

47. This hypothesis receives support from the following factors: (1) the close interrelationship between the Hasideans, Essenes, and Pharisees in terms of *halakoth* (cf. the studies by L.H. Schiffman) and apocalypticism; (2) the more democratic tendencies of the Pharisees (Milik, *Ten Years*, p. 91); and (3) the possible presence of Pharisaic phylacteries at Qumran. Cf. Charlesworth, 'Origin', pp. 223-24. Of course, such a view would have to account for the data in 4QpNah which applauds the 'furious young lion' (= Alexander Janneus) for hanging 'those who seek smooth things' (= the Pharisees; 1.6-8, Vermes).

48. Puech's contention that the whole section from 5.10b onwards refers solely to insincere candidates for community membership (*RevQ* 10 [1979], p. 108) must be rejected as running counter to the natural sense of the text. The object of scorn in 5.10b-11 are the 'men of injustice' who 'have neither inquired nor sought after Him concerning His laws'—a description which does not fit insincere candidates who are trying to learn the community's 'hidden things' without first undergoing an inner repentance. Cf. the distinction between the two cursed groups in 2.4b-10 and 2.11-18.

5.13b-20, 25b–6.1, 3, 6 (negations with אשר לוא and אל plus imperfect);
(2) 5.1-13a flows more naturally into 6.8b-23, eliminating the redundant
discussion of covenant entry and ranking that is found in 5.20b-24 (cf.
5.7b-13a and 6.13b-23); and (3) various examples of vocabulary
common to 5.13b–6.8a and Stage IV material.[49] Nevertheless, Murphy-
O'Connor may have been too hasty in embracing this extension of the
interpolation. Nothing in 5.20b–6.8a indicates a scenario in which the
community has experienced a loss of fervor (the alleged scenario for
Stage IV); and nothing in 5.15b-20a necessarily applies to errant
members (cf. 9.8-9). Pouilly's syntactical arguments do not appear to be
strong enough to compel acceptance of a cohesive interpolation over the
use of different traditional sources by the author of 5.1–6.23.[50]

It is necessary to undertake a fuller discussion of the fourth and final
stage of the literary composition of the Rule: cols. 1-4; the final hymn in
10.9–11.22; and the interpolations in 5.13b-15a (mentioned above), 10.4b,
and 10.6a. According to Murphy-O'Connor, these diverse additions,
while containing independent traditional elements, can all be ascribed to
one and the same writer because they all serve the same function: 'the
desire to rekindle the decreasing fervor of the community'.[51] With
regard to cols. 1-4, the introduction in 1.1-15 aims to stimulate total
devotion to the community's ideals. 1.16–2.25a consists of traditional
liturgical material associated with the annual covenant renewal ceremony
of the community. It is placed here to recall lagging members to the
community ideal and zeal which once characterized their intent and to
do so in the context already outlined in the introduction (cf. especially
2.11-18). 2.25b–3.12 (framed chiastically) has the 'catechetical purpose'
of warning members against a legalistic performance of ritual which
skirts the demand for inner transformation.

The teaching on the two spirits (3.13–4.26) is not a 'literary unity',

49. Cf. Pouilly, *La règle*, pp. 45-50.

50. Puech calls the arguments from vocabulary 'à peu près inexistants'; see his
arguments in *RevQ* 10 (1979), p. 107. Puech also correctly notes the difficulty of
separating 5.18 ('for all those not reckoned in his covenant') from 5.11b ('for they
are not reckoned in his covenant'); and the close connection between 5.7 and 5.20, the
latter quite naturally picking up the discussion which had been temporarily suspended
by the digression in 5.10b-20a (p. 108). Cf. Knibb (*The Qumran Community*,
pp. 110-11) who embraces the suggestion of an interpolation in 5.13b-15a but not for
5.13b–6.8a.

51. 'La genèse', p. 537.

but a text that has passed through three stages of literary development, each of which reflects a different attitude towards dualism.[52] Since the summary introduction in 3.13-15a only covers the material to 4.15 (where a new paragraph begins in the text), it is natural enough to view 3.13–4.14 as the first stage of development. Its emphasis is on a clear-cut cosmological and sociological dualism in which all humanity is ruled either by the Angel of Light or the Angel of Darkness. However, in 4.15-23a the individual human partakes of both domains, although ultimately confidence is expressed in the preponderance of the spirit of truth and consequently eschatological vindication for God's own. Finally, in 4.23b-26 the dualism comes full circle, placing the emphasis squarely on anthropological dualism and concomitant responsibility of humans to choose good over evil. Confidence in the eschatological acquittal of community members has been replaced by a 'veiled warning' framed in view of the unknowability of God's judgment until the End.[53] It is this last view which accounts for the insertion of this block of teaching by the composer of Stage IV.[54] The entirety of cols. 1-4 can thus be viewed as a 'préface exhortative à une *Règle* préexistante dont l'esprit avait été perdu du vue'.[55]

As for the final hymn in 10.9–11.22, Murphy-O'Connor notes the similarities between this hymn and the 'hymns of the community' (as

52. First proposed by P. von der Osten-Sacken, *Gott und Belial*, pp. 17-27.

53. Unfortunately, Murphy-O'Connor never explains how this uncertainty about the outcome of eschatological judgment in 4.23b-26 correlates with the abounding confidence in God's mercy expressed in the hymn in 10.9–11.22 (e.g., 11.12-15), which after all is supposed to come from the same stage of development.

54. For Murphy-O'Connor it is a moot point 'whether 4.23b-26 has been added to adapt the dualistic document to its present context or whether the document has been inserted into this place because its tenor had already been modified by the addition of 4.23b-26' ('La genèse', p. 543). With regard to the significance of 4.23b-26 for explaining the insertion of the Teaching of the Two Spirits into the Rule, Murphy-O'Connor seems to overstate his case somewhat to fit his proposed *Sitz im Leben* for Stage IV. It is difficult to believe that the writer incorporated an entire document simply to make use of the final one-tenth of the text! Cosmological and anthropological dualism are hardly antitheses in apocalyptic thought.

55. 'La genèse', p. 543. The recent attempt of D.C. Allison to identify the Teacher of Righteousness as the author of the teaching on the two spirits ('The Authorship of 1QS III, 3-IV 14', *RevQ* 10 [1980], pp. 257-68) has not met with enthusiastic support but it does raise the question of whether Murphy-O'Connor's reconstruction provides an adequate response.

opposed to 'hymns of the *maskîl*') in 1QH and concludes that the former shares with the latter the same *Sitz im Leben*—that of the covenant renewal ceremony (the same setting as that of 1QS 1.16–2.25a; cf. 1.22-23 with 11.9). Because the hymn in cols. 10-11 lacks the soteriological confession found in other 'hymns of the community' and stresses more human promises to God, Murphy-O'Connor contends that 10.9–11.22 was recited only by new converts at the covenant renewal ceremony and would thus evoke the same kind of visceral reaction as that suggested for cols. 1-4: an emotional remembrance of a once intense commitment. Taken as a whole, Stage IV material responds to a perceived dilution of religious intensity that followed, perhaps, the expansion of an original zealous core of believers at the beginning of Period 1b 'only a few years after Stage III'.[56]

As already mentioned, Murphy-O'Connor's most ardent supporter is J. Pouilly whose work (*La règle de la Communauté de Qumrân* [1976]) buttressed that of Murphy-O'Connor with only minor fine tuning. Elsewhere only partial agreement has been forthcoming. M. Delcor[57] calls Murphy-O'Connor's reconstruction 'brilliant' and is enthusiastic about the identification of an early, 'pre-Qumranic' nucleus of material in cols. 8-9 and of pre-existing, traditional materials (liturgy of the covenant renewal ceremony, treatise on the two spirits, and the closing hymn). He is more skeptical, however, about the chronological arrangement of the material beyond Stage I and, in particular, the correlation of such material with archaeological phases. E. Puech[58] argues for three stages in the development of the Rule (cols. 8-10, 5-7, 1-4). For him, cols. 8-10 are tied together (and thus without a second stage in 8.16b–9.2), written at the beginning of the founding of the community at Qumran in 152 BCE during the reign of Jonathan. Likewise, cols. 5-7 are not interpolated in 5.13b-6.8a or even in 5.13b-15a, but constitute a literary unity. Puech is highly critical of the way Pouilly dissects texts through reliance on minute shifts in vocabulary and syntax.[59] Milik[60]

---

56. 'La genèse', p. 549.

57. Mathias Delcor, 'Littérature essénienne', *DBSup* 9 (1978), col. 854.

58. *RevQ* 10 (1979), pp. 103-11.

59. 'C'est une pétition de principe que de vouloir trouver à tout prix dans les nuances et variétés de vocabulaire différents stades de composition...Il faut d'autres tensions pour que la preuve soit convaincante' (*RevQ* 10 [1979], p. 105).

60. 'Milki-Sedeq', p. 135.

thinks that the oldest form of the Rule comprises 'more or less 1QS V I-IX 11', and that this section was composed by the Teacher of Righteousness 'at the beginning of his activity, between 150–145 BC. A little later, the copyists have enlarged this Rule by making some long additions at the beginning and at the end of the original document'. Knibb[61] concurs with Murphy-O'Connor's analysis and relative dating of 8.1–9.26a, but beyond this is reluctant to arrange any of the originally independent units within the major sections (for example, 5.13b-15a), or even the major sections themselves in any kind of chronological sequence.

Therefore, there is, as yet, no consensus about the chronological stages in which the Rule was composed,[62] although there seems to be widespread agreement that at least most of cols. 8-9 belong to the earliest stage of the composition of the Rule.[63] In view of the doublets (the three distinct introductions which describe the program of the community at the beginning of cols. 1, 5, and 8, for example), the contradictions between major sections (for example, the consolidation of power in the hands of the priests in 9.7 versus the democratization of authority in 5.2-3), and the literary allusions between major sections (for example, cf. 5.1b-2a with 8.13; 5.6 with 8.6), it is likely that the Rule has taken shape in progressive stages of literary development. Murphy-O'Connor's reconstruction has much to commend it but at present the question must remain open as to whether at some points it oversimplifies what was really a more complex process of development (for example, the neat equation

61. *The Qumran Community*, pp. 77-78.

62. This remark stands despite Murphy-O'Connor's assessment of Pouilly's work ('it would appear that his conclusions should be accorded a very high degree of probability') in his own review of the state of research in 'The Judean Desert', *Early Judaism and Its Modern Interpreters* (ed. R. Kraft and G. Nickelsburg; Atlanta: Scholars Press, 1986), pp. 119-56, esp. pp. 128-29.

63. This is not to say, however, that there are not significant dissenters even at this point. Guilbert's position has continued to receive qualified support from J. Licht, *The Rule Scroll* (Jerusalem: Bialak, 1965 [Hebrew]) and D. Dimant ('Qumran Sectarian Literature', esp. pp. 501-502). Dimant acknowledges the composite character of the Rule, but insists that the document was written with a unified plan in mind. For her, doublets do not reflect 'different life situations', but the literary skill of the writer who organized the document in a chiastic pattern. Notwithstanding, it should be borne in mind that since the chiastic pattern primarily develops from the placement of cols. 1-4 and 10-11, Dimant's demonstration of chiasm does not militate against Murphy-O'Connor's hypothesis (which can accomodate a single author/compiler for the material in these columns).

of large blocks of material with limited data drawn from archaeological reconstructions; or the ascription of all detailed regulations to later periods) and at other points makes more complex what is really quite simple (the alleged interpolations in cols. 5-6 and 8-9, for example).

THE RECHABITES OF JEREMIAH 35:
FORERUNNERS OF THE ESSENES?

Chris H. Knights

It has occasionally been proposed, perhaps most notably by Matthew Black, that the Essenes, or Qumran Community, were the descendants of the Rechabites, found in the Bible in Jeremiah 35. This proposal is one that has received little attention from scholars, but it is worthy of investigation and analysis. The purpose of this article is to examine the material concerning the Essenes in Philo and Josephus, in the Qumran literature and in the Damascus Document,[1] and to examine the material in comparison with that about the Rechabites, in order to ascertain whether there are indeed any links between the two groups and, if so, what sort.

Matthew Black's theory, first proposed in 1961 and restated in 1965,[2] was that the Essenes developed out of the *Hasid* movement which emerged in Judaism at the time of the Seleucid persecution. The Hasidim, however, did not represent a complete innovation in the history of Israel. Rather,

> the basic elements in Hasidic Judaism which eventually crystallized into the sect or order of Essenes go very far back into Israel's religious past. I refer to their asceticism, which is undoubtedly to be traced to an ultimate origin in the ancient tribal asceticism, in particular that of the Rechabites or Kenites.[3]

---

1. P.R. Davies, *The Damascus Covenant: An Interpretation of the 'Damascus Document'* (JSOTS, 25; Sheffield: JSOT Press, 1983), has made a strong case for the non-Qumranic origin of CD, so it is treated here as an independent witness to the life and beliefs of the Essenes.

2. M. Black, *The Scrolls and Christian Origins* (Edinburgh: Nelson, 1961); *idem*, 'The Traditions of Hasidaean-Essene Asceticism: Its Origins and Influence', in *Aspects du Judéo-Christianisme* (Paris, 1965), pp. 19-33.

3. *Scrolls and Christian Origins*, p. 15.

For Black, this 'ancient tribal asceticism' stems ultimately from the desert origins of Yahwism, the Rechabites and the Kenites representing 'reactionary revivals of "old nomad customs"'.[4]

Since Black advanced his opinions over 25 years ago, his view of the Rechabites has been firmly and decisively challenged. That there was ever a 'Nomadic Ideal' in ancient Israel is unlikely, as is the idea that the Rechabites were ascetic nomads; moreover, the link between the Rechabites and the Kenites is not universally accepted.[5] It may, nevertheless, still be possible to find links between the Rechabites and the Essenes, but a different method from that proposed by Black is required. What is needed is a recounting of the distinctive Rechabite practices, and then an examination of the literature by and about the Essenes for possible parallels.

At the start of this exercise it should be stated quite clearly that not one of the Dead Sea Scrolls so far published makes any reference to the Rechabites. Neither do the references in Philo and Josephus. Admittedly, Josephus makes mention of the ancient origins of the Essenes, as he does of the ancient origins of the Sadducees and Pharisees, but that is hardly equivalent to saying that they developed from the Rechabites. In his analysis of CD, Philip Davies argues that it reflects an origin for the pre-Qumran Essenes in the Babylonian Exile[6]—surely an 'ancient origin' from Josephus' point of view!

This lack of explicit mention of the Rechabites in the Scrolls and in the Greek authorities should make the assertions that the Rechabites were some sort of proto-Essene group, or that the Essenes used the biblical texts about the Rechabites as part of their own self-understanding dangerous ones. This caution is further borne out by a comparison of the practices of the Rechabites and those of the Essenes.

The Rechabites were married, and produced offspring within their community (cf. Jer. 35.6, 8). The evidence of the Dead Sea Scrolls and of the Greek writers on the Essenes is not unambiguous on this subject,

---

4.   'Hasidaean-Essene Asceticism', p. 20.

5.   See, for example, P.A. Riemann, *Desert and Return to Desert in the Pre-Exilic Prophets* (PhD thesis Harvard University, 1964); S. Talmon, 'The Desert Motif in the Bible and Qumran Literature', in *Biblical Motifs: Origins and Transformations* (ed. A. Altmann; Cambridge, MA: Harvard University Press, 1966), pp. 31-63; F. Frick, 'The Rechabites Reconsidered', *JBL* 90 (1971), pp. 279-87; S. Klein, 'Die Schreiberfamilien: 1Chronik 2.55', *MGWJ* 70 (1926), pp. 410-16.

6.   *The Damascus Covenant, passim.*

however. 1QSa and 1QM certainly imply married sectaries, and the community reflected by CD is also a married one, but 1QS is completely silent on the matter, and may reflect a celibate, male community. Josephus believed that there were two orders of Essenes, one of which was celibate, the other of which practised marriage, but for the sole purpose of procreation (*War* 2.8.2, 2.8.13). There is no evidence that the Rechabites married solely to maintain their race. Philo also thinks that the Essenes were celibate (*Hypothetica* 11, 14).

The Rechabites were commanded by Jonadab to live in tents (Jer. 35.7). While it seems that all the buildings at Qumran were intended for communal use, and that the members of the community there lived in caves, tents, huts or other temporary structures, the term אהל, 'tent', appears but rarely in the Scrolls, and when it does, it apparently does not refer to the dwelling-places of the Essenes. The term מחנה, 'camp', is, however, fairly frequent as a designation of the community, so if a מחנה was made up of tents, then its occurrence could be an indication that a tent-dwelling community was meant. It is, however, by no means certain that מחנה in the Dead Sea Scrolls implies tents. Helfmeyer argues that מחנה denotes '"communities" or "separate settlements" with their own specific rules', and not 'collections of tents'.[7] Num. 13.19 presents a biblical usage of מחנה in the sense of 'unfortified towns'. CD speaks of ערים, 'cities', and בית, 'house', as well as מחנה, so it seems unlikely that the Essenes had a 'tent ideology' like the Rechabites. There is nothing in Philo or Josephus to contradict this conclusion.

It is interesting to note that Abbot Nilus of Ancyra does seem to connect the Essenes with the Rechabites, on the basis of a common tent-residency and wine-avoidance, when he writes,

> Moreover, a group of Jews honoured this kind of life; they are the descendants of Jonadab. They approve of all who wish to live thus, and they introduce them to this polity, living in tents forever, abstaining from wine and delicate food, leading a frugal life…They therefore take special care of their moral conduct, remaining constant in contemplation to a very great extent, whence they are called *Iessaioi* ('Ιεσσαιοι), this name indicating that they are skilled in words.[8]

Whether this monk, who died c. 430 CE, had access to any firm historical data is doubtful. More probably, he had access to much the same

---

7. Article חנה, *TDOT*, V, p. 6.
8. *De Monastica Exercitatione*, ch. 3 (Greek text and Latin translation in PG, vol. 79, cols. 721-22).

material as is available today (though not to the Dead Sea Scrolls) and concluded that, as the Rechabites and the Essenes both represented Jewish ascetical groups, they were connected with each other, and wrote his treatise on the origins of Christian monasticism accordingly.[9]

The Rechabites also prohibited the sowing of seed and planting of a vineyard, and so were non-agricultural (Jer. 35.7, 9). Philo says that some of the Essenes laboured on the land (ὧν οἱ μὲν γεωπονουντες, *Quod Omnis Probus* 76), CD 13.10 mentions threshing-floor and wine-vat (ומגורנו ומגתו) and 1QS seems to imply that the community at Qumran did practice agriculture; hence, once again, the practices of the Rechabites and the practices of the Essenes were different.

The same seems to apply with wine. The Rechabites were com-manded not to drink יין, most probably 'all intoxicants' (Jer. 35.6, 8). The term יין is uncommon in the Scrolls. For instance, in CD it is only used in the quotation of Deut. 32.33 and its explanation, 8.9-10 = 19.22-23 is related to the 'rebels', and so is not really a reference to literal wine to be drunk. תירוש, 'must', is, however, common in the Scrolls other than CD. Whether תירוש represents fermented or unfermented juice of the grape in the Essene writings is still a matter for scholarly debate, but the general consensus seems to be that it denotes an unfermented liquid.[10] If the Qumran community *was* abstinent, this could stem from their evident self-conception as a priestly community, and need not be related to the Rechabites. Philo's account of the Therapeutae of Egypt, who may have been related to the Essenes, speaks of their avoidance of wine, and explicitly relates it to priesthood (*De Vita Contemplativa* 73f.). Despite Jerome's statement (*Adv. Iovinianum* 2.14), it is not clear whether Josephus intends that the Essenes abstained from meat and wine.[11]

The Rechabites and the Essenes also seem to stand at variance with each other in their attitudes to the Land, האדמה/הארץ. The Rechabites

---

9. H.-J. Schoeps, *Theologie und Geschichte des Judenchristentums* (Tübingen, 1949), pp. 250-51, is similarly sceptical about the historical reliability of Nilus's statements.

10. See, e.g., E.F. Sutcliffe, 'Sacred Meals at Qumran?', *HeyJ* 1 (1960), p. 50; G. Vermes, *The Dead Sea Scrolls: Qumran in Perspective* (London: Collins, 1977), p. 94.

11. See E. Schürer, *The History of the Jewish People in the Age of Jesus Christ* (ed. G. Vermes, F. Millar, M. Black and P. Vermes; Edinburgh: T. & T. Clark, rev. edn, 1979), II, p. 571 n. 60.

lived in it (Jer. 35.7, 11), and not in the desert. 1QS 8.13-14, 9.20, 1QM 1.2-3, 4QpPs37 2.1, however, all indicate that the Qumran community deliberately chose to live in the desert, and 1QH 4.8 and 8.4 may also indicate this. מדבר, 'desert', is, however, virtually absent from CD, being found only in 3.7, which referred to the Israelites in the wilderness of Sinai. While Pliny spoke of the Essene encampment by the shores of the Dead Sea (*Naturalis Historia* 5.15/373), Philo spoke of them being resident in villages, but not in the desert (*Quod Omnis Probus* 76), and Josephus said that they settled in large numbers in every town (*War* 2.8.4).

The purpose of the Rechabite practices was, according to Jer. 35.7, to secure long life in the land where the Rechabites were sojourners (גרים). Words associated with גור are, however, not common in the Scrolls. The stem is used in 'sojourning in the land of Damascus' in CD 6.5 (cf. 4.6). There are two uses of the verb in 1QH (3.25, 5.5), but neither are very helpful. The noun גר appears once in 4QFlor (1.4) and three times in CD (6.21, 14.4, 6), where it denotes the 'alien' or the 'convert'—none of which provides a parallel with the Rechabites.

It is clear that the material dealing directly with the Qumran community, that is, the Dead Sea Scrolls other than CD, offers little in the way of possible parallels to the Rechabites. It might have been thought that the non-Qumran material, CD and the accounts in Philo and Josephus, would have been more fruitful, especially if Davies is correct in concluding that the original community represented by CD came into existence during the Exile,[12] but this is not the case. By isolating the distinctive features of Rechabite practice, marriage, tent-residence, non-agriculturalism, wine-avoidance and living in the Land as 'sojourners', and by comparing them in turn with the variegated material we have concerning the Essenes, the initial caution, voiced because of the lack of occurrences of 'Rechabites' in the Qumran literature, is further strengthened. Not one of the Rechabite practices is unambiguously found in the literature concerning the Essenes. In particular, evidence for Essene tent-residency and agriculture-avoidance is non-existent. Rather, there is evidence to the contrary. The Essenes were not influenced by the Rechabites or by the biblical texts dealing with the Rechabites.

Some scholars, such as Schoeps and Kohler, have attempted to find a connection between the Rechabites and the Essenes on the basis of the

---

12. *The Damascus Covenant.*

rabbinic literature.[13] Both these scholars, however, were writing before the impact of the discovery of the Dead Sea Scrolls was fully realized, so their information about the Essenes was limited. The rabbinic references to the Rechabites[14] remain, however, and a number of them stand at variance with the biblical data about them, yet at the same time close to what is known about the Essenes. Hence, the views of Schoeps and Kohler are understandable, but it has now been shown that a direct connection between the Rechabites and the Essenes is unlikely.

Another possibility is that some of the rabbinic texts which mention the Rechabites were, in fact, alluding to the Essenes, but, as I have shown elsewhere in connection with some of these texts,[15] this is unlikely. The Pseudepigraphon variously titled the Story of Zosimus or the History of the Rechabites also represents a post-biblical use of the material about the Rechabites,[16] which one modern scholar has attempted to link with the Therapeutae, who may have been connected with the Essenes.[17] If the connection between the History of the Rechabites and the Therapeutae could be sustained, there may be a hint of a connection between the Essenes and the Rechabites of Jeremiah 35. The date, provenance and literary history of the History of the Rechabites remain uncertain, however, so it is impossible to use it as evidence for a claim that the Qumran community was either descended from, or modelled on, the biblical Rechabites. The conclusion seems inescapable: the biblical Rechabites were not forerunners of the Essenes as they are known through the Dead Sea Scrolls, the Damascus Covenant, and the ancient Greek authors.

13. Schoeps, *Theologie und Geschichte*, pp. 247-55; K. Kohler, 'The Essenes and Apocalyptic Literature', *JQR* 11 (1920–21), pp. 160-63.

14. E.g., *m. Taan.* 4.5; *b. Sotah* 11a; *b. Sanh.* 106a; *Mekhilta of Rabbi Ishmael* and *Mekhilta of Rabbi Simeon* to Exodus 18.27; *Sifre Numbers* 78; *Sifre Zutta to Numbers* 10.29, etc. There are no explicit references to the Essenes in the rabbinic literature.

15. 'Jethro Merited that his Descendants should sit in the Chamber of Hewn Stone', *JJS* 41 (1990), pp. 247-53.

16. M.R. James, 'On the Story of Zosimus', in *Apocrypha Anecdota* (Texts and Studies 2.3; Cambridge: Cambridge Univesity Press, 1893), pp. 86-108; J.H. Charlesworth, 'The History of the Rechabites' (*The Old Testament Pseudepigrapha*, II, pp. 443-61). Compare, C.H. Knights, '"The Story of Zosimus" or "The History of the Rechabites"?', *JSJ* 34 (1993), pp. 235-45.

17. B. McNeil, 'The Narration of Zosimus', *JSJ* 9 (1978), pp. 68-82.

PREDICTIONS OF THE DESTRUCTION OF THE HERODIAN
TEMPLE IN THE PSEUDEPIGRAPHA, QUMRAN SCROLLS,
AND RELATED TEXTS

Craig A. Evans

Although scholarly opinion remains divided as to whether or not lying
behind Mk 13.2 and parallels is a genuine dominical prophecy of the
destruction of the Herodian Temple,[1] the balance in recent years seems
to be tipping in favor of its authenticity. Some scholars have had and still
have reservations. G. Hölscher concluded that the saying preserved in
Mk 13.2 is a *vaticinium ex eventu*.[2] On redaction-critical grounds
W. Marxsen concluded that in Mark, the earliest gospel, 'the risen Lord
is contrasted with the Temple' and that the evangelist 'is the first to
speak of an actual destruction'.[3] R. Pesch is among the most influential
who hold that this prediction is a *vaticinium ex eventu*. He believes that
'the evangelist formed a new logion out of Mark 14.58 [where "false
witnesses" accuse Jesus of having threatened the Temple]' and out of
nothing else.[4] Elsewhere he avers that 'the evangelist already had
knowledge of what happened' and so relates details approximating the
description found in Josephus.[5] J. Lambrecht likewise suspects that the

1. Uncertain himself, R. Bultmann (*The History of the Synoptic Tradition*
[Oxford: Blackwell, 1972], pp. 125, 128) suspected that the prediction of the
Temple's destruction probably originated prior to 70 CE, but may have been ascribed
to Jesus by the Church.

2. G. Hölscher, 'Der Ursprung der Apokalypse Mk 13', *TBl* 12 (1933),
pp. 193-202.

3. W. Marxsen, *Mark the Evangelist* (Nashville: Abingdon, 1969), p. 168.

4. R. Pesch, *Naherwartungen: Tradition und Redaktion in Mk 13* (Düsseldorf:
Patmos, 1968), pp. 83-96. In his commentary, cited in the following note, he modifies
his position by allowing for the possibility that pre-Marcan Christian tradents may
have handed on some form of the tradition.

5. R. Pesch, *Das Markusevangelium* (HTKNT; 2 vols.; Freiburg: Herder, 1984,

prediction does not derive from Jesus.[6] And finally, many of the redaction critics of the seventies despaired of finding certain genuine material in Mark 13 as a whole.[7]

But there have been many scholars who were persuaded that in all probability Jesus did predict the destruction of the Herodian Temple and that the saying found in Mk 13.2 represents authentic dominical tradition.[8] With changing assumptions and refinements in method the

3rd edn), II, p. 271. He specifically has in mind Josephus' report that 'Caesar ordered the whole city and the Temple to be razed to the ground' (*War* 7.1.1 §1-4). Pesch (*Markusevangelium*, pp. 271-72) does believe that Jesus in fact said something, probably in the tradition of the classical prophets, against the Temple as 'the accusation at the trial [14.58] and his mockery on the cross [15.29] make probable'.

6.   J. Lambrecht, *Die Redaktion der Markus-Apokalypse* (AnBib, 28; Rome: Pontifical Biblical Institute, 1967), pp. 68-79, 88-91.

7.   See for example, N. Perrin, *Rediscovering the Teaching of Jesus* (New York: Harper & Row, 1976), p. 155: 'We omit Mark 13 and its parallels, because this is, at best, a version of something which Jesus taught that has been so severely apocalypticized that we have no present means of recovering an authentic teaching directly from it'. Perrin, of course, has in mind the entire chapter, and not simply the prediction found in v. 2. This kind of skepticism is endemic in W.H. Kelber (ed.), *The Passion in Mark: Studies on Mark 14–16* (Philadelphia: Fortress Press, 1976). J. Gnilka, (*Das Evangelium nach Markus* [EKKNT, 2; 2 vols.; Neukirchen: Neukirchener Verlag, 1978–79], II, p. 184) avers that the prophecy in Mk 13.2 'goes back to Jesus with difficulty...it too plainly describes the situation which the Temple landscape reflected after the Roman-Jewish war'.

8.   For a sampling of older studies see J. Klausner, *Jesus of Nazareth* (London: Allen & Unwin, 1925), p. 322; M. Goguel, *The Life of Jesus* (London: Allen & Unwin, 1933), pp. 507-50; V. Taylor, *The Formation of the Gospel Tradition* (London: Macmillan, 1935), p. 73; *idem, The Gospel according to St. Mark* (London: Macmillan, 1952), p. 501; W. Manson, *Jesus the Messiah* (London: Hodder and Stoughton, 1943), p. 67; J. Schniewind, *Das Evangelium nach Markus* (NTD, 1; Göttingen: Vandenhoeck & Ruprecht, 1947, 4th edn), p. 181; E. Klostermann, *Das Markusevangelium* (HNT, 3; Tübingen: Mohr [Paul Siebeck], 1950, 4th edn); E. Lohmeyer, *Das Evangelium nach Markus* (MeyerK, 2; Göttingen: Vandenhoeck & Ruprecht, 1951, 11th edn), p. 268; W.G. Kümmel, *Promise and Fulfillment* (SBT, 23; London: SCM, 1957), pp. 94-95; L. Hartman, *Prophecy Interpreted: The Formation of Some Jewish Apocalyptic Texts and of the Eschatological Discourse Mark 13 Par.* (CB/NTS, 1; Lund: Gleerup, 1966), pp. 239-40; E. Haenchen, *Der Weg Jesu: Eine Erklärung des Markus-Evangeliums und der kanonischen Parallelen* (Berlin: de Gruyter, 1968), p. 433 (though with some hesitation); H. Braun, *Jesus of Nazareth: The Man and His Time* (Philadelphia: Fortress Press, 1969), p. 58.

number of scholars today who accept the authenticity of the prophecy is large and is increasing.[9]

The purpose of this study is to examine the literary, historical, and religious contexts against which the prediction of Jesus should be assessed. The primary point is not to argue for the authenticity of the prophecy found in Mk 13.2, though, as it happens, the results of the study do support its authenticity, but to try to determine as precisely as possible the significance of Jesus' prophecy and the way it would have been understood by his contemporaries. The study will investigate four aspects of the problem: (1) predictions of the Temple's destruction; (2) scriptural/prophetic backgrounds of the predictions; (3) perceived corruption in the first-century Temple as the principal occasion for the predictions; and (4) the Herodian origin of the first-century Temple as a possible contributing factor in the predictions.

---

9.   L. Gaston, *No Stone on Another: Studies in the Significance of the Fall of Jerusalem in the Synoptic Gospels* (NovTSup, 23; Leiden: Brill, 1970), p. 66; E. Schweizer, *The Good News according to Mark* (Atlanta: John Knox, 1970), p. 262; H. Anderson, *The Gospel of Mark* (NCB; Grand Rapids: Eerdmans, 1976), p. 290; C.E.B. Cranfield, *The Gospel according to St. Mark* (Cambridge: Cambridge University Press, 1977), p. 392; C.F.D. Moule, *The Gospel according to St. Mark* (Cambridge: Cambridge University Press, 1977), p. 392; B.F. Meyer, *The Aims of Jesus* (London: SCM Press, 1979), p. 181; F.F. Bruce, 'The Date and Character of Mark', in E. Bammel and C.F.D. Moule (eds.), *Jesus and the Politics of His Day* (Cambridge: Cambridge University Press, 1984), pp. 69-89, esp. p. 80; G.W.H. Lampe, 'A.D. 70 in Christian Reflection', in Bammel and Moule (eds.), *Jesus and the Politics of His Day*, pp. 153-71, esp. p. 161; K. Schubert, 'Biblical Criticism Criticized: With Reference to the Markan Report of Jesus's Examination before the Sanhedrin', in Bammel and Moule (eds.), *Jesus and the Politics of His Day*, pp. 385-402, esp. p. 398; M. Hengel, *Studies in the Gospel of Mark* (Philadelphia: Fortress Press, 1985), pp. 16, 146 n. 39; E.P. Sanders, *Jesus and Judaism* (Philadelphia: Fortress Press, 1985), p. 75; C.S. Mann, *Mark* (AB, 27; Garden City: Doubleday, 1986), p. 510; R.A. Horsley, *Jesus and the Spiral of Violence: Popular Jewish Resistance in Roman Palestine* (San Francisco: Harper & Row, 1987), p. 162; R. Leivestad, *Jesus in His Own Perspective: An Examination of His Sayings, Actions, and Eschatological Titles* (Minneapolis: Augsburg, 1987), p. 146; M.N.A. Bockmuehl, 'Why Did Jesus Predict the Destruction of the Temple?', *Crux* 25/3 (1989), pp. 11-18; G.N. Stanton, *The Gospels and Jesus* (Oxford and New York: Oxford University Press, 1989), p. 183; B. Witherington, *The Christology of Jesus* (Minneapolis: Fortress Press, 1990), p. 111.

Predictions of the Destruction of the Second/Third Temple

There are several traditions, most of which are likely pre-70 CE, that apparently predict, or at least anticipate, the destruction of the post-exilic or Herodian Temple. Although every case is not certain, there is little evidence that these predictions represent *vaticinia ex eventu* (no more than the prophecies of Jeremiah [26.6, 18] and Micah [3.12], for example, should be so regarded).

Testaments of the Twelve Patriarchs

The Testaments of the Twelve Patriarchs contain several predictions of destruction, either of the Temple, or of Jerusalem, or of both:

> And you shall act lawlessly in Israel, with the result that Jerusalem cannot bear the presence of your wickedness, but the curtain of the Temple will be torn, so that it will no longer conceal your shame. (T. Levi 10.3)
>
> And now, my children, I know from the writings of Enoch that in the end-time you will act impiously against the Lord, setting your hands to every evil deed; because of you, your brothers will be humiliated and among all the nations you shall become the occasion for scorn...the impieties of the chief priests...You plunder the Lord's offerings; from his share you steal choice parts, contemptuously eating them with whores. You teach the Lord's commands out of greed for gain...With contempt and laughter you will deride the sacred things. Therefore the sanctuary which the Lord chose shall become desolate through your uncleanness, and you will be captives in all the nations. And you shall be to them a revolting thing, and you shall receive scorn and eternal humiliation through the just judgment of God. All who hate you will rejoice at your destruction. (T. Levi 14.1–15.3)
>
> Now I have come to know that for seven weeks you shall wander astray and profane the priesthood and defile the sacrificial altars. You shall set aside the Law and nullify the words of the prophets by your wicked perversity. You persecute just men: and you hate the pious; the word of the faithful you regard with revulsion. A man who by the power of the Most High renews the Law you name 'Deceiver', and finally you shall plot to kill him...on account of him your holy places shall be razed to the ground. You shall have no place that is clean, but you will be as a curse and a dispersion among the nations until he will again have regard for you, and will take you back in compassion. (T. Levi 16.1-5)
>
> My grief is great, my children, on account of the licentiousness and witchcraft and idolatry that you practice...and you will become involved in revolting gentile affairs. In response to this the Lord will bring you famine and plague, death and the sword, punishment by a siege, scattering by

enemies like dogs, the scorn of friends, destruction... slaughter...
plunder...consumption of God's sanctuary by fire, a desolate land, and
yourselves enslaved by the gentiles. And they shall castrate some of you as
eunuchs for their wives, until you return to the Lord in the integrity of
heart...then the Lord will...free you from captivity under your enemies.
(T. Judah 23.1-5)[10]

Probably written in the second century BCE, these passages likely
have in mind the Hasmoneans. There are several predictions of the
destruction of the Temple and/or holy places. T. Levi 10.3, if genuine,
could be a prediction of the Temple's destruction. H.C. Kee suspects
that a Christian scribe has tampered with the text, changing 'garment'
to 'curtain'.[11] T. Levi 14 predicts the desolation of the Temple, possibly
reflecting the very tradition found in Daniel 9. T. Levi 15.3, however,
understands this desolation as 'destruction', thus in all probability
implying the destruction of the Temple. T. Levi 16, evidently reworked
by a Christian,[12] contains an explicit reference to the razing of the 'holy
places'. This prediction is probably not an interpolation (whether
Christian or Jewish) based on the destruction of the Temple in 70 CE.
Although many inhabitants of Jerusalem were taken to Rome as
prisoners (cf. Josephus, *War* 6.9.3 §420; 7.1.3 §21 7.2.1 §24; 7.5.5
§138), there was not a general dispersion of the people, such as occurred
following the defeat of Bar Kochba. Rather, the language is traditional,
probably echoing the exile following the destruction of Jerusalem and
the Temple in 586 BCE. T. Judah 23, however, parallels the disaster of
70 so closely that one may suspect an interpolation. Siege, plunder,
destruction of the Temple 'by fire', and enslavement are all prominent
features in Josephus' account. However, some features, such as
witchcraft, idolatry, and what sounds like a general dispersion, do not
reflect the events of the first century, but have more of a ring of the
first destruction and exile. Therefore, the passage 'may be an authentic
prediction on the analogy of Dan[iel] 9'.[13]

---

10. Translations based on H.C. Kee, 'Testaments of the Twelve Patriarchs', in
J.H. Charlesworth (ed.), *The Old Testament Pseudepigrapha* (2 vols.; Garden City:
Doubleday, 1983–85), I, pp. 793, 794, 801.

11. Kee, 'Testaments', I, p. 792, n. b.

12. Kee ('Testaments', I, p. 794, n. a) rightly says that v. 13 is not an interpolation, but a Christian revision.

13. Kee, 'Testaments', I, p. 800, n. a.

1 Enoch

1 Enoch apparently contains two prophecies of the destruction of the second Temple:

> Then I stood still, looking at that ancient house being transformed: All the pillars and all the columns were pulled out; and the ornaments of that house were packed and taken out together with them and abandoned in a certain place in the South of the land. I went on seeing until the Lord of the sheep brought about a new house, greater and loftier than the first one, and set it up in the first location which had been covered up—all its pillars were new, the columns new; and the ornaments new as well as greater than those of the first, (that is) the old (house) which was gone. All the sheep were within it. (90.28-29)
>
> ...the roots of oppression shall be cut off. Sinners shall be destroyed; by the sword they shall be cut off (together with) the blasphemers in every place; and those who design oppression and commit blasphemy shall perish by the knife.
>
> Then after that there shall occur...the week of righteousness. A sword shall be given to it in order that judgment shall be executed in righteousness on the oppressors, and sinners shall be delivered into the hands of the righteous. At its completion, they shall acquire great things through their righteousness. A house shall be built for the Great King in glory for evermore. (91.11-13)
>
> ...a royal Temple of the Great One in his glorious splendor, for all generations, forever. (4QEn^g=1En. 91.13b)[14]

Elsewhere Enoch claims to predict the destruction of the Solomonic Temple and the building of the second Temple (1En. 89.72-73). This prediction, of course, is a *vaticinium ex eventu*. But in the passages cited above, which probably date from the Maccabean, even pre-Maccabean period,[15] the destruction of the second Temple and its replacement with a new, eschatological Temple seem to be envisioned. According to L. Gaston the 'ancient house' of 90.28 is not in reference to the Temple itself, but to Jerusalem (otherwise, how can 'all the sheep' be 'within it'?). He rightly points out that the Temple is normally called a 'tower' (cf. 89.50, 54, 56, 73).[16] Since Enoch describes the second Temple as

---

14. Translations based on E. Isaac, '1 (Ethiopic Apocalypse of) Enoch', in Charlesworth (ed.), *The Old Testament Pseudepigrapha*, I, pp. 71, 73 and n. f2.

15. Isaac, '1 Enoch', p. 7, following R.H. Charles, 'Book of Enoch', in R.H. Charles (ed.), *The Apocrypha and Pseudepigrapha of the Old Testament* (2 vols.; Oxford: Clarendon Press, 1913), II, pp. 170-71. 90.28-29 is dated 165–161 BCE; 91.11 105–104 BCE; and 91.12-13 pre-Maccabean.

16. Gaston, *No Stone on Another*, p. 114; cf. P. Volz, *Die Eschatologie der*

polluted (89.73), it is probably correct to understand that it will be removed, along with the old pillars and ornaments, and that it will be rebuilt, along with the new pillars.

The second passage speaks of building a house for the 'Great King'. Does the building of this 'house' (which in the parallel found in 4QEn^g is 'royal Temple'!) imply that the second Temple will first be destroyed? Perhaps logic alone requires this, but it is also possible that the reference to the destruction of the 'towers' in v. 9 is what drew the later material found in vv. 12-17 to ch. 91. Accordingly, the scribe who added vv. 12-17 and its prediction of the building of a house for God may have thought that the destruction of the 'towers' in v. 9 implied that the second Temple, as one of the 'towers', will be destroyed and thus will be in need of rebuilding.

Sibylline Oracles

The Sibylline Oracles appear to contain, if not a prediction of the Temple's destruction, at least a prediction of an attempt to destroy the Temple:

> But again the kings of the peoples will launch an attack together against this land, bringing doom upon themselves, for they will want to destroy the Temple of the Great God and most excellent men when they enter the land. The abominable kings, each one with his throne and faithless people, will set them up around the city. (3.665)[17]

It is unlikely that this oracle is based on the events of 70, or was colored by them (as is the one found in 5.398-402), for there were no 'kings' who assaulted the Temple during that conflict (cf. Jer. 34.1). J.J. Collins believes that it is a part of a much larger section written in the period 163–145 BCE.[18] The oracle probably alludes to various Ptolemaic and Seleucid monarchs, among them Antiochus IV. It is, of course, possible that the oracle continued to be interpreted, well past the Greek period, as prophetic and, therefore, as yet to be fulfilled.

---

jüdischen Gemeinde im neutestamentlichen Zeitalter nach den Quellen der rabbinischen, apokalyptischen und apokryphen Literatur dargestellt (Tübingen: Mohr [Paul Siebeck], 1934), p. 217.

17. Translation based on J.J. Collins, 'Sibylline Oracles', in Charlesworth (ed.), *Old Testament Pseudepigrapha*, I, p. 377.

18. Collins, 'Sibylline Oracles', I, pp. 354-55.

Qumran

Several writings of Qumran predict the destruction of the High Priest, and probably his supporters, but it is unclear if the Temple itself was expected to be destroyed:

> And as for that which he said, 'Because you have plundered many nations, all the remnant of the peoples will plunder you' [Hab. 2.8], the explanation of this concerns the last priests of Jerusalem who heap up riches and gain by plundering the peoples. But at the end of days, their riches, together with the fruit of their plundering, will be delivered into the hands of the army of the Kittim [i.e., the Romans]; for it is they who are 'the remnant of the peoples'. (1QpHab 9.2-7)
>
> The explanation of this word [i.e., Hab. 2.17] concerns the Wicked Priest inasmuch as he will be paid his reward for what he has done to the Poor...For God will condemn him to destruction even as he himself planned to destroy the Poor. (1QpHab 12.3-5)
>
> 'For a lion went to enter in, a lion cub' [Nah. 2.12]. [The explanation of this concerns Deme]trius king of Yawan who sought to enter Jerusalem on the counsel of those who seek smooth things [in 88 BCE; cf. Josephus, *Ant.* 13.14.2 §379-83; *War* 1.4.5 §93-95]. [But he did not enter, for] from Antiochus until the rising of the commanders of the Kittim [God did not deliver it] into the hand of the kings of Yawan [i.e., the Ptolemies and Seleucids]. But afterwards it will be trampled under foot [by the Kittim]. (4QpNah 1.1-3)[19]
>
> And I shall sanctify my [sanc]tuary with my glory for I shall cause my glory to dwell upon it until (?) the day of blessing(?) on which I shall create (anew) my san[ctuary (?)] to prepare it for myself for all [t]ime according to the covenant which I made with Jacob at Bethel. (11QTem. 29.8-10)
>
> ...I shall sanctify...and ma[ke]...house which you shall build... (11QTem. 30.1-4)[20]

It is not clear whether the plundering and destruction of the Wicked Priest entails destruction of the Temple as well. (In 1QpHab 9.9-11 he is 'delivered into the hands of his enemies to humble him with a destroying blow'.) It might be, especially if 11QTemple's hope for a new sanctuary, a 'house which [the righteous] will build', was understood to imply that the old building was to be destroyed. J. Maier, however, thinks that 11QTemple is speaking only of the Temple that Israel was to

19. Translation based on A. Dupont-Sommer, *The Essene Writings from Qumran* (Gloucester: Peter Smith, 1973), pp. 264, 267, 268.

20. Translation based on J. Maier, *The Temple Scroll: An Introduction, Translation & Commentary* (JSOTSup 34; Sheffield: JSOT Press, 1985), p. 32.

build in the promised land;[21] others think that it is eschatological.[22] E.P. Sanders finds in 'until [עַד] the day of blessing' a hint that the Temple will come to an end.[23] But there is also the possibility that this new building approximates the 'sanctuary of men', or spiritual Temple, mentioned in 4QFlor 1.6,[24] in which case the text probably implies nothing of the fate of the Temple. The pesher on Nahum may be referring to Pompey's conquest of Jerusalem in 63 BCE, which is what A. Dupont-Sommer thinks.[25] This may be correct, but it is also possible that this exegesis came to be regarded as a yet-to-be fulfilled prophecy of a Roman trampling of Jerusalem.

Jesus of Nazareth

Jesus of Nazareth predicted the destruction of Jerusalem and its Temple:

> O Jerusalem, Jerusalem, killing the prophets and those who are sent to you! How often would I have gathered your children together as a hen gathers her brood under her wings, and you would not! Behold, your house is forsaken. (Lk. 13.34-35a par.)
>
> And when he drew near and saw the city he wept over it, saying, 'Would that even today you knew the things that make for peace! But now they are hid from your eyes. For the days shall come upon you, when your enemies will cast up a bank about you and surround you, and hem you in on every side, and dash you to the ground, you and your children within you, and they will not leave one stone upon another in you; because you did not know the time of your visitation'. (Lk. 19.41-44)
>
> And as he came out of the Temple, one of his disciples said to him, 'Look, Teacher, what wonderful stones and what wonderful buildings!' And Jesus said to him, 'Do you see these great buildings? There will not be left here one stone upon another, that will not be thrown down'. (Mk. 13.1-2 par.)
>
> But when you see Jerusalem surrounded by armies, then know that its desolation has come near. Then let those who are in Judea flee to the

21. Maier, *The Temple Scroll*, p. 86.

22. B. Thiering, '*Mebaqqer* and *Episkopos* in the Light of the Temple Scroll', *JBL* 100 (1981), pp. 59-75, esp. pp. 60-61; B.Z. Wacholder, *The Dawn of Qumran: The Sectarian Torah and the Teacher of Righteousness* (Cincinnati: Hebrew Union College, 1983), pp. 21-23.

23. Sanders, *Jesus and Judaism*, p. 85. On עַד as the correct reading, see p. 370 n. 18.

24. For a discussion of this question, see Gaston, *No Stone on Another*, pp. 127-28, 164; and Sanders, *Jesus and Judaism*, pp. 84-85.

25. Dupont-Sommer, *The Essene Writings*, p. 268 n. 3.

mountains, and let those who are inside the city depart, and let not those who are out in the country enter it; for these are days of vengeance, to fulfill all that is written. Alas for those who are with child and for those who give suck in those days! For great distress shall come upon the earth and wrath upon this people; and they will fall by the edge of the sword, and be led captive among all nations; and Jerusalem will be trodden down by the Gentiles, until the times of the Gentiles are fulfilled (Lk. 21.20-24 par.)

And there followed him a great multitude of the people, and of women who bewailed and lamented him. But Jesus turning to them said, 'Daughters of Jerusalem, do not weep for me, but weep for yourselves and for your children. For behold, the days are coming when they will say, "Blessed are the barren, and the wombs that never bore, and the breasts that never gave suck!" Then they will begin to say to the mountains, "Fall on us"; and to the hills, "Cover us". For if they do this when the wood is green, what will happen when it is dry?' (Lk. 23.27-31)

As has already been stated, more scholars have concluded that Jesus did predict the Temple's destruction. Usually most are willing to accept the version found in Mk 13.2, 'There will not be left here one stone upon another, that will not be thrown down', but many suspect that much of the remaining material has been heavily redacted by early Christians, either shortly before or after the Temple's destruction.

Lives of the Prophets
The Lives of Prophets, probably pre-70,[26] contains two prophecies of the destruction of the first-century Temple:

And he [Jonah] gave a portent concerning Jerusalem and the whole land, that whenever they should see a stone crying out piteously the end was at hand. And whenever they should see all the gentiles in Jerusalem, the entire city would be razed to the ground. ([LivPro] 10.10-11)[27]

And concerning the end [συντέλεια] of the Temple he [Habakkuk] predicted, 'By a western nation it will happen'. 'At that time', he said, 'the curtain [ἅπλωμα] of the Dabeir [i.e., the Holy of Holies] will be torn into

---

26. On the date of the Lives of the Prophets C.C. Torrey (*The Lives of the Prophets* [SBLMS, 1; Philadelphia: Society of Biblical Literature, 1946] p. 11) concluded that 'the probability is very strong...that the work was composed and given out before the year 80'. D.R.A. Hare ('The Lives of the Prophets', in Charlesworth [ed.], *Old Testament Pseudepigrapha*, II, p. 381 n. 11) dates much more of the material before 70.

27. Translation based on Hare, 'The Lives of the Prophets', II, p. 393.

small pieces, and the capitals of the two pillars will be taken away and no one will know where they are; and they will be carried away by angels into the wilderness, where the Tent of Witness was set up in the beginning'. ([Liv Pro] 12.11)[28]

D.R.A. Hare believes that these prophecies are not based upon the events of 70 CE. In reference to the prophecy credited to Jonah, he thinks that rather than the Romans, the prophecy seems 'to reflect uneasiness regarding the increasing number of gentile visitors and/or residents, which threatened to change the character of Israel's holy city'.[29] He adds that the 'prophecy of 10.11 is best taken as reflecting an earlier situation, not the bitter experience' of 70 CE.[30] In reference to Habakkuk's prophecy of the Temple's destruction at the hands of a 'western nation', Hare similarly concludes that the 'prediction of 12.11 that the Temple will be destroyed by a Western nation was probably understood as referring to the Romans, but nothing requires that it be taken as a prophecy after the fact; the accompanying statements have the ring of unfulfilled predictions'.[31]

I think that Hare is correct. But what about the tearing of the curtain? Could this be a *vaticinium ex eventu*? Probably not, for Josephus says nothing of the Temple veil(s) being torn to pieces. Rather, the veils (καταπετάσματα), vestments of the priests, and several items belonging to the Temple were surrendered intact to the Romans (*War* 6.8.3 §389-91) and were probably among the items carefully put on display in the newly constructed 'Temple of Peace' (*War* 7.5.7 §158-62). Even Mk 15.38, which says that 'the veil [καταπέτασμα] of the Temple was torn in two from top to bottom', does not likely reflect either Josephus or Lives of the Prophets. Nor does it seem likely that the latter work is dependent here on Mark.

Josephus
Josephus himself, who evidently prophesied Vespasian's elevation to Roman emperorship (*War* 3.8.9 §400-402; cf. Tacitus, *Histories* 1.10; 2.1; Dio Cassius, *Roman History* 66.1; Suetonius, *Vespasian* §5), also claims to have predicted the destruction of the Temple and the defeat of the Jewish rebels:

28. Translation based on Hare, 'The Lives of the Prophets', II, pp. 393-94.
29. Hare, 'The Lives of the Prophets', II, p. 393 n. 1.
30. Hare, 'The Lives of the Prophets', II, p. 381 n. 11.
31. Hare, 'The Lives of the Prophets', II, p. 381 n. 11.

> But as...Josephus overheard the threats of the hostile crowd, suddenly
> there came back into his mind those nightly dreams, in which God had
> foretold to him the impending fate of the Jews and the destinies of the
> Roman sovereigns...he was not ignorant of the prophecies in the sacred
> books. (*War* 3.8.3 §351-52)

This prophecy clarifies Josephus' occasional fatalistic statements: 'That
building, however, God, indeed long since, had sentenced to the flames'
(*War* 6.4.5 §250). But what 'prophecies in the sacred books' did
Josephus have in mind? He relates two of them, albeit in very cryptic
terms:

> Who does not know the records of the ancient prophets and that oracle
> [χρησμός] which threatens this poor city and is even now coming true?
> For they foretold that it would then be taken whenever one should begin to
> slaughter his own countrymen. (*War* 6.2.1 §109)
>
> Thus the Jews, after the demolition of Antonia, reduced the Temple to a
> square, although they had it recorded in their oracles that the city and the
> sanctuary would be taken when the Temple should become foursquare
> (τετράγωνος). (*War* 6.5.4 §311)[32]

There is some speculation that the first passage, the one alluding to an
'oracle' that speaks of fratricide, may have been dependent on SibOr
4.115-18: 'An evil storm of war will also come upon Jerusalem from
Italy, and it will sack the great Temple of God, whenever they put their
trust in folly and cast off piety and commit repulsive murders in front of
the Temple'.[33] But this prophecy is clearly a *vaticinium ex eventu*, for
the lines that follow (ll. 119-27) unmistakably describe Nero, the bloody
imperial succession, the arrival of Titus, the burning of the Jerusalem
Temple, and the slaughter of the Jewish people. The allusion to the
eruption of Vesuvius in 79 CE (ll. 128-29) only confirms that these lines
were written sometime after 80.[34] But is this the oracle that Josephus
had in mind? Probably not, for chronological reasons, if for no other.
The Jewish War was written between 75, when the Temple of Peace
was completed, and 79, the year that Vespasian died. Near the end of his
account Josephus mentions the Flavian Temple (*War* 7.5.7 §158), whose
completion Dio Cassius (*Roman History* 66.15) dates to 75. Thus, *War*

---

32. Translation based on H. St. J. Thackeray, *Josephus* (LCL, 2-3; Cambridge,
MA: Harvard University Press, 1927–28), II, p. 675; III, pp. 407, 447, 467.

33. Thackeray, *Josephus*, III, pp. 406-407 n. b. Translation based on Collins,
'Sibylline Oracles', I, p. 387.

34. See Collins, 'Sibylline Oracles', I, p. 382.

itself was later than 75, but it is known that Vespasian was presented with a copy before his death.[35] It is not likely, therefore, that Josephus had seen the prophecy now preserved in the Sibylline Oracles. More likely Josephus had in mind an oracle based on the Jewish scriptures (see below).

Perhaps the most remarkable oracle is that attributed to one Jesus, son of Ananias, who for seven and a half years proclaimed the doom of Jerusalem and her Temple. According to Josephus:

> Four years before the war...one Jesus, son of Ananias ['Ιησοῦς...τις υἱὸς 'Ανανίου]...who, standing in the Temple [ἱερόν], suddenly began to cry out:
> 'A voice from the east,
> 'A voice from the west,
> 'A voice from the four winds,
> 'A voice against Jerusalem and the Sanctuary [ναός],
> 'A voice against the bridegroom and the bride,
> 'A voice against all people' (*War* 6.5.3 §301)
> 'Woe to Jerusalem!' (*War* 6.5.3 §306)
> 'Woe once more to the city and to the people and to the Sanctuary [ναός]...and woe to me also' (*War* 6.5.3 §309)[36]

Josephus tells that this Jesus, a 'rude peasant', was arrested by leading citizens and severely chastised. When he continued to cry out as before, he was taken before the Roman governor, who had him 'flayed to the bone with scourges' (*War* 6.5.3 §302-304). Albinus decided that he was a maniac, and so released him (§305). Jesus continued to proclaim his foreboding oracle, until he was killed by a siege stone catapulted over the city walls (§309).

Yohanan ben Zakkai and Zadok
Apparently two tannaim predicted the destruction of the first-century Temple:

> Forty years before the destruction of the Temple the western light went out, the crimson thread remained crimson, and the lot for the Lord always came up in the left hand. They would close the gates of the Temple by night and get up in the morning and find them wide open. Said Rabban Yohanan ben Zakkai [1st century] to the Temple, 'O Temple, why do you

---

35. Thackeray, *Josephus*, II, p. xii.
36. Translation based on Thackeray, *Josephus*, III, pp. 463-67.

frighten us? We know that you will end up destroyed. For it has been said, "Open your doors, O Lebanon,[37] that the fire may devour your cedars" [Zech. 11.1]'.[38] (*y. Sota* 6.3)

During the last forty years before the destruction of the Temple the lot [for the Lord] did not come up in the right hand; nor did the crimson-colored strap become white; nor did the westernmost light shine; and the doors of the Temple would open by themselves, until Rabbi Yohanan ben Zakkai rebuked them, saying: 'Temple, Temple, why will you be the alarm yourself? I know that you will be destroyed, for Zechariah ben Ido has already prophesied concerning you: "Open your doors, O Lebanon, that the fire may devour your cedars" [Zech. 11.1]'.[39] (*b. Yoma* 39)

[When Vespasian objected to Yohanan ben Zakkai's greeting, 'Vive domine Imperator', Johanan explained:] 'If you are not the king, you will be eventually, because the Temple will only be destroyed by a king's hand; as it is said, "And lebanon shall fall by a mighty one" [Isa. 10.34]'.[40] (*Lam. Rab.* 1.5 §31)

Rabbi Zadok [1st century] observed fasts for forty years in order that Jerusalem might not be destroyed, [and he became so thin that] when he ate anything the food could be seen [as it passed down his throat].[41] (*b. Git.* 56a)

It says, 'Open your doors, O Lebanon, that the fire may devour your cedars' [Zech. 11.1]. This refers to the high priests who were in the Temple, who took their keys in their hands and threw them up to the sky, saying to the Holy One, blessed be he, 'Master of the Universe, here are

37. 'Lebanon' is understood to refer to the Temple: '"And Lebanon", meaning the Temple, as in the passage: "Open your doors, O Lebanon" [Zech. 11.1]' (*Mekilta, Amalek* §2 [on Exod. 17.14]). This equation is based on a word-play between לבנון ('Lebanon') and לבן ('white'); see *Tg. Hab.* 2.17 where 'Lebanon' = the Temple. Cedars from Lebanon were used, of course, in the construction of the Temple (1 Kgs 5.6). Elsewhere Lebanon was closely associated with the Temple (cf. Isa. 60.13). For further discussion see G. Vermes, *Scripture and Tradition in Judaism* (SPB, 4; Leiden: Brill, 1983, 2nd edn), pp. 26-39; Bockmuehl, 'Why Did Jesus Predict the Destruction of the Temple?', pp. 13-14.

38. Translation from J. Neusner, *Messiah in Context: Israel's History and Destiny in Formative Judaism* (Philadelphia: Fortress Press, 1984), p. 112.

39. Translation based on L. Jung, 'Yoma', in I. Epstein (ed.), *The Babylonian Talmud* (18 vols; London: Soncino, 1978), IV, p. 186.

40. Translation based on J. Neusner, *A Life of Rabban Yohanan ben Zakkai* (Leiden: Brill, 1962), p. 40.

41. Translation based on M. Simon, 'Gittin', in Epstein (ed.), *The Babylonian Talmud*, IX, p. 257.

your keys which you handed over to us, for we have not been trustworthy custodians to do the King's work and to eat of the King's table'.[42] (*'Abot R. Nat.* [A] §4)

Yohanan ben Zakkai and other rabbis apparently tried to persuade the rebels to surrender to the Romans. Nearly murdered for his failure to support the rebellion, Yohanan finally escaped the city, being carried out in a coffin (*Lam. Rab.* 1.5 §31; *b. Git.* 56a-b; *Abot R. Nat.* [A] §4). According to the tradition in *Lamentations Rabbah* Zadok's life was spared at Yohanan's request.

The Scriptural/Prophetic Backgrounds of the Predictions

Virtually every prediction of the destruction of the Temple and/or the city of Jerusalem is based upon the Jewish scriptures. The significance of this observation will become clear.

Testaments of the Twelve Patriarchs

The prophetic tradition has supplied much of the imagery of the other predictions found in the Testaments. Indeed, the author makes explicit reference to 'the writings of Enoch', which speak of 'the end-time'. He could hardly make such an explicit reference to Israel's classical prophets without being guilty of a gross anachronism. Nevertheless, the predictions do contain important allusions to the writings of these prophets.

The prediction in T. Levi 10.3 that 'the curtain of the Temple will be torn' is probably an authentic but redacted tradition. Kee has suggested, as noted above, that the text originally read 'garment', or something to that effect, perhaps based on Hos. 2.9-10: 'I will take away my wool and my flax, which were to cover her nakedness. Now I will uncover her lewdness in the sight of her lovers, and no one will rescue her out of my hand'.

The reference to humiliation and scorn among the nations (T. Levi 14.1; 15.2) may be to Ezek. 23.25-35, which because of lewdness and harlotry Israel will be scorned by the nations. The reference to theft of the sacrifices and consorting with whores (T. Levi 14.5) probably is an allusion to the wickedness of the sons of Eli, described in 1 Samuel (see esp. 2.12-17; 22-25), whose wickedness becomes eschatologized and

---

42. Translation based on J. Goldin, *The Fathers according to Rabbi Nathan* (Yale Judaica, 10; New Haven and London: Yale University, 1955), p. 37.

typological (cf. *Tg. 1 Sam.* 2.17, 29; *b. Pesah.* 57a). The reference to teaching for gain (T. Levi 14.6a) may be to Mal. 3.11, which accuses the priests and teachers of the Law of the same thing. The reference to becoming 'like Sodom and Gomorrah' (T. Levi 14.6b) obviously alludes to the wicked cities that were destroyed (Genesis 18–19) and which later became a symbol frequently used by the prophets, often to describe Israel's wickedness (Isa. 1.9; 3.9; Jer. 23.14; Amos 4.11). The reference to taking gentile women for wives (T. Levi 14.6c) is reminiscent of the problem faced by Ezra (Ezra 10.18-24; cf. Neh. 13.23-29), where Levites and priests had married foreign women. Contempt for the 'sacred things' (T. Levi 14.8) may allude to Malachi's complaint (Mal. 1.7, 12). The reference to the desolation of the sanctuary (T. Levi 15.1) may be to the brutal activities of Antiochus IV, also described in Daniel 9 (see esp. vv. 24-27).

There are more allusions to the prophetic tradition in T. Levi 16. Profaning the priesthood and defiling the sacrificial altars (v. 1) once again recalls Malachi (1.7, 12). Disobeying the Law and the prophets (v. 2) recalls the similar complaint of Jeremiah (26.4-5), a complaint which ends with a prediction of the Temple's destruction (Jer. 26.6). Persecution of the just (v. 2) recalls another common prophetic complaint (Isa. 1.23; 5.23; Amos 5.12). The warning that Israel will suffer the loss of her holy places and be made a curse (vv. 4-5) recalls again the language of Jeremiah (Jer. 26.6; cf. 25.18), while the threat of 'dispersion among the nations' (v. 5) appears often in the prophets (Deut. 28.37; Jer. 25.34; 29.18; Ezek. 6.9; Hos. 9.17). The promise of exiled Israel being taken back (v. 5) is also a prophetic commonplace (Deut. 30.3; Jer. 12.15; 32.37; Mic. 2.12).

The prediction of destruction found in T. Judah 23 also appears to reflect the prophetic tradition concerned with the Babylonian destruction. Licentiousness and witchcraft (v. 1) were among the sins of the leading citizens of Jerusalem prior to the city's destruction (2 Chron. 33.6; Isa. 8.19; Jer. 7.9; 23.10; 14; 27.9; Ezekiel 16). Becoming 'involved in revolting gentile affairs' (v. 2) probably alludes primarily to the political intrigues of the Hasmoneans, but it is also reminiscent of earlier prophetic criticisms (Isa. 28.14-15; 30.1-5). The grim features associated with war (vv. 3-4) all find expression in the prophets, particularly in reference to the Babylonian destruction: famine (Jer. 11.22; Ezek. 6.11), plague (Jer. 21.7; Ezek. 6.11), death (Jer. 9.21-22; 21.8-9), sword (Jer. 11.22; Ezek. 6.11), siege (Isa. 29.3; Jer. 19.9; Ezek. 5.2), scattering

(Jer. 9.16; Ezek. 22.15), destruction (Jer. 4.20; 6.1), slaughter (Jer. 7.32; 12.3; Ezek. 21.10), plunder (Jer. 15.13; 17.3; Ezek. 7.21), enslavement (Jer. 5.19; 27.1-11; Ezek. 34.37), and being made eunuchs (Isa. 39.7; 2 Kgs 20.18). In some instances several of these words occur in a single verse (cf. Jer. 15.2). Even the expression, 'consumption of God's sanctuary by fire', does not necessarily reflect the destruction in 70, for the Solomonic Temple was also burned (2 Kgs 25.9; Jer. 52.13). Finally, release from captivity (v. 5) was a widely-held prophetic hope (Isa. 40.11; Jer. 23.3; 31.10; Ezek. 20.41-42).

Jesus of Nazareth

Jesus' predictions, like those of others, were based on the prophetic tradition that had addressed itself to the destruction of the first Temple. All five passages are indebted to the language of the Old Testament, principally to that of the prophets.

Lk. 13.34-35a. The tradition is derived from Q (cf. Mt. 23.37-39) and has a good claim to authenticity.[43] Whether or not it foresees the destruction of the city or the Temple depends upon the interpretation of v. 35a. Let us consider the lament phrase by phrase.

'killing the prophets and stoning [λιθοβολοῦσα] those sent to you!': In the Old Testament there is only one example of a prophet stoned or killed by other means. In 2 Chron. 24.20-21 Zechariah, son of the priest Jehoida, is stoned to death for the speaking the word of the Lord: 'at the command of the king they stoned [ἐλιθοβόλησαν] him in the court of the Lord' (cf. Lk. 11.50-51, where this Zechariah is mentioned). Jeremiah, who was placed in stocks (Jer. 20.1-2) and cast into a pit (38.6), is the only example in the Old Testament of a prophet who was persecuted. Nevertheless, an imaginative and colorful tradition arose that assumed that deadly persecution of the prophets was frequent, if not the norm. For example, it was believed that the prophet Isaiah was placed in a hollow log and sawed in two by order of Manasseh (*MartIs.* 5.1-14; cf. Heb. 11.37). According to the Lives of the Prophets (cf. 1.1; 2.1; 3.1-2; 6.2; 7.2) Isaiah, Jeremiah, Ezekiel, Micah, and Amos were martyred by fellow Israelites. One haggadah gives expression to Jeremiah's reluctance to enter the prophetic vocation: 'O Lord, I cannot go as a prophet to

---

43. So I.H. Marshall, *Commentary on Luke* (NIGTC; Grand Rapids: Eerdmans, 1978), p. 574; J.A. Fitzmyer, *The Gospel according to Luke X-XXIV* (AB, 28 28a; Garden City: Doubleday, 1985), p. 1034. The spelling of Jerusalem ('Ιερουσαλήμ) reflects Aramaic (יְרוּשְׁלֵם) and so argues for antiquity and a Palestinian setting.

Israel, for when lived there a prophet whom Israel did not desire to kill? Moses and Aaron they sought to stone with stones [cf. Josephus, *Ant.* 2.15.4 §327]; Elijah the Tishbite they mocked...'[44] Jesus' statement is a brief summary that echoes similar, and usually longer, summaries in the Old Testament: 'The Lord...sent persistently to them by his messengers...but they kept mocking the messengers of God, despising his words, and scoffing at his prophets, till the wrath of the Lord rose against this people, till there was no remedy' (2 Chron. 36.15-16; cf. Lam. 4.13; Pss. 78, 105, 106). These Old Testament summaries are likely what gave rise to the tradition of the stoning and persecution of the prophets (cf. Mk 12.2-8). Significantly, the Chronicler goes on to speak of the Babylonian destruction of the city and the Temple (2 Chron. 36.17-21).

'...as a hen gathers her brood under her wings': Probably the closest parallel in the Old Testament is found in Deut. 32.11, which speaks of God's love and protective care of his people: 'Like an eagle that stirs up its nest, that flutters over its young, spreading out its wings, catching them, bearing them on its pinions'. Again, it is interesting to observe that Moses' song goes on to describe Israel's disobedience (vv. 15-18) and destruction (vv. 25-27). Elsewhere in the Old Testament there is the image of coming under the protective wing of God (Ruth 2.12; Pss. 17.8; 36.7; 57.1; 61.4).

'Your house [οἶκος] is forsaken [ἀφίεται]': Two passages from Jeremiah (12.7; 22.5) are usually mentioned as lying behind this statement. The second passage, which speaks of desolation (ἐρήμωσις)[45] is probably not primary, but the second one, which in the Greek uses the very verb found in Luke, probably is: 'I have abandoned my house [οἶκος], I have forsaken [ἀφῆκα] my inheritance, I have given the beloved of my life into the hands of her enemies' (LXX Jer. 12.7).[46] What 'house' means is not certain. Fitzmyer thinks that it might be 'seed' or 'offspring',[47] which is probably the meaning in Jeremiah (in

---

44. From L. Ginzberg, *The Legends of the Jews* (7 vols.; Philadelphia: Jewish Publication Society, 1909), IV, p. 295.

45. The cognate ἔρημος occurs in Mt. 23.38 (but omitted in B L and some versions and a few fathers).

46. The Greek is a very literal rendering of the Hebrew.

47. Fitzmyer, *Luke X-XXIV*, p. 1037; cf. F.D. Weinert, 'Luke, the Temple, and Jesus' Saying about Jerusalem's Abandoned House (Luke 13.34-35)', *CBQ* 44 (1982), pp. 68-76.

both passages). But that is not necessarily what Jesus meant. It is not likely that 'house' means either Jerusalem or its people; the context militates against such an interpretation. Perhaps it means the Temple, as Marshall thinks.[48] If it does, then this lament may contain a prediction of the Temple's destruction.

Lk. 19.41-44; Mk 13.2. Jesus' lament for the city of Jerusalem is unique. Not surprisingly Bultmann regards it as 'a *vaticinium ex eventu*', which betrays Christian tendencies.[49] But Fitzmyer does not think so, since one would expect a prophecy after the fact to be more specific in its terminology.[50] As it turns out, the terminology has been drawn from the prophets, especially from Jeremiah.[51] Luke knows of the city's destruction, of course, and this knowledge has influenced his presentation of the tradition. But the tradition itself has not been developed from the events of 70 CE. Thus there really is no reason for not accepting the passage, reworked and contextualized as it may be, as a genuine prediction of Jerusalem's destruction. Again a phrase by phrase analysis will be undertaken.

'seeing the city, he wept [ἔκλαυσεν] for it': Jeremiah had wept for Judah: 'O that my head were waters, and my eyes a fountain of tears, that I might weep [κλαύσομαι] day and night for the slain of the daughter [i.e., Judah] of my people' (Jer. 9.1 [Hebr. and LXX 8.23]; cf. Jer. 14.17). One is also reminded of Elisha who wept (ἔκλαυσεν) as he looked upon Hazael, who was to become king of Syria and who would inflict terrible sufferings on Israel (2 Kgs 8.11-13).

'If you had known on this day, even you, the things that make for peace [εἰρήνη]': Again we are reminded of Jeremiah: 'Be warned, O Jerusalem...saying "Peace, peace [εἰρήνη εἰρήνη]", when there is no peace' (Jer. 6.8, 14; cf. Isa. 48.18; 'O that you had hearkened to my commandments! Then your peace [εἰρήνη] would have been like a river'). Recall the lament in Lk. 13.34: 'O Jerusalem, Jerusalem...'.

'days will come [ἥξουσιν ἡμέραι]': This echoes Isaiah's warning to

48. Marshall, *Luke*, p. 576.

49. Bultmann, *History of the Synoptic Tradition*, pp. 36, 123, 127.

50. Fitzmyer, *Luke X-XXIV*, p. 1255.

51. See C.H. Dodd, 'The Fall of Jerusalem and the "Abomination of Desolation"', *JRS* 37 (1947), pp. 47-54; repr. in C.H. Dodd, *More New Testament Studies* (Grand Rapids: Eerdmans, 1968), pp. 69-83; Gaston, *No Stone on Another*, p. 359; D. Tiede, *Prophecy and History in Luke-Acts* (Philadelphia: Fortress Press, 1980), pp. 65-96.

Hezekiah: 'Behold, the days are coming [ἡμέραι ἔρχονται], when all that is in your house, and that which your fathers have stored up till this day, shall be carried to Babylon; nothing shall be left' (2 Kgs 20.17; cf. Jer. 7.32: 'Behold, the days are coming [ἡμέραι ἔρχονται], says the Lord'; and see the warning given to Eli: 'Behold, the days are coming [ἡμέραι ἔρχονται], when I will cut off your strength...so that there will not be an old man in your house'; 1 Sam. 2.31).

'your enemies will throw up an embankment [παρεμβαλοῦσιν... χάρακά σοι] about you': Jeremiah warned his contemporaries of the coming enemy which will 'cast up a siege mound against Jerusalem' (Jer. 6.6). Similarly Ezekiel warned the inhabitants of Jerusalem by acting out what was coming: 'Put siegeworks against it, and build a siege wall against it, and cast up a mound against it [περιβαλεῖς ἐπ᾽ αὐτὴν χάρακα]' (Ezek. 4.2). Another close verbal parallel is found in Isaiah who warned apostate Jerusalem: 'I will encircle you, O David, throw up an embankment [βαλῶ περὶ σὲ χάρακα], and set towers about you' (Isa. 29.3).

'and will encircle you [περικυκλώσουσίν σε]': The threat of encirclement was a common feature in ancient warfare and is found in some of the very oracles already considered: 'I will encircle [κυκλώσω...ἐπὶ σὲ] you' (Isa. 29.3; cf. 37.33: μὴ κυκλώσῃ ἐπ᾽ αὐτὴν χάρακα); 'and plant battering rams against it round about [κύκλῳ]' (Ezek. 4.2); 'and [the king of Syria and his army] came by night, and surrounded the city [περιεκύκλωσαν τὴν πόλιν]' (2 Kgs 6.14).

'and will hem you in on every side [συνέξουσίν σε πάντοθεν]': One of the few passages that uses a cognate of συνέχω ('to press' or 'hem in'), also employs much of the key vocabulary already noted: 'Nebuchadrezzar king of Babylon came with all his army against Jerusalem, and they laid siege [περιεχαράκωσαν] to it, and built siegeworks around about it [κύκλῳ], and the city came to be pressed [συνοχή]' (Jer. 52.4b-5a). This phrase may echo parts of other passages (Ezek. 4.2; 21.22; cf. 2 Macc. 9.2: '[Antiochus]...attempted... to control the city [τὴν πόλιν συνέχειν]').

'They will dash you and your children [ἐδαφιοῦσίν σε καὶ τὰ τέκνα σου] within you [ἐν σοί] to the ground': Various texts describe little ones being dashed in pieces: '...mothers were dashed in pieces with their children [μητέρα ἐπὶ τέκνοις ἠδάφισαν/רֻטָּֽשָׁה]' (Hos. 10.14; cf. Nah. 3.10; Ps. 137.9); 'Hazael said, "Why does my lord weep?" [Elisha] answered, "Because I know the evil that you will do to the people of

Israel; you will set on fire their fortresses, and you will slay their young men with the sword, and dash in pieces [וּטֹשׁ] their little ones, and rip up their women with child"' (2 Kgs 8.12). For the oracular style of addressing the city of Jerusalem in the second person singular see Ezek. 22.4-16. For several examples of ἐν σοί see vv. 6-12.

'and they will not leave a stone on a stone [οὐκ ἀφήσουσιν λίθον ἐπὶ λίθον] in you [ἐν σοί]': This part of the lament closely parallels the prediction in Mk 13.2: 'There will not be left here a stone upon a stone [οὐ μὴ ἀφεθῇ ὧδε λίθος ἐπὶ λίθον] which will not be thrown down'. But it is probably independent of Mark.[52] The Lucan evangelist avoids doublets, so it is not likely that he has enriched 19.41-44 by borrowing from Mk 13.2 (only to repeat the Marcan material in Lk. 21.6). It is, of course, possible that Mk 13.2 influenced the transmission of the oracle. The language is reminiscent of Hushai's counsel to Absalom: 'If [David] withdraws into a city, then all Israel will bring ropes to that city, and we shall drag it into the valley, so that not even a stone will be left there [μὴ καταλειφθῇ ἐκεῖ μηδὲ λίθος]' (2 Sam. 17.13; cf. Ezek. 26.12 where the prophet predicts that the stones and timbers of Tyre will be picked up and thrown into the sea).

With respect to the origin of the prophecy found in Mk 13.2, it is unlikely that it reflects the description of what happened in 70 CE. Consider the passage that Pesch and others have cited from Josephus: 'Caesar ordered the whole city and the temple to be razed' (κελεύει Καῖσαρ ἤδη τήν τε πόλιν ἄπασιν καὶ τὸν νεών[53] κατασκάπτειν[54]). The feature in the report of Josephus that stands out is that the Temple and the city were destroyed by fire (*War* 6.2.1. §110 ['It is God himself who with the Romans is bringing the fire to purge his Temple']; 6.2.9 §165-67; 6.4.1 §228 ['Titus...issued orders to set the gates (of the Temple) on fire']; 6.4.2 §232-35; 6.4.5 §250-53; 6.4.6-5.2 §254-87; 6.6.3 §354-55; 6.7.2 §363; 6.8.5 §407). 'The Romans, thinking it useless, now that the Temple was on fire, to spare the surrounding buildings, set them all alight...these also they subsequently razed to the ground [κατασκάπτειν]. They further burned the treasury-chambers' (*War* 6.5.2 §281-82). In my judgment the prophecy that not one stone would be left upon another is a genuine prophecy uttered by Jesus.

52. Marshall, *Luke*, p. 719.
53. Νεώς is Attic for ναός.
54. Κατασκάπτειν means 'to dig up' or 'demolish'. Josephus uses it to describe the destruction of Antonia (*War* 6.2.1 §93).

'because you did not know the time of your visitation [καιρὸν τῆς ἐπισκοπῆς]': 'Time of visitation' is clearly an allusion to the threatening oracle of Jeremiah: 'at the time of their visitation [ἐν καιρῷ ἐπισκοπῆς] they will perish' (LXX Jer. 6.15; cf. Jer. 10.15 where the statement is repeated). Fitzmyer correctly notes that ἐπισκοπή frequently translates פְּקֻדָּה (or related forms of פקד), meaning 'visitation', 'inspection', or 'punishment' (cf. Isa. 10.3; Wis. 3.7). It can have either a positive or negative reference.

Lk. 21.20-24. Both Marshall and Fitzmyer think that Lk. 21.20-24 represents a heavily redacted version of Mk 13.14-20. They may be right, for the passage's location (following the Marcan sequence) and some common vocabulary could suggest this. But it is also possible, C.H. Dodd thinks probable,[55] that the material took shape much earlier. I suspect that this material is pre-Lucan and has possibly been redacted in light of the Marcan material. But does it go back to Jesus? Dodd thinks that it was an oracle, based upon Old Testament materials, circulating in Palestine before the Roman war, which Christians mistakenly thought originated with Jesus.[56] This is, of course, possible. But its coherence with Lk. 19.41-44, a lament which likely derives from Jesus, supports the claim of dominical origin. The evangelist replaced the Marcan oracle with his oracle, but not without editing the latter in the light of the former. Like the oracle reviewed above, Lk. 21.20-24 draws heavily upon the prophetic tradition.[57]

'When you see Jerusalem ['Ιερουσαλήμ] surrounded by armies [στρατοπέδον]': Mark (13.14a) has 'When you see the abomination of desolation...' Luke was not interested in the explicit reference to Daniel, but he picked up Mark's opening words. The surrounding of Jerusalem recalls Lk. 19.43 (cf. Isa. 29.3), but 'armies' may echo Jeremiah's description of the siege of Jerusalem: 'Nebuchadrezzar king of Babylon and all his army [στρατοπέδον] and all the kingdoms of the earth under his dominion and all the peoples were fighting against Jerusalem ['Ιερουσαλήμ] (LXX Jer. 41.1 [Heb. 34.1]).

'know that her desolation [ἐρήμωσις] has drawn near': This is an allusion to Mark's 'abomination of desolation', which in turn is drawn from Dan. 12.11 (βδέλυγμα τῆς ἐρημώσεως).

---

55. Dodd, 'The Fall of Jerusalem', pp. 52-54.
56. Dodd, 'The Fall of Jerusalem', p. 52.
57. The oracle consciously draws on the prophetic tradition, as v. 22b makes clear: 'to fulfill all that is written'.

'let those who are in Judea flee [φευγέτωσαν] to the mountains [εἰς τὰ ὄρη]': This material is taken from Mark (13.14b). Investigation into the origin of this warning to flee is complicated by the existence of the well known Pella oracle. According to Eusebius (312 CE), 'the people of the church in Jerusalem were commanded by an oracle [χρησμός] given by revelation before the war to those in the city who were worthy of it to depart and dwell in one of the cities of Perea, which they called Pella, to which those who believed on Christ migrated from Jerusalem' (*Hist. Eccl.* 3.5.3). At this point in his narrative Eusebius makes no reference to Mk 13.14 of Lk. 21.21, which should come as no surprise since his point is the dispersion of the persecuted Church. There is nothing in the Marcan or Lucan oracles that commands flight to Pella, so the passages are not mentioned. When Eusebius later does discuss the fulfillment of Lk. 21.20-24, along with Lk. 19.42-44, in the fall of Jerusalem, he says nothing of the Pella tradition (*Hist. Eccl.* 3.7.3-6). Eusebius gives no indication that the Pella oracle derives in any way from the gospels. If not one of the gospels, then what was Eusebius' source? G. Lüdemann thinks that his source was Ariston of Pella, a Jewish Christian of the second century, the very source that Eusebius drew upon in narrating the events surrounding Bar Kosiba (cf. *Hist. Eccl.* 4.6.3).[58] Epiphanius (367 CE) also knows of this tradition: 'the disciples settled in Pella, Christ having told them to quit Jerusalem and to depart, on account of the fact that it was about to suffer siege' (*Panarion* 29.7.8); '[the disciples] had returned from the city of Pella to Jerusalem...For when the city was about to be seized by the Romans, being forewarned [προχρηματίζειν] by an angel [or messenger], all the disciples withdrew from the city, which was about to be destroyed' (*Treatise on Weights and Measures* §15). His version seems to be independent of Eusebius, but it is not dependent on the gospels either.[59] In my judgment the Pella oracle is not a piece of variant synoptic tradition and so cannot derive from Jesus. It is referred to as an oracle,

58. G. Lüdemann, 'The Successors of Pre-70 Jerusalem Christianity: A Critical Evaluation of the Pella Tradition', in E.P. Sanders, *et al.* (eds.), *Jewish and Christian Self-Definition* (3 vols.; Philadelphia: Fortress Press, 1980–82), I, pp. 161-73, esp. pp. 165-66.

59. C. Koester, 'The Origin and Significance of the Flight to Pella Tradition', *CBQ* 51 (1989), pp. 90-106, esp. pp. 92-97. There apparently is a vague allusion to the Pella oracle in the Pseudo-Clementine *Recognitions* (1.37, 39). See Koester, pp. 97-103.

given by revelation (by Christ or an angel—more likely a Christian prophet), but not as a word of Jesus. But it may owe its inspiration in part to the dominical tradition, such as that in Mk 13.14 and Lk. 21.21, passages which give no clear indication of familiarity with the Pella oracle.[60] In other words, a well known dominical tradition that warns the faithful to flee the grim fate that awaits Jerusalem may have prompted a later prophetical utterance that tells the faithful *where* to flee. The scriptural antecedents of the dominical tradition are vague, but they lend a measure of support to this analysis. Three times Jeremiah tells the people to 'flee [φεύγετε/סנו] from the midst of Babylon' (Jer. 51.6; cf. 50.8; 51.45). Ezekiel says that there will be famine in the city and if people survive, 'they will be on the mountains [ἐπὶ τῶν ὀρέων]' (Ezek. 7.15-16). But the prophet says nothing about flight. According to Zechariah in the day of the Lord people will flee (סנו) and then the Lord will come (Zech. 14.5). The common feature is the warning to flee; what is not common is advice as to where one should go. This coheres with the dominical tradition, not with the Pella oracle (which never speaks of 'fleeing').

'let those in her midst [ἐν μέσῳ αὐτῆς] depart [ἐκχωρεῖν]': These words and phrases are derived from the same contexts already considered: Jeremiah's warnings to flee 'from the midst' (ἐκ μέσου/מתוך) of the city (Jer. 50.8; 51.6, 45); the warning that only those who depart [προσχωρεῖν] and surrender to the Chaldeans will live (Jer. 21.8; cf. Ezek. 9.4: ἐν μέσῳ αὐτῆς [i.e. Jerusalem]). In the first century the 'Chaldeans' would probably have been understood as the Romans. Epiphanius used the word ἀναχωρεῖν (*Panarion* 29.7.8), one of the few agreements between the Pella oracle and the dominical tradition.

'these are the days of vengeance [ἡμέραι ἐκδικήσεως]': This clause is taken from Hos. 9.7: 'The days of vengeance [αἱ ἡμέραι τῆς ἐκδικήσεως] have come, the days of recompense have come, and Israel shall know it [LXX: suffer harm]'. This coheres from the parallel from Jer. 51.6 (LXX 28.6): 'Flee from the midst of Babylon...for this is

---

60. *Pace* J.M. Creed, *The Gospel according to St. Luke* (London: Macmillan, 1930), p. 256. Koester ('Pella Tradition', pp. 104-105) is undecided. Since the whole point of the Pella oracle is to send the faithful to a specific place of safety, and the whole point of Mk 13.14/Lk. 21.21 is to escape Jerusalem, and since the respective traditions have very little common vocabulary, I think that it is doubtful that the synoptic tradition is dependent upon the Pella oracle, or even betrays knowledge of it.

the time of the Lord's vengeance [καιρὸς ἐκδικήσεως] (cf. 46.10 [LXX 26.10]; Deut. 32.35).

'Alas for those who are with child [ταῖς ἐν γαστρὶ ἐχούσαις]': recalls Elisha's lament: 'you will...rip up their women with child [τὰς ἐν γαστρὶ ἐχούσας αὐτῶν] (2 Kgs 8.12).

'great distress [ἀνάγκη] shall be on the earth and wrath [ὀργή] upon this people': Fitzmyer suspects that Luke composed this line.[61] Perhaps, but it is one more phrase from the prophetic tradition: 'That day will be a day of wrath [ὀργή], a day of tribulation and distress [ἀνάγκη]...a day of trumpet blast and battle cry against fortified cities' (Zeph. 1.15-16).

'they will fall by the edge of the sword [πεσοῦνται στόματι μαχαίρης]': Sirach provides the closest Greek parallel: 'Many have fallen by the edge of the sword [ἔπεσαν ἐν στόματι μαχαίρης]' (Sir. 28.18). Elsewhere in the MT the Hebrew equivalent is found: 'and all the army of Sisera fell [וַיִּפֹּל] by the edge of the sword [לְפִי־חָרֶב]' (Judg. 4.16; cf. Josh. 8.24). Jeremiah was told not to take a wife because 'by the sword they shall fall [ἐν μαχαίρᾳ πεσοῦνται] and by famine they shall come to an end' (Jer. 16.4).

'led captive [αἰχμαλωτίζειν] among all nations [εἰς τὰ ἔθνη πάντα]': The first part recalls the warning of the Deuteronomist: 'You shall beget sons and daughters, but they shall not be yours; for they shall go into captivity [ἐν αἰχμαλωσίᾳ/בַּשֶּׁבִי]' (Deut. 28.41), as well as the later prophecy of Jeremiah: 'Those who are for pestilence, to pestilence, those who are for the sword, to the sword, those who are for famine, to famine, and those who are for captivity [αἰχμαλωσίᾳ/לַשְּׁבִי], to captivity [αἰχμαλωσίᾳ/בַּשֶּׁבִי]' (Jer. 15.2; cf. Tob. 1.10: αἰχμαλωτίζειν). The second part alludes to Deut. 28.64: 'and the Lord your God will scatter you among all the nations [εἰς πάντα τὰ ἔθνη/בְּכָל־הָעַמִּים] of the earth' (cf. LXX Ezra 9.7: 'In our iniquities we, our kings, and our sons have been given into the hand of the kings of the nations, to the sword, to captivity [ἐν αἰχμαλωσίᾳ/בַּשֶּׁבִי], to plundering, and to utter shame, as this day').

'Jerusalem will be trodden down by the Gentiles [πατουμένη ὑπὸ ἐθνῶν], until the times of the Gentiles [καιροὶ ἐθνῶν] are fulfilled': The first clause is an allusion to Zech. 12.3 and similar texts: 'and it will come to pass on that day that I shall make Jerusalem a stone trampled

---

61. Fitzmyer, *Luke X-XXIV*, p. 1346.

upon by all the nations [καταπατούμενον πᾶσιν τοῖς ἔθνεσιν]' (cf. Isa. 5.5: εἰς καταπάτημα; Ezek. 26.11; PssSol 17.22: 'purge Jerusalem from Gentiles who trample [ἐθνῶν καταπατούντων] her to destruction'; 1 Macc. 3.45: 'Jerusalem was uninhabited...the sanctuary was trampled down [καταπατούμενον]'). The second clause is reminiscent of Tobit's prophecy: 'And God will again show them mercy, and God will return them to the land of Israel; and they will again build the house, but not as the first, until which time the time of the seasons is fulfilled [πληρωθῇ ὁ χρόνος τῶν καιρῶν]. After these things all will return from their captivity [αἰχμαλωσία] and will build Jerusalem in splendor. And the house of God will be rebuilt in it, just as the prophets of Israel spoke concerning it' (Tob. [א] 14.5; B: ἕως πληρωθῶσιν καιροὶ τοῦ αἰῶνος). Jeremiah uses similar language with respect to the period of time in which Nebuchadrezzar would enjoy ascendancy among the nations (Jer. 27.7). Ezekiel also prophesied that there would come a day of reckoning for the gentile powers (Ezek. 30.3). These traditions, including the dominical tradition under review, are what lie behind Paul's hope (Rom. 11.25).

Lk. 23.27-31. This pericope is unique to Luke. Because Lucan redaction is minimal Fitzmyer suspects that it was derived from L,[62] which I think is correct. Bultmann thinks that it is a Christian prophecy.[63] There are, however, four factors that support a claim for authenticity: (1) The likelihood that it was uttered in Aramaic argues for its antiquity,[64] if not for its authenticity; (2) the fact that this pericope, in which persons weep for Jesus, and in which Jesus himself makes reference to weeping, does not contain a hint of Zech. 12.10 ('when they look on him whom they pierced, they shall mourn'), a prophetic text that Christians would later interpret christologically (Mt. 24.30; Jn. 19.37; Rev. 1.7), also tells in favor of authenticity; (3) the oracle parallels language and imagery found in the oracles already considered (Lk. 19.41-44; 21.20-24), oracles which have reasonable claim to authenticity; (4) the obscure saying in v. 31 argues for something authoritative and genuine, but probably not understood. It does not sound like something a later Christian would invent, nor is it an allusion to the burning of Jerusalem.[65]

---

62. Fitzmyer, *Luke X-XXIV*, p. 1494.
63. Bultmann, *History of the Synoptic Tradition*, p. 37.
64. Marshall, *Luke*, p. 862.
65. *Pace* Fitzmyer, *Luke X-XXIV*, pp. 1498-99. Jesus' wooden cross and the timbers of Jerusalem are hardly in mind. It is not likely either that the evangelist had

'Daughters of Jerusalem': Again, the language and context are reminiscent of Jeremiah's prophecy: 'Hear, O women, the word of the Lord...teach your daughters a lament' (Jer. 9.20; cf. 2 Sam. 1.24: 'Ye daughters of Israel, weep over Saul').

'weep for yourselves and for your children': Jesus tells the weeping women to weep for themselves in light of the coming terrors: 'they will dash your children to the ground' (Lk. 19.44; cf. Hos. 10.14); 'Alas for those who are with child and for those who give suck in those days' (Lk. 21.23; cf. 2 Kgs 8.12).

'days are coming [ἔρχονται ἡμέραι]': The earlier oracles of Jesus are once again echoed (Lk. 19.43: 'the days shall come'; Lk. 21.22: 'days of vengeance'; cf. Jer. 7.32: ἡμέραι ἔρχονται).

'Blessed are the childless [στεῖρα], the wombs that have never given birth and the breasts that have never given suck': Such a tragic beatitude stands in shocking contrast to conventional wisdom (Gen. 21.6-7; 30.23; Lk. 1.25). It is a deliberate and meaningful allusion to Isa. 54.1: 'Sing, O barren one [στεῖρα], who did not bear; break forth into singing and cry aloud, you who have not been in travail'.[66] But Jesus says that the barren of his generation are blessed for a reason entirely different from that of the joyous oracle of Isaiah 54. They will be fortunate because their suffering will be less. Here is an example of the hermeneutics of prophetic criticism, hermeneutics which Jesus employed in assessing Israel's assumptions and interpretation of its sacred tradition (e.g., Lk. 4.16-30).[67] Proliferation, one of many blessings in the messianic age, will be a curse in times of judgment.

'Then they will begin to say to the mountains, "Fall upon us", and to the hills, "Cover us up"': This is a paraphrase of Hos. 10.8: 'and they shall say to the mountains, "Cover us", and to the hills, "Fall upon us"'. The words of Hosea are addressed to an apostate Israel. When God

in mind such a notion, for he never hints at the burning of Jerusalem or the Temple. Note that Lk. 14.15-24, in contrast to its parallel in Mt. 22.1-14, says nothing of the city being burned down (cf. Mt. 22.7).

66. Fitzmyer (*Luke X-XXIV*, p. 1498) is correct to observe that the whole of Isa. 54.1-10 has relevance for the oracle in Luke.

67. See for example, J.A. Sanders, 'The Ethic of Election in Luke's Great Banquet Parable', in J.L. Crenshaw and J.T. Willis (eds.), *Essays in Old Testament Ethics* (New York: Ktav, 1974), pp. 245-71, esp. pp. 253, 266; *idem*, 'From Isaiah 61 to Luke 4', in J. Neusner (ed.), *Christianity, Judaism and Other Greco-Roman Cults* (Part One: New Testament; Leiden: Brill, 1975), pp. 75-106, esp. pp. 99-101. In another study I will explore more fully Jesus' employment of these hermeneutics.

judges them, destroying their 'high places' of idolatry, Israelites will be so filled with shame and terror that they will wish to be buried and out of God's sight. In Jesus' oracle the 'high places' may have been intended as a critical and ironical allusion to Jerusalem's Temple mount. For rejecting God's anointed one, Jesus, the religious establishment of Jerusalem will face a terrifying judgment.

'If they do these things when the wood is green, what will happen when it is dry?': The language of this curious proverbial statement parallels the vocabulary of Ezek. 17.24, which speaks of green wood (ξύλον χλωρόν) and dry wood (ξύλον ξηρόν), but not its meaning. Several interpretations have been offered.[68] It probably means if God is willing to permit such a disaster as the death of the innocent Jesus, how much more severe will be guilty Jerusalem's coming disaster.

One last detail should be discussed briefly. When he took action in the Temple precincts (Mk 11.15-17 par.), Jesus is said to have alluded to Jer. 7.11: 'You have made it [the Temple] a "cave of robbers [σπήλαιον ληστῶν]"' (Mk 11.17). Discussion about whether or not it is intelligible for Jesus to have spoken of robbers, who take by force, as opposed to thieves and swindlers (e.g., κλέπται), who steal by stealth or trickery, misses the point.[69] The allusion to Jeremiah 7 carries with it an indictment and threat against the Temple establishment. It is in this light that Jesus' action should be understood. Jeremiah says that the Lord told him to 'stand in the gate of the Lord's house, and proclaim there this word' (v. 2). The prophet told his contemporaries to 'mend their ways' (v. 3) and do not say, 'This is the Temple of the Lord, this is the Temple of the Lord' (v. 4), as if that will somehow guarantee their safety (cf. v. 14: 'in which you trust'). Jeremiah calls for justice and an end to the oppression of the disenfranchised, such as orphans and widows (vv. 5-6). He calls the Temple a cave of robbers (v. 11), which will be destroyed, as had the sanctuary at Shiloh (vv. 14-15). He tells them to go ahead and offer more sacrifices (v. 21), but they are of no value without obedience (vv. 22-24). Although God has sent many prophets, including Jeremiah, Israel has not listened (vv. 25-27). The nation is therefore rejected and forsaken (v. 29). Therefore, 'the days are coming' when the places of their idolatrous worship will become places of slaughter (vv. 30-32). The voice of joy and the voice of bridegroom and bride will no longer be heard in Jerusalem (v. 34). The oracle

68. See Fitzmyer, *Luke X-XXIV*, p. 1498.
69. As seen, for example, in Sanders, *Jesus and Judaism*, pp. 66-67.

continues into ch. 8 with the grim pronouncement that 'death shall be preferred to life' (v. 3; cf. Hos. 10.8).

Jesus' actions, prophecies, and pronouncements parallel many of the details of Jeremiah 7. As had Jeremiah centuries before, Jesus stood in the Temple precincts and condemned the religious establishment and in all probability at the same time uttered at least one of the prophecies of the Temple's destruction (perhaps as seen in the accusation of the 'false' witness of Mk 14.58).[70] Interestingly enough, this is what Jesus, son of Ananias would do a generation later (*War* 6.5.3 §301). As had Jeremiah, Jesus called for justice and an end to the oppression of the disenfranchised (Mt. 11.5 par.; Lk. 14.13), such as orphans and widows (Mk 12.38-40, 41-44). As had Jeremiah, Jesus also called the Temple a cave of robbers, which was in danger of destruction (Mk 11.17; 13.2). As had Jeremiah, Jesus teaches that sacrifices are of no value in themselves (Mt. 5.23-24; 9.13; 12.7). As had Jeremiah, Jesus also complained that though many prophets had been sent, Israel would not listen (Mt. 23.27 par.). Israel is now forsaken (Mt. 23.38 par.). 'Days are coming' when Jerusalem, the place of worship, will be destroyed, when the barren will be blessed (Lk. 19.42-44; 21.20-24; 23.29), or, as Jesus son of Ananias said, when the 'voice' will be 'against the bridegroom' and 'against the bride' (*War* 6.5.3 §301), when the people will prefer death (Lk. 23.30). Finally, as had those of Jeremiah, the predictions of both Jesus of Nazareth and Jesus son of Ananias, predictions uttered with Jeremiah 7 in mind, occasioned opposition from the religious establishment, not from the laity.[71]

Lives of the Prophets

Both predictions recorded in the Lives of the Prophets are reminiscent of the prophetic traditions of the Jewish scriptures. The prediction that Jerusalem 'would be razed to the ground [ἠφάνισται]'[72] (LivPro 10.11) echoes the language of the prophetic tradition that described the

---

70. So Sanders, *Jesus and Judaism*, pp. 89-90.

71. R.A. Horsley ('"Like One of the Prophets of Old": Two Types of Popular Prophets at the Time of Jesus', *CBQ* 47 (1985), pp. 435-63, esp. p. 451) notes the significance of the fact that when Jesus son of Ananias prophesied the doom of Jerusalem and the Temple (*War* 6.5.3 §300-309) only the priestly aristocracy tried to silence him.

72. Torrey (*Lives of the Prophets*, p. 28 n. 48) suggests the emendment ἀφανισθήσεται.

impending Babylonian destruction of the holy city. Jeremiah warned that God 'will make this city a desolation [ἀφανισμός]' (19.8; cf. 10.22; 12.10-11). Similarly, Ezekiel prophesied to his people: 'Wherever you dwell your cities shall be waste and your high places ruined [ἀφανισθήσεται], so that your altars will be waste and ruined' (6.6; cf. 6.14; 12.19-20).

Habakkuk's prophecy, 'By a western [δυτικός] nation it will happen' (LivPro 12.11), could be based on Dan. 8.5-7, which describes the irresistible advance of the he-goat 'from the west [δυσμή] across the face of the whole earth'. Although the symbol originally applied to Greece, under the rule of Alexander the Great, it could easily have been applied to Rome (as Josephus in fact may have done; *Ant.* 10.11.7 §276).[73] Even the reference to the removal of the 'pillars [στύλους]' in the prophecy credited to Habakkuk is reminiscent of the prophetic tradition: 'And the Chaldeans broke in pieces the bronze pillars [στύλους] that were in the house of the Lord...and carried the bronze away to Babylon' (Jer. 52.17).

Josephus

According to Josephus the prophet Jeremiah predicted the Roman as well as the Babylonian capture of Jerusalem (*Ant.* 10.5.1 §79). Likewise in reference to Daniel, he says that the Roman defeat of Israel had been foretold (*Ant.* 10.11.7 §276). It is not surprising, therefore, to find that the various oracles of Jerusalem's destruction reported by Josephus are based on the Jewish Scriptures.

The oracle about the Jews slaughtering their own countrymen (*War* 6.2.1 §109) could be echoing Mic. 7.5-6: 'Put no trust in a neighbor, have no confidence in a friend...for the son treats the father with contempt, the daughter rises up against her mother...a man's enemies are the men of his own house'. This passage is cited in *m. Sota* 9.15 as part of the woes that will precede the coming of Messiah. Among the woes that are described in this context are murder (*m. Sota* 9.9) and violence (9.15). Several times there is reference to the destruction of the Temple (9.12, 13, 15). Although this mishnaic tradition is obviously post-70, the interpretation of Micah 7 that it presupposes is earlier. A similar prophetic oracle, based on Mic. 7.6, appears in Mark (13.12) and Q

---

73. Bockmuehl ('Why Did Jesus Predict the Destruction of the Temple?', p. 14) suggests that underlying the prophecy found in the Life of Habakkuk is Hab. 1.14-17, where the Chaldeans (cf. 1.6) are described as fish from the sea.

(Mt. 10.35-36/Lk. 12.52-53), and if it does not derive from Jesus himself (as I suspect it does), it at least existed prior to 70. Therefore, Mic. 7.5-6, as interpreted in some eschatological sense, perhaps as seen in Mishnah and in the Synoptic tradition, could have been the oracle to which Josephus alludes.

The four-square prophecy (*War* 6.5.4 §311), mentioned also by Tacitus (*Histories* 5.13) and Suetonius (*Vespasian* §4), though apparently independently of Josephus, may have had something to do with Ezekiel's vision of the restored Temple, which will be situated in the middle of a court one hundred cubits 'foursquare' (τετράγωνος) (Ezek. 45.2; cf. 40.27; 48.16, 17, 20), an apocalyptic concept that probably contributed to the idea of the foursquare (τετράγωνος) heavenly city described in Revelation (21.16). When the Temple precincts were reduced to a square, some may have imagined that this was preparatory to the destruction of the old Temple, in order to make way for the Temple of the end-time.

Even Josephus' prophecy of the accession of Vespasian (*War* 3.8.9 §401) was based on the Jewish scriptures, probably Gen. 49.10 or Num. 24.17, or both:

> But what more than all else incited them to the war was an ambiguous oracle [χρησμός], likewise found in their sacred scriptures, to the effect that at that time one from their country would become ruler of the world. This they understood to mean someone of their own race, and many of their wise men went astray in their interpretation of it. The oracle, however, in reality signified the sovereignty of Vespasian, who was proclaimed emperor on Jewish soil. (*War* 6.5.4 §312-13)

Josephus claims to have understood this 'ambiguous oracle' more accurately than many of his contemporaries. The popular view, probably pretty much consistent with what we find in the targums, was that of the Jewish messianic king 'from the house of Judah' (*Tgs. Onq.*, *Neof.*, *Ps.-J.*, and *Frag.* on Gen. 49.10 and Num. 24.17). Although these targums post-date Josephus, the exegesis preserved in them probably was in circulation in the first century (cf. 4QPatrBless 1-5). For it is likely that the messianic 'star out of Judah' (Num. 24.17) is what lies behind the Matthean story of the visit of the magi (Mt. 2.1-2; cf. Rev. 22.16). In any case, Josephus makes it clear that the oracle was found in the Jewish 'sacred scriptures'.

The oracle attributed to Jesus, son of Ananias, appears to have been based on Jeremiah 7, particularly v. 34: 'And I will make to cease from the cities of Judah and from the streets of Jerusalem the voice of mirth and the voice of gladness, the voice of the bridegroom and the voice of the bride; for the land shall become a waste'.[74] An oracle based on Jeremiah 7 is contextually appropriate, since this chapter is directed against the Temple establishment. Just as Jeremiah of old stood 'in the gate of the Lord's house' and proclaimed his word of judgment (Jer. 7.2), so Jesus, son of Ananias, stood 'before the Temple' and began to proclaim his oracle of woe (*War* 6.5.3 §301).

Yohanan ben Zakkai and Zadok
Yohanan ben Zakkai's prophecy of the destruction of the Temple is based upon two principal passages: Zech. 11.1 ('Open your doors, O Lebanon, that the fire may devour your cedars') and Isa. 10.34 ('and Lebanon shall fall by a mighty one'). There is no specific prophecy credited to Zadok, but since he was one of ben Zakkai's disciples, it is reasonable to assume that he shared his master's views. Ben Zakkai's prophecy is based upon various word-plays by which Lebanon was equated with the Temple (see above). In view of this equation, 'it is not unreasonable', as M.N.A. Bockmuehl has recently put it, 'to grant that the Old Testament judgement oracles applying to Lebanon might therefore have been transferred to the Temple as well'.[75] Such oracles would include Isa. 2.12-16; 33.9; 40.16.

Perceived Corruption in the First-Century Temple

Sin and corruption constituted the most common explanation for the Temple's destruction in 70 CE. Lamenting the fate of Jerusalem, Baruch says: 'You, priests, take the keys of the sanctuary, and cast them to the highest heaven, and give them to the Lord and say, "Guard your house yourself, because, behold, we have been found to be false stewards"' (2 Bar. 10.18).[76] Although ostensibly describing the destruction of the First Temple, the author of this early second-century pseudepigraphon is

---

74. Recall that Josephus said that Jeremiah was one of the prophets who had predicted the Roman capture of Jerusalem (*Ant.* 10.5.1 §79).

75. Bockmuehl, 'Why Did Jesus Predict the Destruction of the Temple?', p. 14.

76. Translation from A.F.J. Klijn, '2 (Syriac Apocalypse of) Baruch', in *Old Testament Pseudepigrapha*, II, p. 624. There were literal keys of the Temple (cf. Josephus, *Against Apion* 2.8 §108), but they also had taken on a symbolic value (see also Mt. 16.19; Rev. 3.7). Further references are considered below.

describing the destruction of the Second Temple in 70 CE (cf. 1.4; 32.2-4).[77] It is significant that the priests are characterized as 'false stewards', a characterization that coheres with some of Jesus' parables (cf. Mt. 24.45-51 par; Mk 12.1-9 par; Lk. 16.1-8). An interpolation in Life of Adam and Eve (in several mss. following 29.3) reads: 'and again they will build a house of God, and the latest house of God shall be exalted more highly than before. And once again iniquity will surpass equity' (late first century).[78] Lack of equity implies criticism of the rulers, as opposed to the people in general. In one writing at least, however, the priesthood itself is blamed for the catastrophe.

The Targums also yield some evidence, principally from Targum Jonathan to the Prophets, that the first-century Temple establishment was remembered as corrupt. This is seen especially in 1 Samuel, Isaiah, and Jeremiah. Containing traditions that antedate, as well as post-date, the destruction of the Second Temple,[79] *Tg. 1 Samuel* yields significant evidence of the belief that the priests of the Second Temple were regarded as corrupt. Chapter 2 contains many editorial insertions and expansions of an apocalyptic nature. Hannah's Song of Praise (vv. 1-10) is transformed, in the Targum, into an apocalypse. She foresees Sennacherib's siege of Jerusalem (v. 2), Nebuchadnezzar (v. 3), the kingdoms of Greece (v. 4), Mordecai and Esther (v. 5a), Rome (v. 5b), eschatological judgment of wicked and righteous (vv. 6-10ab), and the appearance of the Messianic Kingdom (v. 10c). The apocalyptic orientation of the narrative, however, does not end with Hannah's Song. In the verses that follow the sins of the sons of Eli the priest are described. We are told that they 'robbed the sacrifices of the Lord' (v. 17; Heb: 'treated the sacrifices of the Lord with contempt'). They are later asked: 'Why are you robbing my temple?' (v. 29; Heb: 'Why do you kick at my sacrifices and offerings that I commanded?').[80] It is likely that the sons of Eli should be understood as examples of the priesthood of the Second Temple, if not the priesthood of the first century (as is the case in *b. Pesah.* 57a). The prophecy of the demise of Eli's sons and family gives way, in v. 32, to a prediction of the demise of

77. Klijn, '2 Baruch', pp. 615-18.

78. Translation from M.D. Johnson, 'Life of Adam and Eve', in *Old Testament Pseudepigrapha*, II, p. 270 n. 29b.

79. See D.J. Harrington and A.J. Saldarini, *Targum Jonathan of the Former Prophets* (Aramaic Bible, 10; Wilmington: Glazier, 1987), p. 13.

80. Harrington and Saldarini, *Former Prophets*, p. 107.

the Temple establishment: 'And you will be seeing the sorrow that will come upon the men of your house because of the sins that you have sinned in my Temple. And afterwards prosperity will come over Israel' (Heb: 'Then in distress you will look with envious eye on all the prosperity which shall be bestowed on Israel').[81] It is likely that the meturgeman is here alluding to the first-century priesthood, the priesthood that was destroyed. This is likely the case in light of the promise in v. 35 to raise up a faithful priest who will serve the Messiah: 'I will raise up before Me a trustworthy priest, who will minister according to my word, my will, and I will establish for him an enduring kingdom and he will serve my Messiah all the days' (Heb: 'I will raise up for myself a faithful priest...and I will build him a sure house, and he shall go in and out before my anointed for ever').[82] After the corrupt priesthood has been swept away in judgment, a new and faithful priesthood will be established in the Eschaton.

There are at least three major passages in the Isaiah Targum where criticism is directed against the first-century priesthood. The first example is seen in the rewriting of Isaiah's Song of the Vineyard (5.1-7), where the focus has been narrowed from a threat against Judah at large to a threat against the Temple establishment. In place of the Hebrew text's 'tower' and 'wine press', the Targum reads 'sanctuary' and 'altar', respectively (v. 2). Because of the moral failing of the ruling priests (v. 7: 'oppressors'), God will destroy the 'sanctuaries' and the altar (v. 5).[83] This interpretive tradition carries over into the rabbinic literature, where the tower is specifically identified as the Temple, and the wine press the

---

81. Harrington and Saldarini, *Former Prophets*, p. 108.

82. Harrington and Saldarini, *Former Prophets*, p. 108. It is, of course, possible that none other than David and Zadok are in view (as is likely the case in the Hebrew). But judging by Hannah's apocalypse and the redaction of vv. 17, 29, and 32 (including an explicit reference to the Temple), thus making the sins of the priests in Samuel's time conform more closely to those of the first-century priests, it is likely that here also the meturgeman is thinking of some future righteous priest who will faithfully serve the Messiah (compare also *Tg. Zech.* 6.13); Chilton, *The Glory of Israel: The Theology and Provenience of the Isaiah Targum* (JSOTSup, 23; Sheffield: JSOT Press, 1983), pp. 23-24; S.H. Levey, *The Messiah: An Aramaic Interpretation* (MHUC, 2; Cincinnati: Hebrew Union College-Jewish Institute of Religion, 1974), p. 36.

83. Chilton (*Glory of Israel*, p. 18) is probably correct when he notes that the plural 'sanctuaries' refers to the Temple and the synagogues.

altar (*t. Meila* 1.16; *t. Sukka* 3.15).[84] The second example is Isa. 28.1-13,
which has been paraphrased to reflect the leadership of the Herodian
Temple.[85] Whereas the Hebrew of v. 1 reads, 'Woe to...the fading
flower of its glorious beauty', the Targum reads, 'Woe to...the foolish
master of Israel [who] gives the headgear to the wicked of the
sanctuary'. The 'foolish master' (i.e., the High Priest) will be trampled
by the Romans (v. 3).[86] In his place will arise the Lord's Messiah who
will make the 'house of judgment' (i.e., the Temple and/or the Sanhedrin)
pass 'true judgment' (vv. 5-6). Similarly in 42.7 it is anticipated that
Messiah will 'open the eyes of the house of Israel, who have been blind
to the Torah' (Heb: 'to open blind eyes').[87] The first-century priests and
scribes have gone astray, not one of them is 'innocent of oppression'
(28.7-8; cf. *Tg. Isa.* 5.7). In vv. 10-13 the meturgeman goes on to
criticize the priests for disregarding the Law and for holding the Temple
in contempt. This is probably the idea in 53.5, where Messiah 'shall build
the Temple, which was profaned because of our sins, and which was
surrendered because of our iniquities'.[88] The reference to 'the service of
idols' (28.10) is likely hyperbolic ('referring to cooperation with Gentile
power'[89]), and is an attempt to criticize the first-century Temple
establishment as sharply as possible. The third example is seen in the
oracle concerning the faithful priest Eliakim (Isa. 22.20), who becomes in
the Isaiah Targum a portrait of Israel's tragedy. Although he is 'exalted'
(v. 20), and is appointed a 'faithful officer ministering in an enduring
place' (v. 23; the Hebrew reads, 'And I will fasten him like a peg in a
sure place'), and into his hand is placed 'the key of the sanctuary and
the authority of the house of David' (v. 22; the MT reads, 'And I will
place on his shoulder the key of the house of David'), he nevertheless

---

84. Chilton, *A Galilean Rabbi and His Bible: Jesus' Use of the Interpreted
Scripture of His Time* (Wilmington: Glazier, 1984), p. 113. The Temple was referred
to as a 'tower' prior to the first century CE (cf. 1 En 89.56-67). See Mk. 12.1-9
where Jesus criticizes the ruling priests, making use of this very passage from Isaiah.

85. Chilton, *Glory of Israel*, pp. 20, 23; *idem, Isaiah Targum*, pp. 55-57 (and
notes).

86. *Tg. Isa.* 29.1 probably alludes to the Roman siege and destruction of
Jerusalem, while *Tg. Isa.* 25.2 seems to reflect the confidence and hope in the period
between the two Jewish wars. See Chilton, *Glory of Israel*, p. 130 n. 10; *idem, The
Isaiah Targum* (Aramaic Bible, 11; Wilmington, DE: Glazier, 1987), p. 57 (and notes).

87. Levey, *The Messiah*, p. 60.

88. Levey, *The Messiah*, p. 64.

89. Chilton, *Glory of Israel*, p. 23.

'will be cut down and fall, and the oracle of the prophecy that was concerning him will be void' (v. 25).[90] It is possible that the positive elements of the Eliakim oracle (vv. 20-24) derive from the period before 70 CE, while the negative elements of v. 25 reflect disillusionment following the destruction of the Temple.[91] In fact, it appears that most of the contents in ch. 22–24, according to Bruce Chilton, have been rewritten in view of the Roman defeat, with the criticisms leveled chiefly at the 'Temple hierarchy' (see *Tg. Isa.* 17.11: 'you forsook my service...you put off... repentance'; 24.5: 'annulled the feasts'; 24.6: 'deceit' [cf. 5.23]).[92]

In *Tg. Jer.* 7.9 the religious leaders are explicitly called 'thieves'. In 23.11 the Targum accuses the priests of having 'stolen their ways', instead of being 'ungodly', as the Hebrew text reads. Frequently the Targum pejoratively refers to 'scribe and priest', instead of 'prophet and priest', as in the Hebrew text. On other occasions they are called 'robbers of money' (8.10; 6.13: 'robbers of wealth'). The reference to scribe and priest is noteworthy, for these are the very persons who take exception to Jesus' action in the Temple (see Mk 11.18). Commercialism seems to be the point behind the subtle change in *Tg. Jer.* 14.18: 'both scribe and priest devote themselves to trade' (MT: 'both prophet and priest ply their trade'). In reference to coming judgment, *Tg. Jer.* 23.33 says that the scribe and priest will be driven out (instead of being cast off, as it is in the Hebrew). The thrust of the passage seems to be directed at the religious leaders (and not at the people, as it is in the Hebrew).[93] Robert Hayward suspects that these criticisms, which coincide with similar ones found in the writings of Josephus and Qumran, reflect attitudes in Palestine before 70 CE.[94]

Charges of corruption in the first-century Temple are also found in

90. Translation from Chilton, *Isaiah Targum*, pp. 44-45.

91. See Chilton, *Glory of Israel*, p. 19; Chilton, 'Shebna, Eliakim, and the Promise to Peter', in J. Neusner, P. Borgen, *et al.* (eds.), *The Social World of Formative Christianity and Judaism* (H.C. Kee Festschrift; Philadelphia: Fortress Press, 1988), pp. 311-26.

92. Chilton, *Isaiah Targum*, pp. 36, 42-48.

93. R. Hayward, *The Targum of Jeremiah* (Aramaic Bible, 12; Wilmington, DE: Glazier, 1987), p. 37. He observes Targum Jeremiah frequently criticizes the priests: they are accused of robbery, being overly concerned about money, failing to enquire of God or showing compassion for the sick, and of having lack of concern for the people.

94. Hayward, *Jeremiah*, pp. 37-38, cf. 101 n. 14 (on 18.18), 189 n. 38 (on 51.53).

Tannaitic traditions. On one occasion R. Simeon ben Gamaliel (c. 10–80 CE) vigorously protested, because the price of a pair of doves had been raised to one gold denar, a price some twenty-five times the proper charge (*m. Ker.* 1.7). It should be remembered that the dove was the poor man's sacrifice (Lev. 5.7; 12.8). Such a charge would be bitterly resented. R. Yohanan ben Zakkai condemned the priests' claim that they were exempt from the half-shekel temple tax (*m. Šeq.* 1.4). It was 'in the interests of peace' that no one insisted that the priests pay the tax. This statement probably alludes to the violence sometimes suffered by those who opposed the ruling priests. Horsley avers that the 'half-shekel tax was almost certainly a late development in second Temple times, and its payment was controversial at the time of Jesus'.[95] Such controversy is likely what lies behind Mt. 17.24-27, and perhaps also 4Q159 (which, if true, means that the Qumran community also took exception to the tax).

There is also Tannaitic tradition claiming that the family of Annas did not tithe their produce, and for this reason their property was destroyed three years before the rest of Israel. Their refusal to tithe was apparently based on an exegesis of Deut. 14.22-23, an exegesis for which the rabbis had little sympathy (*Sifre Deut* §105 [on 14.22]). A similar tradition is found in *y. Pe'a* 1.6 and *b. B. Mes.* 88a-b. It is possible that the addition in *Tg. Isa.* 5.10 ('because of the sin that they did not give the tithes') alludes to this failure to tithe. Apparently the high priestly families profited in ways that the rabbis considered at best questionable (*m. Šeq.* 4.3-4) and at other times clearly oppressive (*Sifre Deut* §357 [on 34.1, 3]; *Mek. Amalek* 2 [on Exod. 17.14-16]).[96]

The Tannaitic rabbis also preserve tradition, in part corroborated by Josephus (see below), that the office of High Priest was often secured through bribery. Commenting on Lev. 16.3 ('with this shall Aaron come'), R. Berekiah (second century CE) is reported as saying: 'But the verse [i.e., Lev. 16.3] does not apply to the Second Temple [as it does

---

95. Horsley, *Jesus and the Spiral of Violence*, pp. 280, and 345 n. 7. See also S. Freyne, *Galilee from Alexander the Great to Hadrian* (Wilmington: Glazier, 1980), pp. 271-82; W. Horbury, 'The Temple Tax', in Bammel and Moule, eds., *Jesus and the Politics of His Day*, pp. 265-86.

96. See R. Hammer, *Sifre: A Tannaitic Commentary on the Book of Deuteronomy* (Yale Judaica, 24; New Haven and London: Yale University Press, 1986), pp. 378 (and p. 512 n. 4), 380. Employing word-play, 'Gilead' (Deut. 34.1) is understood as a reference to Jerusalem; 'Zoar' (34.3) is understood as a reference to the oppressive establishment in Israel.

to the First Temple], because in its time the priests used to outbid one another for the office of High Priest, so that there were eighty High Priests who served (in disorderly succession) in the Temple. Hence the first part of the verse, "the fear of the Lord prolongs days" (Prov. 10.27a), applies to the priests of the First Temple, and the conclusion of the verse, "the years of the wicked shall be shortened" (Prov. 10.27b), applies to the priests of the Second Temple' (*Pesiq. R.* 47.4).[97] The same tradition also appears in *Lev. Rab.* 21.9 (on 16.3), with a slight variation: 'In the Second Temple, however, because they used to obtain the office of High Priest for money, or, as some say, because they used to kill each other by means of witchcraft...'[98] It is likely that this tradition particularly has in mind the Herodian/Roman period, for some 28 High Priests (only two of which were from families that had any legitimate claim) held office in little more than one century (from 37 BCE to 70 CE).

According to early Amoraic traditions, the High Priests of the first century were always wealthier than the other priests. The High Priest was expected 'to be greater than his brethren in beauty, strength, wealth, wisdom, and good looks'; for this reason, the other priests on one occasion 'filled up [the High Priest's] woodshed with gold denars' (*t. Yoma* 1.6).[99] The High Priests are accused of defiling the Temple: '"Depart hence, ye children of Eli," for they defiled the Temple of the Lord' (*b. Pesah* 57a). 'Children of Eli' alludes to the evil sons of Eli, priest of Shiloh, who profited from the sacrifices, engaged in harlotry, and from those who resisted 'they took it by force' (1 Sam. 2.12-17). It was observed above that *Tg. 1 Samuel* 2 has rewritten the story of these sons, making their sins conform to those of which the first-century priesthood was thought guilty. The sentence, 'they took it by force' (1 Sam. 2.16), virtually functions as a refrain in the talmudic passage under consideration.

Although they are accused of many cultic violations, the most serious charge, so far as the present study is concerned, is that the High Priests

---

97. Trans. based on W.G. Braude, *Pesikta Rabbati* (2 vols.; Yale Judaica, 18; New Haven and London: Yale University Press, 1968), II, p. 808.

98. Trans. based on J.J. Slotki, *Midrash Rabbah: Leviticus* (London and New York: Soncino, 1983), p. 272. In this version R. Aha (third century CE) is given credit for the interpretation of Prov. 10.27.

99. Trans. based on J. Neusner, *The Tosefta* (6 vols.; New York: Ktav, 1977–81), II, p. 186.

took more than what was lawfully required. This is seen in a discussion of the distribution of the hides of the sacrificed animals. 'At first they did bring the hides of Holy Things to the room of *bet happarvah* and divide them in the evening to each [priestly] household which served on that day. But the powerful men of the priesthood would come and take them by force. They ordained that they should divide it on Fridays to each and every watch. But still did violent men of the priesthood come and take it away by force...Beams of sycamore were in Jericho. And strong-fisted men would come and take them by force' (*t. Menah.* 13.18-19; cf. *t. Zebah.* 11.16-17; *b. Pesah,* 57a).[100] Apparently the ruling priests (i.e., the 'powerful men of the priesthood') were stealing the tithes (hides, in this case) to which the lower-ranking priests were entitled.[101] Because of this practice, it was not long 'before the priests covered the face of the entire porch [of the Temple] with golden trays, a hundred by a hundred [handbreadths], with the thickness of a golden denar' (*t. Menah.* 13.18-19); cf. *b. Pesah.* 57a: 'they covered the whole Temple with gold plaques a cubit square of the thickness of a gold denar'; *m. Šeq.* 4.4: 'What did they do with the surplus of the heave offering? Golden plating for bedecking the Holy of Holies').[102]

In the passages under consideration, four sets of 'woes' are recited concerning three of the four principal high-priestly families of the first century: 'Concerning these and people like them...did Abba saul ben Bithnith [first century CE] and Abba Joseph ben Johanan [first century CE?] of Jerusalem say, "Woe is me because of the house of Boethus. Woe is me because of their staves. Woe is me because of the house of Kathros. Woe is me because of their pen. Woe is me because of the house of Hanin. Woe is me because of their whispering. Woe is me because of the house of Ishmael ben Phabi. For they are High Priests, and their sons [are] treasurers, and their sons-in-law [are] supervisors,

100. Trans. from Neusner, *Tosefta,* V, p. 161.

101. It is probably against this inequity that *t. Yoma* 1.5 speaks: 'But in the case of Holy Things...the High Priest and the ordinary priest are the same: each receives an equal portion'. Trans. based on Neusner, *Tosefta,* II, p. 186. Although the laws of the Pentateuch did not, with regard to the offerings and tithes, favor the ruling priests over the lower-ranking priests, from the time of Roman control the ruling priests had such control (Josephus, *Ant.* 14.10.6 §202-203 [44 BCE]).

102. Trans. from Neusner, *Tosefta,* V, p. 161. The talmudic quotation is from H. Freedman, 'Pesahim', in Epstein (ed.), *The Babylonian Talmud,* III, p. 284; the mishnaic quotation is from H. Danby, *The Mishnah* (Oxford: Oxford University Press, 1933), p. 156.

and their servants come and beat us with staves"' (*t. Menah.* 13.21; cf.
b. Pesah. 57a; see also *t. Zebah.* 11.16-17; *y. Maas. Š.* 5.15).[103] Greed,
nepotism,[104] oppression, and violence, according to these rabbinic
traditions, characterized the leading aristocratic priestly families.
'Boethus' is probably the lower-ranking priest from Alexandria,
mentioned by Josephus in *Ant.* 15.9.3 §320, who gave his daughter
Mariamme to Herod as wife, and whose son Simon, in return, Herod
appointed High Priest (22–25 BCE). The rabbis lament his family's
'staves', with which they beat people. This lament, however, is also
expressed in regard to the other families, as the concluding line quoted
above indicates. (From Josephus, moreover, we learn that the beatings
were not perpetrated by the family of Boethus alone [*Ant.* 20.8.8 §181;
20.9.2 §207].) The identity of 'Kathros' is less certain. He may be the
'Simon Cantheras', son of Boethus, of *Ant.* 19.6.2 §297 and 19.6.4
§313, who served as High Priest (41 CE). The rabbis lament his family's
pen, 'with which they wrote their evil decrees'.[105] 'Hanin' is none other
than Annas of the New Testament (Lk. 3.2; Jn. 18.13, 24; Acts 4.6),
who served as High Priest (6-15 CE) and whose five sons, a grandson,
and son-in-law Caiaphas at various times served as High Priests (see *Ant.*
18.2.1 §26; 20.9.1 §198, where he is called Ananus). This family is
particularly criticized by the rabbis (*Sifre Deut* §105 [on 14.22]; *y. Pe'a*
2.16; and possibly *m. Ker.* 1.7). In the present text, the rabbis lament his
family's 'whispering', by which they mean their secret conspiracies to
effect 'oppressive measures'.[106] 'Phabi' (or Phiabi) and his son
'Ishmael' are mentioned in *Ant.* 18.2.2 §34. The family of Phabi is
lamented by the rabbis (according to the parallel passage in *b. Pesah.*
57a) 'because of their fists'. Phabi's son Ishmael, the successor of
Annas, served as High Priest (15-16 CE). Another Ishmael, son of Phabi
II, served as High Priest (59-61 CE), and is specifically mentioned by
Josephus as one of the High Priests whose servants beat the lower-
ranking priests (*Ant.* 20.8.8 §179-81; see also 20.9.2 §207).

It is not likely that this rabbinic tradition has in mind only the excesses

103. Trans. based on Neusner, *Tosefta*, V, pp. 161-62. The reading is modified in
light of the parallel passage in *b. Pesah.* 57a.

104. The Temple treasurer and supervisor (or 'captain') were second and third in
authority to the High Priest himself. Tosefta's claim that these posts were awarded to
relatives is confirmed by Josephus (*Ant.* 20.6.2 §131; 20.9.3 §208; cf. Acts 4.6).

105. Freedman, 'Pesahim', p. 285 n. 4.

106. Freedman, 'Pesahim', p. 285 n. 2.

that took place in the years immediately preceding the war with Rome. The woes are pronounced against three of the principal families that served throughout the first century. The rabbis were also critical of the politics behind the appointment of High Priests. 'When [unacceptable] kings became many, they ordained the practice of regularly appointing priests, and they appointed High Priests every single year' (*t. Yoma* 1.7; cf. *Pesiq. R.* 47.4).[107] The passage goes on to describe the cultic violations and resulting death of one of the High Priests from the family of Boethus (*t. Yoma* 1.8). Moreover, the gold plaques that covered the Temple may be related to the plates of gold that Josephus describes (*War* 5.5.6 §222; cf. *m. Šeq.* 4.4). It is likely that the profiteering and extortion that resulted in the accumulation of so much gold took years, and perhaps had something to do with the refurbishing of the Temple that continued throughout most of the first century.

According to the Tosefta tractate considered above, because of the greed and hatred of the powerful priestly families, the Second Temple was destroyed: 'As to Jerusalem's first building, on what account was it destroyed? Because of idolatry and licentiousness and bloodshed which was in it. But [as to] the latter building we know that they devoted themselves to Torah and were meticulous about tithes. On what account did they go into exile? *Because they love money* and hate one another' (*t. Menah.* 13.22, my emphasis).[108] Whereas hating one another could refer to the bloody fighting between the rebel factions during the war, loving money undoubtedly refers to the greed of the high priestly families. Finally, echoing first-century tradition already cited, a rabbinic tradition reads: 'This verse [Zech. 11.1] refers to the High Priests who were in the Temple, who took their keys in their hands and threw them up to the sky, saying to the Holy One, blessed be He, "Master of the Universe, here are your keys which you handed over to us, for we have not been trustworthy stewards to do the King's work and to eat of the King's table"' (*'Abot R. Nat.* A §4; see also B §7).[109]

---

107. Trans. from Neusner, *Tosefta*, II, p. 187. Tosefta's statement is hyperbolic. High Priests were not appointed 'every single year' (cf. Jn 18.13). Some served less than a year, but most served for longer.

108. Trans. from Neusner, *Tosefta*, V, p. 162.

109. Trans. based on Goldin, *Fathers according to Rabbi Nathan*, p. 37. This tradition is at times applied to the destruction of the First Temple, cf. *b. Ta'an.* 29a; *Lev. Rab.* 19.6 (on 15.25). It should be noted that comparison between the two Temples, their destructions, and the ensuing exiles, is not rare in the Targums and

Much of this critical picture is corroborated by Josephus. Bribery and violence at times characterized the Temple establishment's rule, especially in the 50s and 60s. Josephus tells us that former High Priest Ananias enhanced his reputation by supplying people (such as the newly-appointed Roman governor Albinus) with money. We are also told that when Jesus ben Gamaliel (= Joshua ben Gamala) gained the high priesthood (through bribery according to *b. Yebam.* 61a; *b. Yoma* 18a), a feud arose between him and his predecessor: 'Ananias, however, kept the upper hand by using his wealth to attract those who were willing to receive bribes' (*Ant.* 20.9.4 §213).[110] Josephus himself was victimized by bribes accepted by the High Priest Ananus (*Life* 38-39 §193-96). Describing the 50s and 60s, Josephus reports that the chief priests sent their servants to take by force the tithes from lower-ranking priests, 'beating those who refused to give', with the result that some of the poorer priests starved to death (*Ant.* 20.8.8 §181, 20.9.2 §206-207; cf. rabbinic traditions below). Josephus also tells us that the High Priest Ananus, son of Annas (Lk. 3.2), plotted the death of James, the brother of Jesus, and a few others during the interim between Festus and Albinus (*Ant.* 20.9.1 §197-200).

All of this material, however, dates from periods *after* the destruction of the Temple, and so may not offer a fair and accurate picture of the Temple establishment in the earlier period, especially in the time of Jesus himself. Is there evidence from the early decades of the first century that the Temple establishment was viewed as corrupt?

Qumran may provide some evidence. In the commentary on Habakkuk, and elsewhere, the High Priest is customarily referred to as the 'Wicked Priest' (1QpHab 1.13; 8.9; 9.9; 11.4), who has robbed the poor (1QpHab 8.12; 9.5; 10.1; 12.10), has amassed wealth (1QpHab 8.8-12; 9.4-5), and has defiled the 'Sanctuary of God' (1QpHab 12.8-9). Similarly, 4QpNah 1.11 refers to the 'riches that he [the Wicked Priest?] heaped up in the Temple of Jerusalem'. One passage seems to be specifically related to the Temple:

> 'Woe to him who gets criminal gain for his house, setting his nest on high to be safe from the grasp of misfortune! Thou hast resolved on shame for thy house. Many peoples are in extremeties and the sinner is thyself. For the sto[ne] cries out [from] the wall [and] the beam from the framework

---

writings of the rabbis (see *Tg. Isa.* 51.19; *Tg. Ezek.* 24.6; *Tg. Ps.-J.* Gen. 45.15; *t. Menah.* 13.22; *b. Ta'an.* 28b-29a; *Pesiq. R.* 47.4).

110. Trans. from L.H. Feldman, *Josephus* (LCL, 9; Heinemann, 1965), p. 503.

replies' [Hab. 2.9-10]. [The explanation of this word] concerns the [Prie]st who [...] that its stones might be in oppression and the beam of its framework in robbery. (1QpHab 9.12–10.1)[111]

All these complaints cohere with the criticisms and complaints that have been examined above. But do these criticisms refer to the first-century priesthood or to the Hasmonean priesthood of the last two centuries BCE? It is likely that the 'Wicked Priest' originally did refer to a Hasmonean priest (whether Hyrcanus or someone else). Of course, because of its eschatological perspective, the first-century CE Qumran community may very well have understood the Habakkuk *pesher* to refer to contemporary High Priests. If it was so, how representative was the Qumranian attitude toward Jerusalem's priestly aristocracy? Did Jesus share their attitude?[112]

Another important source is the Testament of Moses. Although some have argued for a Maccabean date, the allusions to Herod and his successors in ch. 6 have led most scholars to conclude that the Testament of Moses was written during the first century.[113] R.H. Charles dated the writing to just prior to 30 CE, a conclusion with which J. Priest agrees.[114] Chapter 5 describes the corruption of the Hasmonean priests, chapter 6 describes the oppression of Herod the Great (for 34 years, see v. 6), and chapter 7 apparently describes the priesthood of the first century CE. The fragmentary chapter reads:[115]

---

111. Dupont-Sommer, *Essene Writings*, p. 265. Bockmuehl ('Why Did Jesus Predict the Destruction of the Temple?', p. 18 n. 38) thinks that the 'beam' refers to the beams of the Temple.

112. In an earlier study (C.A. Evans, 'Jesus' Action in the Temple: Cleansing or Portent of Destruction?', *CBQ* 51 [1989], pp. 237-70, esp. pp. 260-62) I suggested that Jesus may have held to an opinion approximating that of the Qumran community. For further discussion, see C.A. Evans, 'Opposition to the Temple: Jesus and the Dead Sea Scrolls', in J.H. Charlesworth (ed.), *Jesus and the Dead Sea Scrolls* (ABRL; New York: Doubleday, 1982), pp. 235-53.

113. The allusions are obvious: According to 6.2-6 a 'rash and perverse' man [Herod] will rule 'for thirty-four years'. According to 6.7 Herod 'will beget heirs [Archelaus, Herod Antipas, Philip] who will reign after him for shorter periods of time'. These heirs will be subdued by a 'powerful king of the West', i.e., Rome (6.8).

114. R.H. Charles, *The Assumption of Moses* (London: A. & C. Black, 1897), pp. lv-lviii; J. Priest, 'Testament of Moses', in Charlesworth (ed.), *Old Testament Pseudepigrapha*, I, pp. 920-21. Even if a Maccabean date is required, then chs. 6–7 would have to be understood as a later, probably first-century, interpolation.

115. Trans. from Priest, 'Testament of Moses', I, p. 930.

When this has taken place, the times will quickly come to an end. [...]
Then will rule destructive and godless men, who represent themselves as
being righteous, but who will (in fact) arouse their inner wrath, for they
will be deceitful men, pleasing only themselves, false in every way imag-
inable, (such as) loving feasts at any hour of the day—devouring, glut-
tonous.

[Seven-line lacuna] But really they consume the goods of the (poor),
saying their acts are according to justice, (while in fact they are simply)
exterminators, deceitfully seeking to conceal themselves so that they will
not be known as completely godless because of their criminal deeds
(committed) all the day long, saying, 'We shall have feasts, even luxurious
winings and dinings. Indeed, we shall behave ourselves as princes'. They,
with hand and mind, touch impure things, yet their mouths will speak
enormous things, and they will even say, 'Do not touch me, lest you
pollute me in the position I occupy...'.

The passage is clearly directed against a wealthy, powerful priestly
aristocracy. Since the passage apparently follows the demise of Herod's
sons, the setting of this apocalyptic vision must be the first century, and
probably some time in the 30s. If this is indeed the case, then what we
have here is pre-70 evidence, possibly from the time of Jesus, of the
belief that the priestly aristocracy was corrupt. It is significant,
furthermore, that several of the complaints reflect the very ones
observed in the post-70 literature surveyed above.

Taken together, this evidence demonstrates that various groups, such
as some tannaitic and early amoraic rabbis, Qumran sectarians, and
Josephus viewed various priests, High Priests, or priestly families as
wealthy, corrupt, often greedy, and sometimes violent. Of course, just
because the Temple establishment was viewed as corrupt, does not mean
that it actually was. Nevertheless, my concern is with the public
perception, for it is against this public perception that Jesus' predictions
of the Temple's destruction would have been interpreted. Evidence that
the Temple establishment was viewed as corrupt is substantial. This
evidence existed before and after the time of Jesus, and can even be
traced to the very time of Jesus.[116]

---

116. For additional discussion, see C.A. Evans, 'Jesus' Action in the Temple and
Evidence of Corruption in the First-Century Temple', *SBLSemPap* (1989), pp. 522-
39. Sanders's failure (*Jesus and Judaism*, pp. 61-76) to take into account the
evidence of corruption in the first-century Temple is the major weakness of his interpretation of Jesus' attitude toward the Temple. His interpretation has been criticized
by R. Bauckham, 'Jesus' Demonstration in the Temple', in B. Lindars (ed.), *Law*

Several features in the Gospels support these conclusions. The Baptist's scathing prophetic criticism, 'You brood of vipers! Who warned you to flee from the wrath to come?' (Mt. 3.7b; Lk. 3.7b), was likely originally addressed to the priestly aristocracy (and not to the 'Pharisees', as in Matthew, nor to the 'multitudes', as in Luke), and as such is completely in keeping with the social and religious conditions of Palestine.[117] Jesus' parables concerning poor stewardship also reflect these conditions. The Parable of the Wicked Vineyard Tenants (Mk 12.1-9) threatens the priestly aristocracy with the loss of their position and power. The abuses of power and privilege described in the Parable of the Faithless Servant (Mt. 24.45-51 = Lk. 12.42-46) probably reflect how the ruling aristocracy was perceived in the minds of Palestinian peasants. Jesus' pronouncement on the half-shekel Temple tax (Mt. 17.24-27) may have been a 'declaration of independence from the Temple and the attendant political-economic-religious establishment'.[118] Jesus' comment regarding the poor widow and the others who were contributing to the Temple's coffers (Mk 12.41-44) was probably a lament—not a word of commendation—and an implicit criticism of the economic oppressiveness and inequity of the Temple establishment. The condemnation of the 'scribes' who 'devour widows' houses' (Mk 12.38-40) may very well allude to Sadducean scribes and not, as is usually assumed, Pharisaic scribes (see Josephus, *Ant.* 18.1.4 §16).[119] In Jesus' lament for Jerusalem (Mt. 23.37-38 = Lk. 13.34-35) there are significant parallels to Jeremiah, the prophet who had severely criticized Jerusalem's First Temple (Jer. 7.14, 34; 12.7; 22.5; 26.9), whose criticism Jesus may have had in mind when he took action in Jerusalem's Second Temple (Jer. 7.11 in Mk 11.17).[120] Various other details during Passion Week cohere with the criticisms of the priestly aristocracy. The priests demand to know by what authority Jesus acted the way he did (Mk 11.27-33). The ruling

and Religion: Essays on the Place of the Law in Israel and Early Christianity (Cambridge: James Clarke, 1988), pp. 72-89, esp. pp. 86-87; M.D. Hooker, 'Traditions about the Temple in the Sayings of Jesus', *BJRL* 70 (1988), pp. 7-19, esp. p. 17; Evans, 'Jesus' Action in the Temple', pp. 256-69; Bockmuehl, 'Why Did Jesus Predict the Temple's Destruction?', p. 16.

117. R.A. Horsley and J.S. Hanson, *Bandits, Prophets, and Messiahs: Popular Movements at the Time of Jesus* (Minneapolis: Winston, 1985), pp. 178-79.

118. Horsley, *Jesus and the Spiral of Violence*, p. 282.

119. See J. Jeremias, *Jerusalem in the Time of Jesus* (London: SCM Press, 1969), p. 231.

120. Horsley and Hanson, *Bandits*, p. 175.

priests cannot arrest Jesus immediately because of their fear of the multitude (Mk 12.12). Jesus is arrested by 'servants of the ruling priests' who are armed with 'clubs' (Mk. 14.43-50; recall *t. Menah.* 13.21).

The Eschatological Inadequacy of a Temple Built by Herod

Perhaps a significant contributing factor to the expectation that the first-century Temple would inevitably be destroyed was that is was *Herodian* and not *Davidic*. The first-century Temple is often referred to as the 'second Temple', the one that replaced Solomon's Temple after its destruction by the Babylonians (2 Kings 25; Ezra 3–6). Strictly speaking, however, that is inaccurate. The first-century Temple, built by Herod the Great (*War* 1.21.1 §401), was in reality Israel's *third* Temple. Herein lies the problem. By what scriptural precedent or prophetic expectation could the Idumean Herod[121] build the Temple of Jerusalem? According to Nathan's oracle (2 Sam. 7.12-16) the son of David was to build the Temple. Solomon built it, of course (1 Kings 6–7),[122] but in later exegesis Nathan's oracle came to be interpreted eschatologically. We see this in Qumran (4QFlor 1.1-13; 4QpsDan A 1.7-9; 2.1-4; 4QPatrBless 1-2) and in the New Testament (Lk. 1.32-33; Acts 2.30; 2 Cor. 6.18; Heb. 1.5).[123] Since Nathan's oracle had come to be interpreted in an eschatological sense, at least in some circles, it is not difficult to see how the Herodian Temple could have been viewed as prophetically invalid and therefore probably doomed to destruction.

The Scriptures of Israel expected a descendant of David to become king. According to Isa. 11.1-2 a 'branch' was expected to grow out of the stump and roots of Jesse (cf. *Tg.*: 'the Messiah shall be anointed from among his children'). This idea is given expression frequently in the

---

121. Herod's father Antipater is clearly identified as 'an Idumean by race' (*War* 1.5.2 §123) and his mother a member of 'an illustrious Arabian family' (*War* 1.8.9 §181). According to the Testament of Moses 'a wanton king, who will not be of a priestly family, will follow them [i.e., the Hasmonean priest-kings], (6.2); trans. based on Priest, 'Testament of Moses', p. 930.

122. Although David did not build the Temple, he did bring the Ark of the Covenant to Jerusalem and place it in a tent (2 Sam. 6.12-19), and he later built an altar (2 Sam. 24.21, 25).

123. For many of the insights in this section I am indebted to O. Betz, 'Die Frage nach dem messianischen Bewusstsein Jesu', *NovT* 6 (1963), pp. 20-48; *idem*, 'Probleme des Prozesses Jesu', *ANRW* 2.25.1 (1982), pp. 565-647, esp. pp. 625-44.

prophets (Isa. 16.5; Jer. 23.5; 30.9; 33.15, 17, 21; Ezek. 17.22; 34.23-24; 37.24-25; Hos. 3.4-5; Mic. 5.2; Amos 9.11; Zech. 3.8; 6.12-13). The messianic, implication of most of these passages is intensified in the LXX and Targum.

The same hope is expressed in the sectarian writings of the intertestamental period. The author of the Psalms of Solomon awaits a messianic descendant *of David*: 'Lord, you chose David to be king over Israel, and swore to him about his descendants forever, that his kingdom should not fail before you' (17.4; cf. 2 Sam. 7.13-16). 'With pomp they set up a monarchy because of their arrogance; they despoiled the throne of David with arrogant shouting' (17.6). 'See, Lord, and raise up for them their king, the son of David, to rule over your servant Israel in the time known to you, O God' (17.21). These lines, in all probability, were penned shortly before Herod's birth or during his childhood.[124] Similar hopes were expressed at Qumran: '"I wi[ll be] a father to him and he shall be my son" [2 Sam. 7.14a]. This is the Branch of David who will arise with the Seeker of the Law and who will sit on the throne of Zion at the end of days; as it is written, "I will raise up the tabernacle of David which is fallen" [Amos 9.11]'. (4QFlor 1.11-12); 'a monarch will [not] be wanting to the tribe of Judah when Israel rules, [and] a (descendant) seated on the throne will [not] be wanting to David' (4QPatrBless 1-2).[125] As he aspired to Jewish kingship, Herod must have been painfully aware of this traditional and sacred hope. In short, his Temple and kingship were suspect because he was not of the line of David.

Probably in response to some of these objections and criticisms, Herod claimed Davidic ancestry and attempted the deeds expected of a Davidide.[126] It is thus conceivable that Herod the Great wished to be viewed as Israel's messianic and Davidic king.[127] At many points the life

---

124. Cf. also the first-century apocalyptic hope of 4 Ezra 12.31-32: 'And as for the Lion that you saw [cf. 11.37]…speaking to the Eagle [i.e., Rome] and reproving him for his unrighteousness…this is the Messiah whom the Most High has kept until the end of days [cf. 13.52], who will arise from the posterity of David'.

125. Trans. based on Dupont-Sommer, *Essene Writings*, pp. 313, 314.

126. A. Schalit, הורדוס המלך האיש ופעלו (ET: *Herod the King: The Man and His Achievement*) (Jerusalem: Mosad Bialik, 1960), pp. 233-34.

127. The infancy account of Herod's attempt to destroy Jesus may imply that the Matthean evangelist regarded the former as some sort of messianic rival of the latter (Mt. 2.1-18).

of this remarkable ruler paralleled that of David. The Essene Menahem prophesied to Herod that he would become King (*Ant.* 15.10.5 §373). As a youth David received similar tidings from Samuel (1 Sam. 16.12-13). Herod married into the Jewish royal family when he married the Hasmonean Mariamme, 'and thus became kinsman of the king' (*War* 1.12.3 §241), just as David married Michal, the daughter of King Saul (1 Sam. 18.20-29). Herod was appointed King of the Jews[128] by Antony and the Roman Senate (*War* 1.14.4 §282-85), just as David was anointed King by Samuel (1 Sam. 16.13) and later by the men of Judah (2 Sam. 2.4) and the elders of Israel (2 Sam. 5.3). In *conquering* Israel, Herod enjoyed several remarkable, almost miraculous, deliverances (*War* 1.17.4 §331-32; 1.17.1 §340-41), so that he came to be regarded as 'a man beloved of God [θεοφιλέστατος]' (*War* 1.17.4 §331; cf. *Ant.* 14.15.11 §455: Ἡρώδην εἶναι θεοφιλῆ). Similarly David was favored by several narrow escapes (1 Sam. 18.10-11; 19.12; 21.10-15), gaining the reputation of one who enjoyed God's favor and abiding presence (2 Sam. 5.10; 22.51; Ps. 18.50). Herod captured Jerusalem (*War* 1.17.8 §342–1.18.3 §357), as did David (2 Sam. 5.6-9). Like David (1 Sam. 17.19-54; 18.7, 27), Herod was a man of prowess (*War* 1.21.3 §429-30).

But perhaps Herod's greatest claim to fame, and the most significant of his many achievements, was his rebuilding of the Temple. This in itself, in light of Nathan's oracle (2 Samuel 7), would have been Herod's strongest claim to regal legitimacy.[129] According to Josephus Herod built the Temple, with a 'magnificence never surpassed [ἀνυπέρβλητος]' (*War* 1.21.1 §401), thus implying that Herod's Temple was at least equal to, if not in some sense superior to Solomon's. In two other places Josephus compares Herod and Solomon, the builders of the Temple (*War* 5.4.1 §137; 5.51 §185). According to TBenj. 9.2 'the latter Temple will exceed the former in glory' (cf. 1En 90.29; Tobit [B] 14.5). Was this what Herod attempted to do, build the 'latter Temple', whose glory 'will exceed the former'? In his speech, before commencing construction, Herod compared the second Temple with Solomon's noting that the former was smaller. This deficiency Herod wished to remedy by building a new Temple (*Ant.* 15.11.1 §385-87). '[Herod] surpassed his predecessors in spending money, so that it was thought that no one else had adorned the Temple so splendidly' (*Ant.* 15.11.3 §396).

128. βασιλεὺς Ἰουδαίων, which is precisely the wording on the *titulus* affixed to Jesus' cross (Mk. 15.26 par.).

129. Betz, 'Messianische Bewusstsein Jesu', p. 36 n. 1.

Josephus also makes a point of Herod's zeal for the Temple. When gentiles attempted to break into the sanctuary to view its contents, Herod protected the Temple from profanation. According to Josephus Herod deemed 'victory more grievous than defeat, if these people should set eyes on any objects not open to public view' (*War* 1.18.3 §354; cf. 1.7.6 §152: 'Of all the calamaties of that time [Pompey's capture of Jerusalem] none so deeply affected the nation as the exposure to alien eyes of the Holy Place'). This concern for the Temple's sanctity is quite remarkable.

But the most dramatic display of zeal for the Temple is seen in the dedication that followed its completion. Herod celebrated the completion of the Temple by sacrificing three hundred oxen (*Ant.* 15.11.6 §422). This extravagance paralleled that of Solomon, who along with all the congregation of Israel sacrificed innumerable sheep and oxen (1 Kgs 8.5, 63).[130] Josephus reports that during the entire period of the construction of the sanctuary (eighteen months)[131] it never rained during the day, which was regarded as a manifestation of divine power (*Ant.* 15.11.7 §425). Recall that the Chronicler tells us that fire fell from heaven and consumed the sacrifices, filling the Solomonic Temple with God's glory (2 Chron. 7.1-3). Significantly Josephus tells us that 'the day on which the work of the Temple was completed coincided with that of the king's accession' (*Ant.* 15.11.6 §423), a coincidence which in Herod's mind may have lent his claim to rule a measure of legitimacy.[132]

Herod not only rebuilt the Temple, he rebuilt Jerusalem and built for himself a palace (*War* 1.21.1 §401-402). Again, there is comparison with David: 'David built the city' (2 Sam. 5.9) and had a house built for himself (2 Sam. 5.11). 'You raised up for yourself a servant, named

---

130. David also offered sacrifices to celebrate the Ark's arrival in Jerusalem (cf. 2 Sam. 6.17; compare also Josiah's Passover celebration; 2 Chron. 35.1-19; 1 Esdras 1.1-22; 2 Kgs 23.21-23). Two related 'cleansings' of the Temple should be mentioned: (1) Succeeding the idolatrous Ahaz, Hezekiah repaired the Temple doors (2 Chron. 29.3) and ordered the cleansing of the Temple, including altar and utensils (2 Chron. 29.4-19). To consecrate the sanctuary he had seven bulls, rams, lambs, and he-goats offered (2 Chron. 29.20-24). After the consecration service thousands of animals were sacrificed (2 Chron. 29.31-36). (2) Judas Maccabeus and his brothers cleansed the Temple and rebuilt the altar and the interior of the sanctuary (1 Macc. 4.36-51). For eight days sacrifices were offered (1 Macc. 4.52-59).

131. The entire complex, of course, took many years to complete. Work finally ceased sometime between 62 and 64 CE (*Ant.* 20.9.7 §219).

132. Evidently importance was attached to such coincidences (cf. 1 Macc. 4.54).

David. And you commanded him to build a city for your name, and in it to offer you oblations from what is yours' (4 Ezra 3.23-24). Solomon, of course, built himself a palace, built the Temple, and built the wall around Jerusalem (1 Kgs 3.1; 5.5). Solomon built cities (1 Kgs 9.15-19); so did Herod (*War* 1.21.2-10 §403-21). Herod appointed a High Priest—something that was quite rare according to Josephus (*Ant.* 15.3.1 §39-41)[133]—as did Solomon, when he replaced Abiathar with Zadok (1 Kgs 2.27, 35). Herod may also have portrayed himself as Israel's *go'el*, 'redeemer'.[134]

That Jesus was recognized as a Davidide is well supported in the New Testament. With little or no apologetic interest Paul refers to Jesus as descended 'from the seed of David according to the flesh' (Rom. 1.3). It is hard to believe that a man with the education and background that Paul had could have been mistaken in such a matter as this, especially after having persecuted the early Church and, presumably, at that time having gathered what counter-evidence was available. There is no hint anywhere in the New Testament or in other early reliable sources that Jesus' Davidic descent was disputed.[135] From a Christian perspective, because Jesus was understood as much more than a mere physical descendant of David, very little was made of it. The genealogies, which claim to document Davidic descent (Mt. 1.2-16; Lk. 3.23-38), are likely neither literary fictions nor instances of *ad hoc* apologetic. Fake genealogies would only create problems.[136] Moreover, the infancy

133. Herod later appointed Simon son of Boethus to the High Priesthood, in order to marry his daughter (*Ant.* 15.9.3 §320-22).

134. Schalit, הורדוס המלך, pp. 271-72. Schalit's work has been criticized for too readily accepting the biased claims found in the fragments of Herod's biographer Nicholas of Damascus (b. *c.* 64 BCE); cf. J.C. Greenfield, *JBL* 80 (1961), pp. 82-84. For a more critical study of this important historian, whose works (*Historia Universalis* in 144 books) Josephus made use of (esp. in *War* 1 and *Ant.* 15-17), see B.Z. Wacholder, *Nicholas of Damascus* (Berkeley: University of California Press, 1962).

135. This point has been taken by G. Dalman, *The Words of Jesus* (Edinburgh: T. & T. Clark, 1902), pp. 319-24. Rabbinic claims that Jesus was illegitimate or fathered by a Roman soldier are late and wholly unreliable (*b. Sanh.* 106a; *b. Šab.* 104b; cf. *Against Celsus* 1.32.33).

136. Marshall, *Luke*, pp. 157-59. Fitzmyer (*Luke I-IX*, pp. 497-98) comments that although the Matthean and Lucan evangelists have fashioned their respective genealogies, they 'most likely did depend on different existing Davidic ancestry lists'. See also Jeremias, *Jerusalem in the Time of Jesus*, pp. 213-21, 275-302.

narratives do not struggle with the question of Jesus' Davidic descent, as Haenchen thinks,[137] they struggle to explain how Jesus *of Nazareth* could have fulfilled the *Bethlehem* prophecy (cf. Jn. 7.42). And finally, apostolic preaching relating to the resurrection presupposes Davidic lineage (Acts 2.24-36; 13.30-37).[138]

The widespread acceptance of Jesus' Davidic descent probably derives from Jesus himself, as seen in synoptic tradition that has reasonable claim to authenticity. Jesus appealed to David's example to justify the actions of his disciples (Mk 2.25 par.).[139] On at least one occasion Jesus is openly hailed as 'Son of David' (Mk 10.47 par.; cf. Mt. 21.9).[140] Even the question about why David called his son 'lord' (Mk 12.35-37 par.) does not imply Jesus' rejection of Davidic descent, only a particular understanding of it.[141]

137. Haenchen, *Weg Jesu*, pp. 4.16-17.

138. See R. Pesch, *Die Apostelgeschichte* (2 vols.; EKKNT, 5; Neukirchen-Vluyn: Neukirchener Verlag, 1986), I, pp. 122-23; H. Conzelmann, *Acts of the Apostles* (Hermeneia; Philadelphia: Fortress Press, 1987), p. 21.

139. Although vv. 27-28 may originally have been independent, the rest of the pericope (vv. 23-26) in all probability reflects a genuine episode in the life of Jesus; cf. Haenchen, *Weg Jesu*, p. 122: '[There is the possibility that] it really occurred once that Jesus went through a grain field with his disciples hungry, and the Pharisees—it could have been simply a farmer—took offense at the picking of grain'; cf. Taylor, *Mark*, pp. 214-15; Gnilka, *Markus*, I, p. 122. The complexities of the argument militate against the view that this pericope was created by the early Church in order to answer critics of a libertarian approach to the Sabbath (*pace* Bultmann, *History of the Synoptic Tradition*, p. 16; Anderson, *Mark*, pp. 108-109); cf. Marshall, *Luke*, pp. 229-30; Stanton, *Gospels and Jesus*, p. 243.

140. Bultmann (*History of the Synoptic Tradition*, p. 213) doubts the authenticity of the passage because the blind man is named and Jesus is called 'son of David'. Fitzmyer (*Luke X-XXIV*, p. 1213) rightly wonders if such details really are signs of community creation. Cranfield (*Mark*, p. 344) thinks it more probable that the 'narrative is based on the reminiscence of an eye-witness'. Gnilka (*Markus*, II, p. 111) also speaks of the preservation of a 'historische Erinnerung'. Similarly E. Hirsch (*Frühgeschichte des Evangeliums* [2 vols.; Tübingen: Mohr (Paul Siebeck), 1952, 2nd edn], I, p. 117), Lohmeyer (*Markus*, p. 224), and Taylor (*Mark*, pp. 446-47) find marks of historical reality.

141. Haenchen's view (*Weg Jesu*), pp. 416-17) that Mk. 12.35-37 was an attempt on the part of early Christian scribal activity to solve the problem that Jesus was not a Davidide is not satisfactory. If early Christianity had actually struggled with such a problem, how would the creation of Mk. 12.35-37 have helped? It would only have contributed to the problem. Taylor (*Mark*, pp. 490-91) puts it aptly: 'It is difficult to think that the doctrinal beliefs of a community could be expressed in this allusive

There is evidence that Jesus may have viewed Herod as an usurper and rival, and so incorporated this view into some sort of Davidic typology. The principal passage that supports this idea is Lk. 13.31-33: 'Some Pharisees came and said to him, "Get away from here, for Herod wants to kill you". And he said to them, "Go and tell that fox, 'Behold, I cast out demons and perform cures today and tomorrow, and on the third day I finish my course'" '.[142] O. Betz suggests that Jesus may have called Herod a 'fox' as a play on his name: שׁוּעָל ('fox') and שָׁאוּל ('Saul').[143] He thinks that Jesus probably viewed himself in some sort of typological sense as the Davidic rival of Herod/Saul. W. Grimm followed up and elaborated on Betz's ideas by proposing that certain aspects of Jesus' itinerant ministry parallel the period in David's life when the latter was the Lord's anointed, but not yet enthroned king.[144]

manner...Such a denial on [Jesus'] part would have furnished a major ground for an attack against him'. See also Anderson, *Mark*, p. 284; Lohmeyer, *Markus*, pp. 262-63. Fitzmyer (*Luke X-XXIV*, p. 1313), accepting the authenticity of the pericope, suggests that the original 'meaning may be wholly lost to us' (since third-century rabbinic interpretation offers no sure guide), but that it was the springboard for the early Palestinian community's confession that 'Jesus is Lord'. For the suggestion that the pericope is but the remnant of a longer, authentic exchange between Jesus and opponents who had hoped to trap him into making an inflammatory announcement of his Davidic identity, see R.P. Gagg, 'Jesus und die Davidssohnfrage: Zur Exegese von Markus 12.35-37', *TZ* 7 (1951), pp. 18-30.

142. J.B. Tyson ('Jesus and Herod Antipas', *JBL* 79 [1960], pp. 239-46, esp. p. 245) argues that this pericope reflects a genuine episode in the life of Jesus. Fitzmyer (*Luke X-XXIV*, p. 1030) agrees.

143. Betz, 'Messianische Bewusstsein Jesu', pp. 41-42.

144. W. Grimm, 'Eschatologischer Saul wider eschatologischer David: Eine Deutung von Lc. xiii 31 ff,' *NovT* 15 (1973), pp. 114-33. Grimm suggests that lying behind Lk. 13.31-33 is 1 Sam. 23.9-13. There are some parallels (including material not treated by Grimm): We read of David, without home or country, running for his life. The disenfranchised of Israel attach themselves to him (1 Sam. 22.2: 'every one who was in distress, and every one who was in debt') and become his loyal following. On various occasions David is warned of Saul's murderous intentions (1 Sam. 22.5; 23.9-13, 25) and then flees from Saul and wanders in the wilderness (1 Sam. 22.5; 23.13-14, 24-29). Betz ('Messianische Bewusstsein Jesu', pp. 41-42) and Grimm liken Jesus' experience, particularly in relation to Herod Antipas, to these features in the story of David. Debtors, the distressed, and the disenfranchised seek help from Jesus (Mk 2.15-17); Mt. 11.19 = Lk. 7.34); many of them follow him (Mk 2.15; 3.7). Jesus wanders in the wilderness (Lk. 5.16; 7.24) and is warned of Herod's murderous intentions (Lk. 13.31). And, of course, on one occasion (Mk 2.23-26) Jesus defends plucking grain on the Sabbath by an appeal to David's example in

The conflict between Jesus and Herod appears at several points, and seems to have been rooted in the conflict between John, Jesus' predecessor, and Herod. The conflict probably owed its origin to John's condemnation of Herod's marriage to Herodias, his brother Philip's wife (Mk 6.18; Lk. 3.19; Josephus, *Ant.* 18.5.2 §116-19). John's criticism of the marriage was probably based on the prohibition against marrying the spouse of a relative (Lev. 18.16; 20.21), except when the levirate law was applicable. Since Jesus held to a strict halakah regarding divorce and remarriage (Mt. 5.31-32; 19.3-9), it is reasonable to assume that he was in agreement with John's stance toward the Herodian marriage. In response to this preaching Herod imprisoned John (Mk 6.17; Lk. 3.20), which occasions an important communication between the Baptist and Jesus. Sending messengers to Jesus, John inquired of him: 'Are you he who is to come, or shall we look for another?' (Mt. 11.2-3; Lk. 7.18-19).[145] It is likely that John raised this question because Jesus had failed to live up to the expectation of the fiery reformer who would sift the threshing floor (cf. Lk. 3.15-17). In no sense did it appear to the imprisoned Baptist that Jesus was 'one mightier than [John]' (v. 16).[146] From this it may be inferred that John, who had verbally opposed Herod, expected Jesus, who was supposed to be mightier, to take stronger action against the Galilean ruler. But Jesus had not; hence the question. Jesus responded by pointing to his ministry of preaching and miracles (Mt. 11.4-6; Lk. 7.21-23). (On the significance of this answer see below.) For various reasons, personal and political, Herod executes John (Mk 6.17-29; Lk. 3.19-20). Although Josephus emphasizes the political expedient for taking this action (*Ant.* 18.5.2 §118-19), he later describes Herodias' departure 'from a living husband' and marriage to

---

1 Sam. 21.1-6. Finally, Grimm suggests that Luke's grammatically peculiar use of πορεύεσθαι in 13.33 reflects the *hitpaʿel* of הלך in 1 Sam. 23.13. These parallels are suggestive and may reflect a genuine aspect of how Jesus and his followers understood their experience. Grimm, however, goes beyond the evidence in arguing for a Lion (= David/Jesus) v. Fox (= Saul/Herod) typology (as might be supported by the frequent contrast between the two animals in Aesop's fables). Fitzmyer (*Luke X-XXIV*, p. 1031) thinks such a comparison is 'farfetched'. Neither is Marshall (*Luke*, p. 571) convinced. H.W. Hoehner (*Herod Antipas* [SNTSMS, 17; Cambridge: Cambridge University Press, 1972], p. 221), however, accepts the comparison.

145. The authenticity of this question put to Jesus can scarcely be doubted; Kümmel, *Promise and Fulfillment*, pp. 110-11; Marshall, *Luke*, p. 288; Fitzmyer, *Luke I-IX*, pp. 663-64.

146. So Fitzmyer, *Luke I-IX*, p. 665.

Herod Antipas as a 'flouting of (the traditions of) the fathers' (*Ant.* 18.5.4 §136). Thus, at an essential point Josephus corroborates the version found in the Synoptic Gospels.

Sometime after John's death Herod heard of Jesus' remarkable ministry and concluded that the Baptist had been raised from the dead (Mk 6.14-16; Lk. 9.7-9).[147] 'And he sought to see him' (Lk. 9.9). Herod would later get his wish (Lk. 23.7-8). But before Jesus was brought before the ruler of Galilee, he warned his disciples to 'beware the leaven of the Pharisees and the leaven of Herod' (Mk 8.15).[148] What this originally meant is obscured by the context in which the Marcan evangelist has placed it and by the secondary application that he has given it. It is probable that the 'leaven' of the Pharisees was their insistence on receiving a 'sign from heaven' (Mk 8.11), while the 'leaven' of Herod, similarly, was his desire to see Jesus perform a 'sign' (Lk. 23.8).[149]

It is also said that Jesus was opposed by the Herodians (Mk 3.1-6; 12.13-17), a group of influential persons, perhaps overlapping with the Sadducees,[150] who supported Herodian and Roman rule.[151] In the first episode Jesus, on the sabbath, heals the man with the withered hand. The Pharisees then take counsel with the Herodians to find a way to destroy Jesus. It had been wondered why the Herodians would take exception to Jesus healing someone on the sabbath. That the Pharisees would take exception, of course, occasions no surprise. But if some of the Herodians were in fact Sadducees, a party that took the written Torah seriously, then their opposition to Jesus becomes understandable. Moreover, as collaborators with Herod and the Roman authorities they may be expected to oppose someone who was viewed as a threat to the

147. That Herod had in fact actually heard of Jesus' ministry is not at all hard to imagine; cf. R.A. Guelich, *Mark 1-8:26* (WBC, 34a; Waco: Word, 1989), p. 328.

148. Some mss., including ∏45, read 'leaven of the Pharisees and the leaven of the Herodians'. But this is probably harmonization (plural 'Herodians' to go with plural 'Pharisees') suggested by Mk. 3.6; 12.13; Taylor, *Mark*, p. 366.

149. So Guelich, *Mark*, p. 419.

150. Which would explain their close association with the 'Boethusians' (a group that had enjoyed Herodian favor since the days of Herod the Great) and possibly why Matthew (16.1, 6) replaced 'Herodians' with 'Sadducees'; cf. Hoehner, *Antipas*, pp. 336-39.

151. So H.H. Rowley, 'The Herodians in the Gospels', *JTS* 41 (1940), pp. 14-27, followed by Hoehner, *Antipas*, pp. 332-39. Josephus speaks of the 'partisans of Herod' (*Ant.* 14.15.10 §450) and of the 'Herodeioi' (*War* 1.21.6 §319). These may very well be the forerunners of the 'Herodians' found in the gospels.

status quo. One other detail deserves comment. In 3.5 Jesus 'looks around at them with anger [ὀργή], grieved at the hardness of their heart'. For two reasons I suspect that the second phrase is Marcan: (1) it mitigates the harshness of the first phrase (the Matthean and Lucan evangelists elect to omit altogether reference to Jesus' anger) by suggesting that Jesus was angry and saddened by his opponents' spiritual blindness; and (2) it is part of Mark's obduracy theme (cf. 4.11-12; 6.52; 8.17-19). Without the second phrase the picture is altered. Accordingly, in the pre-Marcan tradition there may have been a greater degree of anger and hostility, *on both sides*. In the second episode some Pharisees and Herodians ask Jesus about paying taxes to Caesar.[152] This is precisely the kind of concern we should expect of Herodians. Although Jesus' answer is clever and seems to avoid the trap (cf. 12.13), he was, nevertheless, apparently accused of teaching that it was not lawful to pay taxes to the Roman Empire (cf. Lk. 23.2). What, if any, of this may have been relayed to Herod himself is impossible to say.[153]

The Parable of the Pounds (Lk. 19.11-27) affords us with the intriguing possibility of learning something about Jesus' criticism of the Herodian dynasty. Recently R. Rohrbaugh has suggested that the parable originally had nothing to do with Christian stewardship, but was a criticism of the wrong kind of kingship.[154] Seen in this light, the characters of the parable are completely transformed. The harsh 'nobleman' who expected his servants to make large profits, or at least earn interest (though all of this either directly violated Torah or offended first-century peasant sensitivities), who took what was not his, and who

152. The authenticity of this passage is almost universally accepted; cf. Bultmann, *History of the Synoptic Tradition*, p. 26; Taylor, *Mark*, p. 478: 'Of it genuineness there can be no question'; Haenchen, *Weg Jesu*, p. 406; F.F. Bruce, 'Render to Caesar', in Bammel and Moule (eds.), *Jesus and the Politics of His Day*, pp. 249-63; Horsley, *Jesus and the Spiral of Violence*, p. 307; Witherington, *Christology of Jesus*, pp. 101-104.

153. It may only be a coincidence, but it is intriguing to observe that only in Luke do we have (1) Jesus accused of teaching people not to pay taxes; and (2) Jesus brought before Herod. It is thus possible that the Herodians did report to Herod Jesus' answer regarding the payment of tax to Caesar.

154. R. Rohrbaugh, 'A Peasant Reading of the Parable of the Talents/Pounds: A Text of Terror?' a paper read in New Orleans at the 1990 annual meeting of the Society of Biblical Literature. Although his point was chiefly concerned with a socio-economic reading of the parable, I would like to take up his suggestion and apply it to the present study's concern with Jesus and Herod.

was hated by his citizens who even sent an embassy after him, saying 'We do not want this man to reign over us', does not represent Jesus, but represents a greedy, power-hungry middle eastern monarch. The 'wicked' servant, on the other hand, is in reality the righteous servant, for he refused to engage in profiteering and unlawful usury. This interpretation may in fact enjoy a measure of support from the *Gospel of the Nazoreans*, as quoted and discussed by Eusebius: 'But since the gospel in Hebrew characters [i.e., the *Gospel of the Nazoreans*], which has come into our hands, enters the threat not against the man who had hid (the talent), but against him who had lived dissolutely—for he had three servants: one who squandered his master's substance with harlots and flute-girls, one who multiplied the gain, and one who hid the talent; and accordingly one was accepted (with joy), another merely rebuked, and another cast into prison—I wonder whether in Matthew the threat which is uttered against the man who did nothing may refer not to him, but by epanalepsis to the first who had feasted and drunk with the drunken' (*Theophania* §22 [on Mt. 25.14-15]).[155] The *Gospel of the Nazoreans* might witness a pre-Lucan (and perhaps pre-Q) form of this parable that is actually closer to the point that Jesus had originally scored.[156]

Many commentators have pointed out the similarities between the parable's nobleman and Archelaus, one of the sons of Herod the Great (cf. Josephus, *Ant.* 17.9.3-11.4 §219-320; *War* 2.2.1-6.3 §14-100).[157] It

155. From R.W. Funk, *New Gospel Parallels: Volume One, The Synoptic Gospels* (Philadelphia: Fortress Press, 1985), p. 419.

156. So Rohrbaugh, 'Peasant Reading'.

157. The nobleman went to a far country (v. 12), just as Archelaus went to Rome (*Ant.* 17.9.3 §219); the nobleman hoped to receive a kingdom (βασιλεία) and to return (v. 12), just as Archelaus hoped (*Ant.* 17.9.3 §220: βασιλεία); the nobleman left household instructions to his servants (v. 13), just as Archelaus did (*Ant.* 17.9.3 §219, 223); the nobleman's citizens hated (μισεῖν) him (v. 14), just as Archelaus' subjects hated him (*Ant.* 17.9.4 §227: μῖσος); an embassy (πρεσβεία) is sent after the nobleman (v. 14), as one was sent after Archelaus (*Ant.* 17.11.1 §300: πρεσβεία); the citizens petitioned the foreign country against the nobleman's rule (v. 14), just as the envoys petitioned against Archelaus (*Ant.* 17.11.1 §302); the nobleman slaughtered (κατασφάζειν) his citizens who opposed him (v. 27), just as Archelaus had done before his journey (*Ant.* 17.9.5 §237, 239: σφάζειν); when the nobleman returned as ruler, he collected his revenues (vv. 15-19), just as Josephus notes that Archelaus was to receive 600 talents as his yearly tribute (*Ant.* 17.11.4 §320); and finally, when the nobleman returned, he settled accounts with those who had opposed

has been wondered why the hero of the parable would have been modeled after such a figure. But if the nobleman was not the hero of the parable, but was the villain, modeling him after Archelaus makes perfect sense. If the parable were originally uttered in Judea, instead of Galilee, that could explain why it was modeled after the deposed ruler of Judea, and not after brother Herod Antipas of Galilee. Jesus' point, therefore, may have been to illustrate the wrong approach to rule, as he in fact does in other places: 'You know that those who are supposed to rule over the Gentiles lord it over them, and their great men exercise authority over them. But it shall not be so among you; but whoever would be great among you must be your servant, and whoever would be first among you must be slave of all' (Mk 10.42-44). More to the point, Jesus might not have been simply criticizing the wrong philosophy of kingship; he may have been criticizing the Herodian dynasty itself.

When Jesus and Herod finally met, the latter 'hoped to see some sign done by him' (Lk. 23.8).[158] But Jesus did not cooperate (Lk. 23.9). What specific sign he hoped to see is hard to say. When Herod initially became interested in meeting Jesus, it was after hearing that Jesus' disciples had 'cast out many demons, and anointed with oil many that were sick and healed them' (Mk 6.13; cf. Lk. 9.6). Recall that John had entertained doubts about Jesus and that Jesus tried to satisfy the imprisoned prophet by describing his ministry of miracles (Mt. 11.4-6; Lk. 7.22-23). In other words, the miracles that Jesus was doing were his credentials. It was these credentials that Herod wanted to review

him (v. 27), which parallels Archelaus' settling with Joazar the high priest for having supported the rebels (*Ant.* 17.13.1 §339). Since Herod Antipas also traveled to Rome to press his claim to the throne, and was also opposed, his experience loosely fits the experience of the parable's nobleman. But it is Archelaus who offers the closest match.

158. Although many commentators have thought that this pericope is a Lucan creation (e.g., Creed, *Luke*, p. 280), there are good reasons for regarding it as historical. See Hoehner, *Antipas*, pp. 224-50; idem, 'Why Did Pilate Hand Jesus over to Antipas?', in E. Bammel (ed.), *The Trial of Jesus* (C.F.D. Moule Festschrift; SBT, 13; London: SCM Press, 1970), pp. 84-90; Fitzmyer, *Luke X-XXIV*, p. 1479. Herod's interest in seeing a sign (σημεῖον) may have had more to do with politics than mere entertainment. Recall that many of the messianic/prophetic claimants in this period promised 'signs' of one sort or another. Josephus, describing the unrest of first-century Palestine, says: 'Imposters and deceivers called upon the mob to follow them into the desert. For they said that they would show them unmistakable marvels and signs [σημεῖα]' (*Ant.* 20.7.6 §168; cf. *War* 2.13.4 §259).

personally. But Jesus gave him no opportunity, so Herod and his soldiers mocked Jesus and treated him with contempt, arraying him in a 'shining robe [ἐσθής]' (Lk. 23.11; compare description of the robe worn by King Agrippa; Acts 12.21; Josephus, *Ant.* 19.8.2 §344; cf. *War* 2.1.1 §1-2, in reference to Archelaus dressed in 'white robe [ἐσθής]' and received as king; and Tacitus, *Histories* 2.89, in reference to Vitellius). The mockery, especially as indicated by the robe, probably had to do with Jesus as Israel's legitimate king (cf. Lk. 19.38: 'Blessed is the King').[159] Just as Solomon, David's son, was arrayed in a royal robe (ἐσθής; *Ant.* 8.7.3 §186), so Jesus is thus arrayed. In other words, when Jesus and Herod finally meet, they meet as rival kingly claimants.[160]

Concluding Summary

The results of the study may be summarized by the following four points:

1. As did many others, Jesus predicted the destruction of the Herodian Temple. This tradition is well attested and is corroborated in a variety of ways.
2. As did many others, Jesus employed the language of the classical prophets, particularly Jeremiah and Ezekiel, whose oracles were concerned with the Babylonian destruction of

159. So Betz, 'Probleme des Prozesses Jesu', p. 638 n. 215; Hoehner, *Antipas*, p. 243; E. Schweizer, *The Good News according to Luke* (Atlanta: John Knox, 1984), p. 352. Fitzmyer (*Luke X-XXIV*, p. 1482) disagrees, arguing that to say that the robe has to do with kingship 'is to read a Marcan nuance into it'. On the contrary, taking the robe as a mock sign of royalty fits the Lucan context (Lk. 19.38) and reflects not only his Marcan source (Mk 15.17; cf. *Ant.* 8.7.3 §185), but the scriptural and historical antecedents (as in Josephus cited above) known to the Lucan evangelist. Fitzmyer says that the Lucan context (cf. 23.14-16) argues for understanding the robe as mocking Jesus' guiltlessness. But since, according to Luke, Pilate and Herod do in fact declare Jesus innocent, in what sense was Jesus 'mocked' (23.11) when arrayed in the robe? If Herod and company were *mocking* Jesus' innocence, then Pilate's declaration that he and Herod find no guilt in Jesus makes no sense. Although Luke does not say what color the robe was, as does Mark ('purple'), nor says anything about a crown of thorns, the meeting with Herod, only reported by Luke, probably is meant to contrast the two kings.

160. Remember that it was Herod's ambition to gain officially the title 'king' that led to his banishment (Josephus, *Ant.* 18.7.2 §245-56).

the Solomonic Temple, in predicting the Herodian Temple's destruction. Moreover, Jesus even alluded to some of the same complaints (e.g., Jer. 7.11).

3. There is substantial evidence of corruption in the Herodian Temple establishment. Furthermore, there is evidence of sectarian and peasant resentment toward the ruling establishment (i.e., ruling priests, Roman authorities). Jesus' action in the Temple (the so-called 'cleansing') was in all probability related to, indeed possibly the occasion for, a prophetic word against the Temple.

4. The fact that the first-century Temple was built by Herod may have been a factor in anticipating its destruction. Built by Herod and administered by corrupt non-Zadokite ruling priestly families, the Temple faced certain destruction according to many Jews. However, whether or not this was a factor in Jesus' actions or in his prediction of the Temple's destruction is not certain. It must remain no more than a speculation. That he was critical of the Herodian dynasty and that Herod Antipas took a malevolent interest in Jesus seem likely.

4Q521 'ON RESURRECTION' AND THE SYNOPTIC GOSPEL TRADITION: A PRELIMINARY STUDY[*]

James D. Tabor and Michael O. Wise

Introduction

Among the most intriguing of the Dead Sea Scrolls now available to all interested scholars is one that has been entitled 'On Resurrection'.[1] None of the early descriptions of the Qumran finds mentioned this text. Its very existence is therefore a surprise—a surprise that, in view of the text's potential historical and theological importance, is not entirely pleasant. The text comprises thirteen fragments, the largest of which preserves portions of three columns. The second and best preserved of these columns will be the concern of the present study.

4Q521 appears to be a sort of admonition, although the fragmentary state of the surviving portions precludes any firm decision as to the

[*]   The authors would like to thank James Charlesworth for the opportunity to discuss in a proper forum ideas that have sometimes been distorted when they have appeared in the popular press. Professor Charlesworth also discussed the text with them and made several suggestions which they have adopted. Thanks are due also to Norman Golb for discussing the text with Wise, and to Anthony Tomasino for his several suggestions for the reading and understanding of the text. Wise has prepared the Semitic side of the article, while Tabor is responsible for the discussion of the New Testament implications. [This article antedates E. Puech's *editio princeps* of 4G521. Editor].

1.   The title 'On Resurrection' and the siglum '4Q521' follow the *Dead Sea Scroll Inventory Project: Lists of Documents, Photographs and Museum Plates, Fascicle 8: Qumran Cave 4 (4Q521-4Q575) Starcky*, compiled by S.A. Reed; January 1992. The photographs of the text are PAM 41.676, 41.948 and 43.604. The last number represents the latest photograph, the basis for our transcription. For the photographs see also R. Eisenman and J. Robinson, *A Facsimile Edition of the Dead Sea Scrolls* (2 vols.; Washington, DC: Biblical Archaeology Society, 1991) plates 384, 528 and 1551. A photograph of this text, accompanied by a preliminary translation, was published by R. Eisenman in *BAR* 17 (Nov/Dec 1991), p. 65.

text's genre. A speaker addresses an audience and instructs them on various matters concerning their relationship with God. From time to time, the speaker expresses his own feelings on these matters, so one encounters some first-person verbal forms. In fragment 1 column 2 the teaching centers on the eschaton. What will it be like in the 'Day of the Lord?' The speaker describes that time, drawing on many passages of the Hebrew Bible, particularly on Psalm 146, Isaiah 61 and Isaiah 40. His description is remarkable in many respects, not least in its ideas about a messianic figure. Further, 4Q521 appears to have close connections with important aspects of early Christian tradition, particularly the sayings source known as Q. In the following pages we propose first to discuss the text's meaning and use of the Bible, then to turn to a brief appraisal of some possible implications for the study of the Synoptics.

Text and Translation of 4Q521 1 ii 1-14

1. [c.4   הש[מ]ים והארץ ישמעו למשיחו
2. [הים דא[שר בם לוא יסוג ממצות קדושים
3. התאמצו מבקשי אדני בעבדתו   *vacat*
4. הלוא בזאת תמצאו את אדני כל המיחלים בלבם
5. כי אדני חסידים יבקר וצדיקים בשם יקרא
6. ועל ענוים רוחו תרחף ואמונים יחליף בכחו
7. [י]כבד את חסדים על כסא מלכות עד
8. מתיר אסורים פוקח עורים זוקף כ[פופים]
9. ל[ע]ולם אדבק [בו ע]ל[[מ]שלים ובחסדו [אבטח]
10. ומ[ו]בו לעד משיחו] הקדש לוא יתאחר [לבוא]
11. וכ>בם< דות שלוא היו מעשה אדני כאשר י[בוא]
12. אז ירפא חללים ומתים יחיה ענוים יבשר
13. [c.5]..ש.[c.2]   קד[ושים ינהל ירעה [ב]ם [יעשה
14. [c.16   ] [כ.[ ]וכלי   c.12   [

1.   [The hea]vens and the earth will obey his Messiah,
2.   [the sea and (all) th]at is in them. He will not turn back from the commandment of the Holy Ones.
3.   Take strength in his (mighty) work, all you who seek the Lord.
4.   Will you not find the Lord in this, all you who wait (for him) with hope in your hearts?
5.   Surely the Lord will seek out the pious, and will call the righteous by name.

6.   His spirit will hover over the poor; he will give power to those who believe.

7.   He will glorify the pious with the throne of the eternal kingdom.

8.   He will free the captives, open the eyes of the blind, straighten those be[nt double].

9.   For[ev]er I will cleave [to him aga]inst the [po]werful, and [I will trust] in his loving kindness

10.   [and in his goodness forever. His] holy [Messiah] will not be slow [in coming.]

11.   And as for the glorious things that are not the work of the Lord, when he (i.e., the Messiah) [come]s

12.   then he will heal the wounded, resurrect the dead, proclaim glad tidings to the poor.

13.   ...he will lead the [Ho]ly Ones, he will shepherd [th]em. He will do

14.   ...and all of it...

Analysis

Lines 1-2: For the restoration, cf. Ps. 146.6, עשה שמים וארץ את הים ואת כל אשר בם. This Psalm was very influential on the author's thinking, both verbally and conceptually. Note the general tenor of the Psalm, with its concern for the destitute—precisely the concern of the Qumran text. Further, l. 8 of our text is a slightly modified quotation of vv. 7-8 (see below). Crucial terminology used by both the Psalm and our text includes רוח and צדיקים. Like the Qumran text, the setting of Psalm 146 is the eschaton (ביום ההוא). Thus, this restoration is virtually certain. For משיחו, where the suffix clearly indicates 'his (i.e., God's) Messiah' although God is unmentioned, cf. a fragmentary (previously unpublished) portion of 4Q287, [נח]ה על משיחו רוח קוד[ש], 'the holy spirit rested upon his Messiah'. Note also *Pss. Sol.* 18.5, εἰς ἡμέραν ἐκλογῆς ἐν ἀνάξει χριστοῦ αὐτοῦ, 'for the appointed day when his *Messiah* will reign' (our emphasis).

Line 2: The syntagm נסג מן occurs only in Ps. 80.19, ולא נסוג ממך. Used with various prepositional complements, the usual meaning of נסג is 'to turn back, disobey, apostatize'. The phrase מצות קדושים does not occur in the Bible, but in analogous phrases such as מצות דוד מצות לוים, and מצות המלך (i.e., phrases where the name of God does not occur), the MT points מצות as a singular, 'commandment'. קדושים presumably implies עם קדושים (Dan. 8.24) or קהל קדושים (Ps. 89.6). The substantival use of the adjective does not occur in the Bible.

Line 3: For התאמצו, cf. 2 Chron. 10.18 and 13.7 and 1 Kgs 12.18 (with slightly different nuances). Biblical Hebrew (BH) instances the verb with prepositional complements ל and על, never (as here) ב. For מבקש אדני, note particularly Isa. 51.1, 1 Chron. 16.10, Ps. 105.3 and Prov. 28.5. עבדתו is susceptible of at least three different interpretations, each of which would fit the present context. It can be understood as: (1) יהוה עבדת—God as object, the faithful as subject (cf. Num. 8.11, Josh. 22.27 and 2 Chron. 35.16; (2) עבדת יהוה—God as subject, the faithful as object. Only Isa. 28.21 refers to an action performed by God using the term עבדה. The context there is instructive: God will arise in anger to do his 'work', by which is meant his eschatological work of judgment. This understanding of the term is particularly felicitous in the present context; (3) עבדת משיחו—the Messiah as subject, God or the people as object. Although it is difficult to decide which is the best option in the present context, option (2) has been adopted for this translation.

Line 4: For תמצאו אדני, cf. Hos. 5.6, Job 23.3, Ps. 32.6, Jer. 29.13 and particularly Deut 4.29. Given its verbal juxtaposition, the latter passage (בקשתם אתי ומצאתם) was probably the portion our author had in mind. The phrase כל המיחלים occurs only at Ps. 31.25, where one reads חזקו ויאמץ לבבכם כל המיחלים ליהוה. Given the several other words that biblical portion has in common with 4Q521, the passage's influence seems clear.

Line 5: The meaning of בקר here is 'to seek in order to care for'; cf. Ezek. 34.11-12 (an important informing passage for 'On Resurrection' as a whole). No combination of בקר and חסידים occurs in the Bible, nor does any biblical text that mentions חסידים bear a close resemblance to this phrase in the scroll. The syntagm קרא בשם is rare in the Hebrew Bible, being attested only four times. Only in two of these occurrences does the phrase refer to more than one person: Josh. 21.9 and Isa. 40.26. The passage in Joshua has nothing else in common with the present context, but Isa. 40.26 reads לכלם בשם יקרא. כלם refers to God's צבא, a felicitous term in the context of holy war such as 4Q521 may imply.

Line 6: Concerning ועל ענוים רוחו תרחף, only Gen. 1.2 combines the terms רחף and רוח; further, רוח אלהים appears in Genesis 1, corresponding to רוחו here.[2] The idea of renewal, a new age, is in keeping with the thrust of the scroll. For יחליף בכחו the antecedent text is clearly

---

    2.   For some interesting comments on this portion of 4Q521 see D. Allison, Jr, 'The Baptism of Jesus and a New Dead Sea Scroll', *BAR* 18 (March/April 1992), pp. 58-60.

Isa. 40.31, קוי יהוה יחליפו כח. Note here also the reference to 'waiting on the Lord', reprised (using a different verb, of course) in l. 4 above. As to אמונים, only Pss. 12.2 and 31.24 and 2 Sam. 20.19 use this locution in a manner comparable to the scroll. It is also possible, however, that the ancient exegetes understood Isa. 26.2 to use אמנים with the requisite nuance: שמר אמנים ויבא גוי צדיק. If so, the setting of Isaiah 26 is relevant (ביום ההוא).

Line 7: יכבד את חסידים is not a biblical phrase. For כבד על, cf. Dan. 11.38 ולאלה מעזים על כנו יכבד. חסידים meaning, as here, 'the pious', appears only in the Psalter, and chiefly in what many scholars regard as later Psalms. Note also 1 Macc. 2.42 for συναγωγὴ Ἀσιδαίων, and cf. 1 Macc. 7.13 and 2 Macc. 14.6. כסא מלכות עד is not a biblical phrase, but cf. כסא מלכות in Esth. 1.2, 1 Chron. 28.5, etc.

Line 8: This line is a slightly modified quotation of Ps. 146.7-8, dropping only the Tetragrammaton: יהוה זקף כפופים יהוה מתיר אסורים יהוה פקח עורים. The fact of the quotation makes the restoration at the end of the line certain. For פקח עורים cf. also Isa. 35.3-6 and Isa. 61.1 (in the LXX), and the discussion below.

Line 9: Since דבק usually takes ב as its prepositional complement, the restoration should most likely be either [באדני] or [בו]. The limitations of space and the requirements of sense greatly favor the latter; between אדבק and ל no more than four to five spaces intrude, and one must allow for movement to [שלים. Adopting that restoration, and in view of the spacing, and the reading of [ל, it is probable that the preposition על should also be restored. One might perhaps suggest כ[ול, but that word yields no clear sense in the context. The result is therefore על followed by a partially preserved substantive. Further, spacing apparently allows only one letter between ש and ל, i.e., ל[ ]ש. Thus the substantive must lack only a single letter. What might make sense in this context? The only possible roots seem to be כשל, חשל, נשל, and משל. Neither the first term, 'stumblers', nor the third term, 'those clearing away', is promising. The second root, חשל, is unattested in *Qal* in BH; the *Niphal* does occur once and means 'to be shattered' (Deut. 25.18). Biblical Aramaic uses the verb in the simple stem—again, only once—where it means 'to shatter' (Dan. 2.40). Attestation clearly does not favor this alternative, but it might make sense in the present context. Still, the best option by far seems to be משל. The term occurs in two important informing passages whose influence is apparent throughout 4Q521: Isaiah 40 (v. 10) and Isa. 49 (v. 7; see discussion on l. 13 below).

Further, the term makes better sense in the scroll than do any of the apparent alternatives, and is better attested in Hebrew than are they. Its translation is more problematic; 'rulers' in the sense of foreign war leaders would make sense here, as would the same translation in the sense of corrupt native authorities (cf. Isa. 28.14; Jer. 51.46; Prov. 28.15; Isa. 14.5 and Dan. 11.39). Further, either of these possibilities would be attractive in view of the nationalistic fervor common to many of the Dead Sea Scrolls. We have adopted a less provocative translation because of the general tenor of 'On Resurrection'. The text seems to be rather abstract. We do not expect references to specific historical circumstances, however oblique. Thus we have chosen the translation 'the powerful' (cf. the usage in 2 Chron. 23.30, where the term parallels אדירים). For the restoration at the end of the line, the most likely reading is אבטח— provided, of course, that the restoration of the first half of the line is correct, thus affecting the understanding of the syntax at this point. When speaking of God, BH uses בטח frequently with חסד, more frequently than other reasonable options for the present context such as שמח. Note especially Ps. 13.6, ואני בחסדך בטחתי, and cf. Pss. 21.8, 52.10, etc.

Line 10: The first half of this line is so broken that any reconstruction is speculative. It is possible to make some tentative suggestions. If the first word of the line is to be understood in correlation with the last phrase of l. 9, as the *waw* suggests, then it might be fruitful to consider possible poetic pairings used with חסד. In poetic texts of the Hebrew Bible חסד pairs with אמת, אמונה and רחמים. None of these terms begins with the needed *tet*, of course. The only term that does is טוב, paired once with חסד at Ps. 23.6, ירדפוני טוב וחסד. Given its very limited attestation as a paired term for חסד, our suggestion is not confident. The lack of the preposition ב does not count against it, however, since, when a preposition governs several objects, 'preposition override' may occur and it will not be repeated.[3] If the restoration of טובו is accepted, then one might further restore לעד. The result is a nice *inclusio* when taken with לעולם at the beginning of l. 9. We further propose restoring משיחו at the end of the lacuna. This is a crucial and, admittedly, speculative restoration, but it has several considerations in its favor. First, if it is right that the text returns in ll. 11-13 to the messianic figure it began describing in ll. 1-2, then we would expect an explicit mention of that

---

3. Cf. e.g., 1 Sam. 15.22 for the override of a ב in a very similar syntactic situation. For the terminology, see M. O'Connor, *Hebrew Verse Structure* (Winona Lake, IN: Eisenbrauns, 1980), pp. 310-11.

figure somewhere prior to l. 12. Where was this mention? The options are the present lacuna, the lacuna at the end of l. 10, and the lacuna at the end of l. 11. For syntactic reasons, the last option is unlikely. Thus the messianic figure was presumably mentioned somewhere in l. 10. Perhaps that mention was indeed at the end of the line, following יתאחר. But the reading (admittedly, materially uncertain) of הקדש seems to favor the present lacuna. The proposed phrase is then an attested Qumran description of a messiah—cf. 1Q30 i 1-2, which reads מ]שיח הקודש. And, as a last point in favor of this restoration, it fills out exactly the fourteen letters and spaces missing in this lacuna (provided, of course, that our other restorations for the line approach the truth). Even if this restoration is not accepted, however, the arguments for the movement of the text in ll. 11-13 remain. The author's use of יתאחר is not a biblical usage. The root does not occur in the *Hithpael* either in BH or in Tannaitic Hebrew. The usage here appears to be an Aramaism, for אתאחר appears in Targumic Aramaic meaning 'to be delayed'. The related *Eshtaphal* in Syriac means 'to delay, linger; be tardy, slow'. The meaning required by the present context is nearer the Syriac—a reflexive rather than passive nuance. As with the Syriac and the BH semantics of the (presumably related) אחר, one expects an infinitival complement with this verb. Cf. especially Gen. 34.19, and also Deut. 7.10 and 23.22 and Eccl. 5.3. We have suggested לבוא in line with our previous restorations. For the concept of a Messiah 'coming' in Qumranic texts, note CD 19.10 בבוא משיח אהרן.

Line 11: נכבדות appears in BH only at Ps. 87.3, meaning 'glorious things'. That meaning is certainly a fitting description of the content of ll. 5-8 above. It is surprising to encounter the relative pronoun ש in this text, as it is rarely used in Qumranic Hebrew. Only 4QMMT, some calendrical texts and 4QD use it; otherwise אשר is overwhelmingly the choice. Perhaps the author of this text was influenced by the fact that his informing text, Psalm 146, also uses ש once (at v. 5). מעשה יהוה occurs five times in BH (at Exod. 34.10, Deut. 11.7, Josh. 24.31, Judg. 2.7 and Jer. 51.10). It always refers to God's miraculous intervention in the nation's circumstances, and especially describes his deliverance and judgment. In this meaning מעשה is essentially a collective; thus there is no problem of agreement with היו. Again, this phrase seems to point backward rather than forward in the text. Note that היה sometimes appears in BH where one might expect instead a pure noun clause. This usage is most common when, as in 4Q521, היה functions as the

connecting word between a subject and a participial predicate.[4] The use
of the perfect therefore does not require any particular aspectual or
punctiliar nuance here; the translation 'are' communicates the meaning
best. In order to evaluate כאשר, it is necessary to take that word, the
following (only one word in length) and the first portion of l. 12 as a
unit. כאשר commonly appears in comparative clauses. In such instances
the most frequent usage is כאשר + protasis—כן + apodosis. If that
construction were to be understood in the present context, the two very
difficult letters at the beginning of l. 12 would be restored as כן. If that
was the author's intention at this point, what is being compared? It
might be the situation of the eschaton with 'predictions' about that time
contained in the Bible. Then the natural restoration for the lacuna would
be something like [כתוב] or [אמר]. Yet that understanding seems
incorrect here, since only one of the phrases that follow in l. 12 is found
written in the Bible. The author's claim would be false. It seems better to
understand the usage here not as a comparative clause, but as a temporal clause. In 'contemporary temporal clauses',[5] BH usage ordinarily
requires כאשר + ו. Since one can clearly see the remains of two letters at
the beginning of l. 12, however, the author presumably departed somewhat from biblical idiom.[6] The best proposal for the badly damaged
letters of l. 12 is then אז, 'when'. While that construction is not attested
in BH, the analogous use of כ and אז as coordinate temporal conjunctions
is known; for example, 2 Sam. 5.24 ויהי כשמעך...אז תחרץ.[7] In BH, אז with
the imperfect ordinarily denotes a certain emphasis as opposed to the
simple imperfect (cf. Deut. 4.41, 1 Kgs 8.1, 9.11). However the end of
l. 11 is restored, it is clear that the author intended a disjunction with
what was said earlier. Whereas the miraculous acts of God's eschatological visitation and judgment were described, now the author intends to
move to something else. No other understanding of l. 11 makes any
sense.

Line 12: ירפא חללים is not a biblical phrase, nor does any portion of the
Bible seem close to it in spirit. מתים יחיה does not occur in the Bible

---

4.   See GKC §141 i, and cf. Gen. 3.1, Judg. 1.7 and Job 1.14.

5.   For the terminology and discussion, see B.K. Waltke and M. O'Connor, *An
Introduction to Biblical Hebrew Syntax* (Winona Lake, IN: Eisenbrauns, 1990),
§§38.5 and 38.7.

6.   Further, the first of these two letters does not appear to have been a broad
letter such as כ, a further argument against the 'comparative clause' understanding.

7.   Note also especially 1 Chron. 14.15.

either. The closest text is Isa. 26.19, יחיו מתיך נבלתי יקומן. This biblical text apparently associates resurrection with God's visitation of wrath and judgment 'when he comes from his place' (v. 21), and may have informed our author's thinking. The biblical text does not say precisely who is doing the resurrecting. ענוים יבשר is a modified quotation of Isa. 61.1 and a critical phrase in answering the question of who is the agent responsible for the actions in l. 12. In view of the phrase's importance, it would be well to consider the whole of Isa. 61.1:

רוח אדני יהוה עלי יען משח יהוה אתי
לבשר ענוים שלחני לחבש לנשברי לב
לקרא לשבוים דרור ולאסורים פקח קוח

The language of this portion is certainly in our author's mind at various points in 'On Resurrection'. Particularly noteworthy are the words and phrases רוח אדני, משח, פקח, לבשר ענוים, and אסורים. Further, the temporal setting of Isaiah 61 (דרור) can be understood as the eschaton (cf. the use of דרור in 11QMelchizedek, which is specifically interpreting this portion of Isaiah), and thus equates with that of Psalm 146. Finally, the general concern for comforting the downtrodden appears in Isa. 61.1, Psalm 146 and the Qumran work. With its reference to משח, a Second Temple reader of this portion of Isaiah would almost certainly conclude that it speaks of a Messiah, and it is likely that the author of 4Q521 thought the same. Further, he is elsewhere careful in his use of the Bible. When he is describing the 'glorious things' connected with God's visitation, he relies only on biblical portions that explicitly mention either יהוה or אדני (usually the former). Thus, when describing an activity associated with a messianic figure, the author presumably meant to say that it was this Messiah who would 'proclaim glad tidings', not God himself. (Note that the Bible never uses בשר of God.) This understanding makes sense of the disjunction of l. 11 as well. A new actor arises in l. 12. The identity of that actor is clear by virtue of the biblical quotation: the Messiah. It is presumably this person who is responsible for all the activities of l. 12 (and, as we shall see, l. 13). The Messiah resurrects the dead as God's agent. The author of 4Q521 seems to make that point specifically.

Line 13: For קדושים ינהל, note especially Isa. 49.7-11. The setting of that portion is ביום ישועה. The vocabulary of these verses includes קדוש (i.e., Israel, 49.7), ינהל (49.10), ירעו (49.9) and אסורים (49.9). For ירעה בם, cf. especially Ezek. 34.23, והקמתי עליהם רעה...את עבדי דויד הוא ירעה אתם.[8] In

---

8. Note also Isa. 40.11.

this portion from Ezekiel, it is a messianic figure who 'tends' the flock of Israel. This fact is further support for the inference that all the activities of ll. 12-13 are messianic activities that will take place when the eschaton dawns. For רעה ב, see perhaps Ps. 78.71, reading with the presumed *Urtext* of the LXX.

4Q521 contains a number of interpretive difficulties. It also suffers from lacunae at critical portions in the text. As a result, it would be foolish to claim that we have arrived at a perfect understanding of this fascinating work. It would also be wrong to suppose that our suggested restorations are all correct. Nevertheless, the following points seem secure: (1) In ll. 1-2 (and, perhaps, 3) 'On Resurrection' describes a messianic figure; (2) ll. 4-9 deal with eschatological visitation in which God lifts up the oppressed and rewards his faithful; (3) l. 11 establishes a disjunction with the preceding lines; (4) ll. 12-13 describe activities that are associated with a messianic figure in the Hebrew Bible. The cautious conclusion that it is a Messiah who heals the wounded, resurrects the dead, proclaims glad tidings to the poor, leads the Holy Ones and acts as their shepherd seems reasonable. On that basis, we can now turn to the Synoptic traditions.

4Q521 and the Synoptic Traditions

One of the more significant features of 4Q521 for the study of Christian origins is its striking verbal links with central portions of the Lukan Synoptic tradition—and more particularly, with the Q Source upon which Luke relies. Following Q, Matthew and Luke share a pericope about a deputation that John the Baptist sends to Jesus while John is imprisoned (Lk. 7.18-23/Mt. 11.2-6). John's disciples ask Jesus, 'Are you the coming one, or do we look for another?' The story is thus tightly framed around the question of messianic identity. What will be the signs of the true Messiah? Jesus' answer is formulaic:

> Go and report to John what you have seen and heard: the blind receive sight, the lame walk, the lepers are cleansed, and the deaf hear, *the dead are raised up, the poor have the good news preached to them*, and blessed is he who keeps from stumbling over me (Lk. 7.22-23, our emphasis).

This precise reply, based on Q 7.22 is, verbally, nearly identical to Matthew's version (Mt. 11.5-6). That fact indicates minimal redaction on the part of both writers. The source clearly reflects a pre-Synoptic formula for identifying the Messiah, which likely functioned in disputes between rival messianically oriented groups before 70 CE.

Like the Qumran fragment, this Q saying is based on a complex set of quotations and allusions to texts from the Hebrew Bible. These texts were understood to describe the signs of the Messiah and the arrival of the messianic age. Q 7.22 appears to draw most directly from Isa. 35.3-6 and 61.1. The former passage mentions five elements: (1) the opening of the eyes of the blind; (2) the unstopping of the ears of the deaf; (3) the leaping of the lame; (4) the shouting of the tongue of the dumb; and (5) the breaking forth of water in the Arabah.

The Q saying refers precisely to the first three of these elements, closely paralleling in Greek the LXX translation. The context of Isaiah 35 is that of the appearing of 'the glory of Yahweh' (כבוד יהוה) in the wilderness (במדבר)—specifically, in the region of the Arabah (vv. 1-2). This passage closely parallels Isa. 40.3, 5:

> A voice of one calling,
> Clear the way for Yahweh in the wilderness (במדבר),
> Make smooth in the Arabah a highway for our God...
> Then the glory of Yahweh (כבוד יהוה) will be revealed,
> And all flesh will see it together.

It is well known that this passage from Isaiah 40 was central to the self-understanding of the community behind 1QS (cf. 1QS 8.13-16). The passage is equally central to the Synoptic traditions (e.g., Mt. 3.3; cf. Jn. 1.23).

The dependence of the Q source upon Isa 61.1 is equally direct. The MT clearly speaks of an 'anointed' agent of Yahweh who is to:

> Preach glad tidings to the poor,
> ...To bind up the brokenhearted,
> To proclaim liberty to captives,
> And release to those who are bound (לאסורים פקח קוח)

The phrase in the Q passage, 'the blind receive sight' (τυφλοὶ ἀναβλέπουσιν), though thematically tied to Isa. 35.5 as noted above, is a direct quotation from the LXX translation of Isa. 61.1b. There the Hebrew expression לאסורים פקח קוח is rendered τυφλοῖς ἀνάβλεψιν, and understood to mean 'the opening (of the eyes) of those bound (by blindness)'. This is also Luke's Greek rendering of the phrase when he quotes Isa. 61.1 directly in Lk. 4.18.

Accordingly, of the six signs of the Messiah found in Q 7.22, four come directly from Isa. 35.5 and 61.1. The two remaining phrases, 'lepers are cleansed' and 'the dead are raised' appear to have no such direct basis in these or related passages in the Hebrew Bible. Nevertheless, in both instances the Q saying probably reflects an understanding of John and Jesus as fulfilling the mission of eschatological Elijah/Elisha figures. This understanding was based on the cycle of stories in 1 and 2 Kings together with the prophecy of Mal. 4.5-6, the prophecy predicting that such a figure would arise in the last days.[9] Both Elijah and Elisha are reported to have raised the dead, and Elisha heals Naaman the leper (1 Kgs 17.17-24; 2 Kgs 4.18-37; 2 Kgs 5.1-14).

What is most noteworthy is that the Qumran fragment (ll. 8, 12) not only speaks of 'releasing the captives and restoring the sight of the blind' (directly based, as noted above, on Ps. 146.7-8)—which roughly parallels in theme both Isa. 61.1 and Q 7.22—but also says 'he will raise from the dead' and 'preach glad tidings to the poor'. The last two phrases parallel the last two signs of the Messiah in Q 7.22 (νεκροὶ ἐγείρεται πτωχοὶ εὐαγγελίζονται). Since these lines of the Qumran fragment and Q 7.22 are closely related linguistically and thematically to Isa. 35.5 and 61.1 and Ps. 146.7-8, yet none of these biblical passages speak specifically of raising the dead, we have a most interesting linking parallel between 4Q521 and the early Christian Q source.[10] Both include resurrection of the dead as a key event of the messianic age—indeed, as an identifying tag of the Messiah himself. In the Q passage no firm distinction is made between what God will do, and what his agent the Messiah will do. Isaiah 35 and Psalm 146 seem to have God himself more directly in view, but Isaiah 61 focuses on the Messiah as sent from God.

What might this parallel indicate regarding the early history of the Jesus movement in Palestine as reflected in Q and that of the movement responsible for the Qumran text? It is certainly significant that the Q Source passage is directly linked to discussions about the signs of the

9.   These portions are clearly the sources in the synoptic tradition as a whole (Mk. 9.13/Mt. 17.11-14; Mk. 6.15//Lk. 9.7-9; Mk. 8.28//Mt. 16.14 and Lk. 9.19). All of the Gospels associate the wilderness mission of John the Baptist with both Isa. 40.1 and Mal. 4.5-6. It is particularly noteworthy that Luke makes direct reference to Elisha healing the leper Naaman (2 Kings 5) in the same Nazareth synagogue scene where Jesus claims to fulfill Isa. 61.1-2. He clearly intends the scene to illustrate the general signs of the Messiah and the messianic age based on his Q passage (7.22).

10.   Cf. the Hebrew text of Matthew known as Even Bohan at 11.5, in which this same idea is expressed in the words החיים מתים והענוים מתבשרים (following MSS E and F). For the text and the theory that Even Bohan may preserve portions of a pre-Greek text of Matthew, see G. Howard, *The Gospel of Matthew according to a Primitive Hebrew Text* (Macon, GA: Mercer University Press, 1987), esp. p. 48.

Messiah among the disciples of John the Baptist and the followers of Jesus. All three movements—that of John, of Jesus, and of the Qumran materials—seem to use the same sets of texts to describe the messianic age and its telltale signs. Now, based on the newly released 'On Resurrection', all three groups seem to share the same technical list of criteria for identification of the Messiah.

It is also of note that Luke as a whole has largely cast his redaction of his Markan source in terms of the common elements contained in the Q 7.22 pericope and this Qumran fragment. Although it is unlikely that Luke knew the Qumran text directly, it seems that he shares with its author a common set of messianic expectations. Such interpretive directions evidently influenced Luke. For example, his crucial and dramatic scene of the inauguration of the ministry of Jesus is set in the synagogue at Jesus' hometown Nazareth (Lk. 4.16-30; in sharp contrast to Mk 6.1-6). There Jesus arises and reads Isa. 61.1-2b, the very text that serves as a focus of both the Q saying and 4Q521.[11] In the same passage he mentions the widow whose son Elijah raised from the dead, as well as the cleansing of Naaman the leper—a remarkable concatenation. Luke has another story, found only in his Gospel, of Jesus healing ten lepers on a single occasion (Lk. 17.11-19). With reference to the Messiah raising the dead, Luke relates that Jesus raised the dead son of a widow from Nain (Lk. 7.11-19). This story is again unique to Luke, and he places it immediately before the Q 7.22-23 saying discussed above. He illustrates the theme of raising from the dust those 'bent double' by including a story, once again unique to his Gospel, of a woman who is oppressed by Satan and released through healing by Jesus (Lk. 13.11-16).

As these examples illustrate, the dominant themes of the Q saying and 'On Resurrection' run through Luke's Gospel. They characterize his understanding of the Messiah: care for the poor and outcast, release of the oppressed (blind, deaf, lame, lepers) and raising of the dead. For Luke these activities are nothing less than *the* signs of both the Messiah and the messianic age.

---

11. Luke's quotation is essentially that of the LXX version. In addition to its interpretation of the MT noted above, the LXX adds an additional phrase, ἀποστεῖλαι τεθραυσμένους ἐν ἀφέσει. This phrase is taken from Isa. 58.6. This technique of building thematic parallels from a variety of prophetic texts characterizes both the Q pericope and the Qumran fragment.

LEVI AND THE LEVITES IN THE DEAD SEA SCROLLS[*]

Robert C. Stallman

In 1978 Jacob Milgrom published an article, a collection of studies on the Temple Scroll in which he noticed the prominence given to the Levites; in fact, he labeled the scroll 'innovative' in that it elevated them 'far beyond the status the Levites possessed at any time during their history and even beyond the idealistic demands of the Bible itself'.[1] He interpreted this pro-Levite bias as a protest against the usurpation of Levitic roles and rights by non-Zadokite priests. Although not necessarily consequent, he deduced that the Temple Scroll reflected a degree of conflict within cultic circles. He concluded,

> Thus the scroll gives new grounds for investigating the tensions and struggles among priestly families and between priests and Levites at the end of the Second Temple period.[2]

Since that time, relatively few studies involving Levi or the Levites have been published.

In 1981, however, three articles appeared which examined this tribe in 11QTemple, CD, and 1QS. Based on a comparison of organizational structures, including the Levites in particular, Colin Kruse cut across the grain of majority opinion and argued that 1QS must be dated earlier than CD.[3] Barbara Thiering looked at the Levites and other officials in the Temple Scroll to support her claim that the sect provided the models of leadership for the early Christian communities, the bishop (ἐπίσκοπος)

[*]   James H. Charlesworth read the first draft of this paper and supplied many helpful suggestions; R.B. Dillard subsequently offered insights related to the books of Chronicles. Their assistance and encouragement is gratefully acknowledged.

1.   Jacob Milgrom, 'Studies in the Temple Scroll', *JBL* 97 (1978), p. 501.

2.   Milgrom, 'Temple Scroll', p. 504.

3.   C.G. Kruse, 'Community Functionaries in the Rule of the Community and the Damascus Document: A Test of Chronological Relationships', *RevQ* 10 (1981), pp. 543-51.

specifically being patterned after the overseer (מבקר).[4] In that same year, 1981, Terry Donaldson published a study of Levitical messianology in Late Judaism [*sic*] in which he noted a clear difference between the thoughts of the Qumran community and other so-called intertestamental literature on this subject.[5]

A few major publications on the Levites appeared in the later eighties. In 1984 Roger Beckwith sought to explain the irregular sequence of psalms in the Qumran scrolls together with the presence of 'noncanonical' compositions by considering the liturgical needs of Levitical singers organized in twenty-four courses serving in rotation.[6] In 1988 Carol Newsom noted the special attention given to Levi in 4Q379, the Psalms of Joshua, which she judged as not of Qumran origin.[7] In a volume dedicated to recent Temple Scroll studies, Hans Burgmann argued against Qumran authorship of 11QTemple, choosing instead to read it as an all-round attack written by Sadducean Levites against their three enemies: the priests, Pharisees, and Essenes.[8] Finally, in an article focusing on the exegetical principles of the community, Jacob Milgrom once again addressed the elevated role of the Levites at Qumran, this time reversing his earlier claim regarding the historical tension between the priests and this tribe. Instead, the specific 'homogenizing' kind of biblical interpretation evidenced in the document did itself necessitate the elevation of these people.[9]

In light of these few scattered studies, those individuals with a more general interest in the history and development of the Levites may find it helpful to consider all the references to Levi and the Levites

---

4.   B.E. Thiering, '*Mebaqqer* and *Episkopos* in the Light of the Temple Scroll', *JBL* 100 (1981), pp. 59-74.

5.   T.L. Donaldson, 'Levitical Messianology in Late Judaism: Origins, Development and Decline', *JETS* 24 (1981), pp. 193-207. Donaldson does not explain his use of the phrase 'Late Judaism' to denote the historical period of his study nor does he define its limits. The Judaism from the period c. 250 BCE to 200 CE is commonly designated 'Early'.

6.   R.T. Beckwith, 'The Courses of the Levites and the Eccentric Psalms Scrolls from Qumran', *RevQ* 11 (1984), pp. 499-524.

7.   C. Newsom, 'The "Psalms of Joshua" from Qumran Cave 4', *JSS* 39 (1988), pp. 56-73.

8.   H. Burgmann, '11QT: The Sadducean Torah', in *Temple Scroll Studies* (ed. G.J. Brooke; JSPSup, 7; Sheffield: JSOT Press, 1989), pp. 257-63.

9.   Milgrom, 'The Qumran Cult: Its Exegetical Principles', in *Temple Scroll Studies*, pp. 165-80.

throughout the Dead Sea Scrolls corpus. With the valuable help of the recently published graphic concordance to the scrolls,[10] I have been able to compile a comprehensive set of such references in addition to those regarding Kohath, Gershon and Merari. The various spellings of 'Levi' and 'Levites' supplied by E. Qimron were also taken into account.[11] Altogether some 80 readings were located plus a few lacunae in which editors inserted the names. These findings were then collated according to their respective documents. The ensuing study is a rather straight-forward, largely descriptive consideration of this data. The discussion of the Levites in each major document is followed by an evaluation which summarizes the findings and takes stock of current research on the issues raised. The order in which the documents are taken up is according to the frequency of references to Levi and Levites and thus is disengaged from the complex and debatable issues of dating the materials.

Technically, this study concerns the Dead Sea Scrolls rather than the body of work produced by the Qumran community itself. Determining the latter is a much more subjective matter which includes not only deciding primary authorship but the extent of adaptation and redaction of preexisting materials. 11QTemple is a good example. Although scholarly consensus on basic matters is particularly difficult to achieve in Qumran studies, I am convinced the Qumran community should be identified with the Essenes.[12]

1. *11QTemple*

As already noted, Jacob Milgrom has conveniently collected and evaluated various indications of Levites elevated to a relatively high status in 11QTemple.[13] I will consider them in turn and offer some explanations along the way.

---

10. J.H. Charlesworth and others (eds.), *Graphic Concordance to the Dead Sea Scrolls* (Tübingen: Mohr [Paul Siebeck]; Louisville: Westminster Press/John Knox, 1991).

11. Elisha Qimron, *The Hebrew of the Dead Sea Scrolls* (HSS, 29; Atlanta: Scholars Press, 1986), 200.17.

12. Charlesworth, 'Sense or Sensationalism? The Dead Sea Scrolls Controversy', *Christian Century* (29 January 1992), pp. 95-96.

13. 'Temple Scroll'.

A. *Data*

1. *Gates*. In naming the gates of the middle and outer courts, 11QTemple assigns the central one on the eastern side—the most prestigious—to Levi (39.12; 40.14). In Num. 3.38, the eastern spot in front of the Tent of Meeting was assigned to Moses together with Aaron and his sons. It may be added that the Levites were not included in the counting of Israel and so did not receive a campsite next to the other tribes around the sanctuary; they encircled the Tent to establish a border with the Gershonites to the west, the Kohathites to the south, and the Merarites to the north, thus dividing the tribe as a whole into four divisions: one priestly and three nonpriestly (Num. 2.17, 33; 3.23, 29, 35). Other Levitical references in 11QTemple relating to the gates concern architectural dimensions and distances (39.15, 16; 40.15).

2. *Chambers*. The column of 11QTemple dealing with the assignment of chambers gives each tribe one section, two to the priests, but to the Levites *three*, in accordance with the locations of their aforementioned clan encampments (44.3-45.2).

In the description of Kohath's section of chambers, 44.14 contains a peculiarity. Originally it had stated that the area from the gate of Joseph to the gate of Benjamin was to be allotted to 'the sons of Kohath from the sons of the Levites', but the scribe skillfully and ingeniously erased the *beth* and *yod* from מבני to read simply 'from the Levites' (הלויים {י}נ{ב}מ). The medial *nun* was not altered to a final form.[14] Two accounts of the correction have been conjectured. Yadin's explanation is that the scribe wrote מבני under the influence of the previous designations of tribal members and had originally followed it with הלוי, later emending it to הלויים.[15] Thus he attaches no significant difference to the

14. In his masterful analysis of ancient Jewish scripts, F.M. Cross traces the development of the formal types of medial and final *nuns*, but does not document the use of a medial *nun* in the final position. Cf. 'The Development of the Jewish Scripts', in *The Bible and the Ancient Near East: Essays in Honor of William Foxwell Albright* (ed. G.E. Wright; Garden City, NY: Doubleday, 1961), pp. 143, 151-52, 155-56, 159, 171, 178-79, 186.

15. Yadin says that there is an 'impression' that the scribe originally wrote הלוי without the suffix (Yigael Yadin, *The Temple Scroll* [3 vols.; Jerusalem: Israel Exploration Society, Institute of Archaeology of the Hebrew University of Jerusalem and the Shrine of the Book, 1983, 1983, 1977], I, p. 187). No orthographic features in the word support this claim and technical analysis of the ink(s) used may not distinguish the noun from the suffix. He may be referring to line length. The word in

two phrases 'from the sons of Levi' and 'from the Levites'. Thiering's alternative explanation hinges on there being a substantial difference between 'Levites' and 'sons of Levi' whom she takes to denote priests alone. Thus the scribe's mistake was that he incorrectly designated the Kohathites priests, necessitating a correction to simply (nonpriestly) 'Levites'. Not only is her semantic distinction unfounded, she offers no rationale for the mistake in the first place. For Yadin, it is a simple and rather understandable slip which rightly deserves no further attention. What stands out in this text is not only that the Levites are allocated Temple chambers but also that they receive more space than the priests who, according to Ezekiel, were the only ones assigned rooms (Ezek. 42.1-14).

3. *Offerings*. Next, in the detailed description of the Wood Offering Festival (23.9-24.11) the twelve tribes, two at a time, are to contribute wood on six consecutive days. Levi and Judah start off the routine, presenting wood on the first day. Milgrom states:

> Again, there is no biblical precedent: the tribe of Levi never appears in a ritual in consort with other tribes nor does it ever appear first in a tribal list.[16]

The specific text at issue here, TS 1 i.10, is not formally part of the scroll of 11QTemple.[17] Yadin regarded this and other fragments as authentic remnants from two or three copies of the Temple Scroll and used it to supply missing information in cols. 23–25 which he identified as

---

question stands at the end of l. 14 and without the masculine plural suffix makes the line of average length and not far past the left margin line which is barely visible toward the upper part of the column. With the suffix, however, l. 14 is as long as l. 10 in the same column, therefore unusual but not exceptional. According to Yadin, then, the scribe first penned the grammatically incorrect construction 'from the sons of the Levi' which later received a double correction. I prefer an original reading with two plurals: 'from the sons of the Levites'.

16. Milgrom, 'Temple Scroll', p. 501.

17. This fragment is part of a small group of three designated Rockefeller 43.366 and appears in Plate 40*:1 of Yadin's supplementary volume to his three-part study, *The Temple Scroll*. See also M.O. Wise, 'A Manuscript Join in the "Festival of Wood Offering"', *JNES* 47 (1988), pp. 113-21, and his excursus on Rockefeller 43.366 in *A Critical Study of the Temple Scroll from Qumran Cave 11* (Studies in Ancient Oriental Civilization, 49; Chicago: University of Chicago Press, 1990), pp. 44-60.

instructions for the 'Feast of the Wood Offering' as mentioned in Neh. 10.35.[18] M. Wise, however, expressed concern about this procedure. Noting a quotation from Lev. 23.42–24.2a in the first part of the fragment together with several characteristically Deuteronomic features, he concluded the fragment was a 'Deuteronomized' piece of material from Leviticus.[19] Against Yadin who places the fragment in cols. 23–25 and Qimron who fits it between cols. 28–29, Wise regards the three fragments comprising Rock. 43.366 as a 'proto-Temple Scroll' from which the material in fragment one, part of an original D source, was removed by the final redactor in favor of the Festival Calendar source of 11QTemple 13–29.[20]

The honourable position of the Levites in the procedure for the Wood Offering Festival, then, should not be included with other pro-Levitic data from 11QTemple in its final form. Rather, according to Wise, it should be classified as an element of the D source (300–190 BCE). TS 1 i.6-12 thus contain a pseudepigraphic supplement to the Pentateuch which nowhere obliges the tribes to provide wood.[21]

4. *Sacrifices*. The Levites are further elevated in that they receive a double portion of the sacrifices during the two Feasts of Wine and Oil, getting two pairs of the fourteen animals offered. The priests get a pair, the Levites a pair, and so on for each tribe (21.[1]; 22.12). Though not explicitly stated, the tribe of Levi is considered one of the twelve in this instance, as elsewhere in the scroll.[22] If Yadin's restoration of 21.4 is correct, the Levites are correspondingly honored by consuming the wine after the priest, but before the other tribes.[23]

5. *Judges*. Another example of Levitical preference which exceeds their stature in the Bible is in 11QTemple 61.8-9 which quotes Deut. 19.17 but with the addition of 'and the Levites' so that disputing parties seeking a hearing shall appear before a panel of priests and Levites

18. Yadin, *Temple Scroll*, I, pp. 8, 122-24.
19. In like manner, he claims 1Q22, the Words of Moses, is a 'Deuteronomized' form of Leviticus 16 and 25 (Wise, *Critical Study*, pp. 48-50).
20. Wise, *Critical Study*, pp. 50-51.
21. Wise, *Critical Study*, p. 60.
22. Recall the twelve gates of the middle and outer courts; Manasseh and Ephraim are always subsumed under Joseph.
23. A point not mentioned by Milgrom. See Yadin, *Temple Scroll*, I, pp. 109-10; II, p. 94.

together with judges. No variant readings support this addition, but it harmonizes with the Levitic role in the judicial reforms of Jehoshaphat (2 Chron. 17.7-9; 19.8). Like Deut. 21.5, the Levites are to settle cases regarding dispute and assault (63.4).[24]

6. *Royal Cabinet*. Also, the royal cabinet is to be composed of twelve leaders of his people, twelve priests, and twelve Levites (57.11-13).

7. *Perquisites*. Next, as perquisites the Levites receive a tenth of the grain, wine and oil, the shoulder (שכם) from the sacrifice, a hundredth of the booty, spoil and hunt, a fiftieth of the young pigeons, and a tenth of the honey (60.6-9). These laws are an expansive interpretation of Deut. 18.1-5, the most important difference being the allotment of the shoulder, which also appears in 11QTemple 22.10. Milgrom notes that according to the Bible, 'Neither is the shoulder ever considered a sacred portion nor are the Levites ever awarded sacrificial flesh'.[25]

Whereas in the Bible the 'foreleg' belongs to the priest (Deut. 18.1-3), the extent of this portion is ambiguous depending on whether or not the upper bone, the shoulder, is included. Since Deut. 18.1 stipulates that the Levites along with the priests are to eat the offerings by fire, the Temple Scroll makes a minimalizing interpretation the 'foreleg' (exclusive of the shoulder) assigned to the priests, thus leaving the shoulder for the Levites. One need only consider a cow's anatomy to realize that the Levites would enjoy the choicest cuts. That the priests would also receive the 'jowls and the inner parts' (Deut. 18.3) could hardly have been very reassuring to them.

The Levitical portion of spoil recovered from a victorious battle is like that of the Bible, only the method of calculation differs. In this case, 11QTemple 58.13 follows after the manner of Num. 31.30. Here, the warriors and the rest of the Israelites get half of the spoil each, but in the Bible, the priests get one five-hundredth of the warrior's half and the Levites one fiftieth of the other. In the Temple Scroll, the priests receive one thousandth and the Levites a hundredth, and *then* the rest is divided

24. Not included by Milgrom.
25. Milgrom, 'Temple Scroll', p. 502. The subject of the Levites receiving the shoulder is too detailed for inclusion here. Milgrom wrote an appendix on it in the first volume of Yadin's *Temple Scroll* (Milgrom, 'The Shoulder for the Levites', pp. 169-76). The two differ on several minor points (see Milgrom, 'Temple Scroll', pp. 504-506).

in half. The portions to the priests and Levites is the same in either calculation, but in the Temple Scroll the remaining two halves are equal whereas in the Bible they are not. In the former, the warriors and Israelites each receive 49.45% of the spoil. According to the Bible, they receive 49.9% and 49% respectively.[26] The real interest here centers not on the Levites per se, but on the hermeneutics of the Temple Scroll. The author has cleverly interpreted the rules for spoil allotment in Num. 31.25-30 so as to avoid contradicting 1 Sam. 30.24-25 in which David, without mentioning either priest or Levite, laid down a lasting ordinance that warrior and noncombatant must receive *equal* shares.[27]

8. *Slaughter*. The Levites perform the actual slaughter of the animal for the peace offering (22.4) in contrast to the practice of the priests in Jerusalem near the end of the Second Temple period. This privilege is strictly not an 'innovation', as Milgrom claims,[28] but a reestablishment of the Levitic right to slaughter according to the precedents set during the reforms of Hezekiah and Josiah (2 Chron. 30.17, 22; 35.11-14).

9. *Priestly Function*. Last in Milgrom's list is what he calls the most significant fact of all: priestly functions are assigned to the Levites. Strangely, his references to these duties of offering blessings and curses come not from 11QTemple but from 1QS and 1QSa.[29] The Temple Scroll also assigns duties to Levites based closely on Deut. 18.6-8:

> And if a Levite comes from one of your towns from anywhere in Israel where he is living—and he may come when he desires—to the place on which I will choose to cause my name to dwell, then, like any of his brothers the Levites who stand there before me, he may minister (60.12-14).

In this case, presumably because of the context, Milgrom chooses to translate ירשת as meaning only 'assist', though he recognizes the possibility that it means 'officiate', giving the Levites theoretical permission to officiate in the altar service.[30] The function of officiating (שרת) and

26. Yadin's calculations here are incorrect, as Milgrom has shown ('Temple Scroll', p. 521, regarding Yadin, *Temple Scroll*, I, p. 361).

27. Yadin, *Temple Scroll*, I, p. 361.

28. Milgrom, 'Temple Scroll', p. 503.

29. Milgrom, 'Exegetical Principles', p. 503.

30. Milgrom, 'Temple Scroll', n. 10.

pronouncing blessings is afforded by Deut. 21.5 and carried over in 11QTemple 63.3.[31]

B. *Evaluation*

Milgrom's catalogue of the data clearly shows that 11QTemple elevates the Levites in status above their place according to the Pentateuch and even the pro-Levitic Chronicler. They were distinguished in both cult and court. In the arrangement of the Temple their gate and chamber locations were prominent. In the sacrificial realm they were the first of the twelve to receive atonement, enjoy a double portion of the offerings returned, and perform slaughter in the regular cult. The extent of their perquisites ranged beyond the statutes of the Bible, and included the prized shoulder portion. They served on the judiciary and advised the king, being equally represented among the priests and Israelites. What is at issue, then, is the significance of these facts. Although Milgrom occasionally noted the presumed scriptural basis for these 'innovations', his general explanation for them was a historical background of tension and struggle between priests and Levites in Jerusalem; the scroll polemically argued in favor of the Levites, restoring and extending the range of their employment and entitlements.[32]

Burgmann agreed and went so far as to claim that not only does the scroll defend the Levites, it shows hostility toward the priests, Pharisees, and (most startlingly) the Essenes. It is therefore the product not of the Qumran community, but Sadducean Levites in Jerusalem.[33] Burgmann is right to note the presence of nonsectarian documents in the caves; but he is wrong when he says that the work was found in Cave 11 with other nonsectarian scrolls. The unique form of the psalter found there can only be Qumranic and there is no undeniable proof that 11QTemple came from Cave 11 at all. 11QTemple in its original form is certainly an old work and may predate the settlement of the community at Qumran,[34] but without denying the presence of inevitable intergroup tension, the hostility Burgmann detects hyperextends the data, especially relative to the Essene group.

31. Not included by Milgrom.

32. Milgrom, 'Temple Scroll', pp. 503-504.

33. '11QT', pp. 257-63.

34. Charlesworth, 'The Origin and Subsequent History of the Authors of the Dead Sea Scrolls: Four Transitional Phases among the Qumran Essenes', *RevQ* 10 (1981), pp. 218-22.

Milgrom's subsequent study of the exegetical practices of the community, however, has provided a more cogent explanation for the prominence of the Levites in 11QTemple. He withdrew his earlier judgment that it reflected the existence of tensions and struggles between priests and Levites.[35] Rather, not all the Levitical innovations of the scroll need be based on historical conditions. In his words, as a 'fundamentalistic sect' the community looked to scripture for the resolution of all problems and believed its rules must be followed to the letter.[36] Together with this observation, the exegetical method known as homogenization, a forerunner of rabbinic *binyan 'āb, forced* an interpretation of scripture favoring the Levites as is typical in Deuteronomy and the books of Chronicles, resulting in an unparalleled Levitic windfall. The exegetical principle itself is not unique; its use was. Where the technique was employed by man (Pharisees and rabbis) the result was oral law: subjective, and open to debate. Where it was used by God (as was thought to be the case with 11QTemple) the result was definitive and unalterable.[37] While Milgrom has argued persuasively for an *exegetically* forced elevation of the Levites in specific texts, he nowhere denies the possible existence of tensions in the Second Temple period between priests and Levites which could also partially account for their prominence in a polemical document aimed against an illegitimate priesthood. In what manner and to what degree non-Zadokite priests may have realistically displaced the roles and rights of the Levites, however, is uncertain.

As is often the case, then, an ancient text tells us more about the worldview of its composers and sponsoring community than it does about their actual world itself. The real conditions of the ancient world recede even further from sight when the document in question purports to be laying down prescriptions for the future, in this case, a time when its authors would officiate in the authentic and properly structured Temple of God—a virtual dream come true.

2. *1QM*

A. *Data*

1. *Scroll and Fragments.* Information regarding the Levites in the document known as the War of the Sons of Light against the Sons of

---

35. Milgrom, 'Exegetical Principles', p. 176.
36. Milgrom, 'Exegetical Principles', p. 177.
37. Milgrom, 'Exegetical Principles', p. 178.

Darkness comes from the scroll 1QM and the fragments of 4QM1, 4QM2, 4QM3, and 4QM4.[38] Unlike the main scroll which is relatively well preserved, the fragments associated with it are of dubious value for several reasons. Like the many other fragments associated with 1QM, these are often short and badly damaged, making reassembly quite uncertain. Extensive textual additions must often be posited in order to make even minimal sense of the readings, and anyway, most testify to a different recension than 1QM, or conceivably to a similar but distinct work altogether. While one can always use 'variants' like these to supplement or correct the main text, the problems associated with such a task in this case make it ill-advised. Nevertheless, the evidence from these fragments will be factored into the following discussion where possible for the sake of completeness.

2. *Sons of Light*. The introduction to the scroll describes a coming war between 'the sons of light' and 'the sons of darkness'. Throughout the document each group receives further identification which is not always clear or unambiguous. A case in point, the godly participants are first named as 'the sons of Levi, the sons of Judah, and the sons of Benjamin, the exiles of the wilderness' (1QM 1.2) but elsewhere Israel as a whole is either stated or implied (2.7; 3.13-16; 11.7; 12.13; 13.7-13; 17.7-8; 19.5-8). Careful reading indicates that the two groups are not mutually exclusive, but the whole document characteristically gives prominence to the tribe of Levi, usually divided into 'priests' and 'Levites'.

3. *Sacrificial Function*. Most of column two concerns the chronological plan of the war together with various duties of the participants. In the sanctuary, twelve priests are to serve continuously and twenty-six are to serve in courses. After them, likewise, the Levites are to officiate, twelve chiefs of the Levites serving continuously (one for each tribe), but also chiefs serving in courses (1QM 2.2). Behind these Levites the chiefs of the tribes and the fathers of the congregation stand at the gates.

4. *Banners and Inscriptions*. Of considerable interest to the author of 1QM are the specific preparations for battle. Again, the Levites along with the priests receive much attention. 1QM 3.13–4.17 details the battle banners (אותות). Because the bottom of each column is missing, the list of groups with banners is incomplete, leaving only descriptions of those for

---

38. Also labeled 4Q491, 4Q492, 4Q493, and 4Q494, respectively.

the whole congregation, the chiefs of the camps of the three tribes, the tribe, Merari, the thousand, the hundred, the fifty, and the ten. The mention of Merari, especially after a sizable gap makes it reasonable to assume the other Levitical clans were mentioned also, namely Kohath and Gershon. According to 4.1, Merari's banner was to contain the phrase 'Offering of God' followed by the name of the clan prince (נשׂיא) and the names of its commanders of thousands (אלפים). These names and phrases are to be changed when the participants go out to battle, draw near for battle, and withdraw from battle and, though not perfectly clear, it appears, by the process of elimination, that 4.6-8 details these changes for the Levitical clans, of which there are *four*. The third chapter of Numbers divides the tribe of Levi into three clans who serve the Aaronide priests and CD 10.5 specifies that four judges are to be selected from the tribe (singular) of Levi and Aaron. It may well have been, therefore, that the description of Merari's banner followed details pertaining to those of Aaron, Gershon, and Kohath, though not necessarily in that order.[39] The other tribes are neither considered clan by clan nor even named as such. They are, however, named in an inscription for the prince of the congregation, but only after the name of 'Israel and Levi and Aaron' (5.1). Although the name of the item so inscribed is unreadable, that a banner is not involved is clear from the first letter being a *mem*, making either a shield (מגן) or a staff (מטה) possible.[40]

5. *Battle Sounds (horns).* During the battle itself, the priests and Levites serve as commanders who carry no weapons. The manner of their oversight is the subject of 1QM 7.9–9.9. In preparation for battle, seven priests march between the battle lines, one encouraging the troops and the rest blowing five kinds of trumpets. As the priests march out, 'seven Levites shall go out with them and in their hands seven ram's horns. Three officers from the Levites [shall go] in front of the priests and the Levites (7.14-15). These Levitical officers then accompany successive formations of fifty skirmishers as they march out from the gate (7.16). In the heat of the battle the priest's trumpet blasts actually direct the action; the sound of the Levites appears to function differently. A low sounding of the priestly trumpet signals the advance while a shrill

39. Y. Yadin, *The Scroll of the War of the Sons of Light against the Sons of Darkness* (Oxford: Oxford University Press, 1962), p. 54.
40. Yadin claims the latter is too long and opts for the former (*War Scroll*, p. 278).

staccato sound signals the actual throwing of the spears and continues through seven deliveries. The Levites, however, team up with the whole of the horn band (וכול עם השופרות) in unison to make such a blast as to 'melt the heart of the enemy' (8.9-10). Although the priests continue their signalling throughout the seven-step engagement, the blast of the ram's horns accompanies only its commencement. The trumpets, then, are directed to the troops while the horns intimidate the enemy. Lacunae in the rest of the directions from 8.13 to the end prevent the reading of any more references to the Levites in this section although Yadin posits their role alongside the priests.[41] A similar description of priests and Levites wielding instruments occurs in 16.3-9 with specific mention of the Levites and the whole horn band in 16.7-8. Another section dealing with a battle engagement (17.10-17) almost certainly contained a reference to the Levites in the lacuna of 17.13 just before mention of the horn band. Priests and Levites associated with battle trumpets and horns can also be found in 4QM1 1 i17; 13 i. 6 and 4QM3 1 i.9.

Regarding the place of music in warfare, there are parallels here to the intimidating use of wind instruments in the conquests of Jericho and also the Midianites (Josh. 6.20 and Judg. 7.20), but in neither of those cases were Levites or horns (שׁופרים) mentioned.

6. *Prayer and Exhortation*. Following the organization of the Sons of Light and their tactics, the scroll lists prayers to be recited before, during, and after the war. Yadin calls these two logistical and liturgical segments the 'Battle Serekh Series' (cols. 2-9) and the 'Ritual Serekh Series' (cols. 9-14). In this section the Levites again function alongside the priests. 1QM 13.1-2 states that the priests, Levites, and the elders of the rule (סרך) should accompany the chief priest[42] and together 'they shall bless from their standing place the God of Israel and all His truthful deeds and they shall curse there Belial and all the spirits of his lot'. Extended rubrics follow. This same collection of people occurs again in 15.4 in the third major section which deals with the war against the Kittim (cols. 14-20). In this text the chief priest reads a prayer before battle and the rest exhort the troops to be strong and brave. The Levites

41. Yadin, *War Scroll*, pp. 296-99. His restoration of three words in l. 15 seems reasonable enough; his restoration of two complete lines at the end of the column, however, does not.

42. Because the bottom of col. 12 is missing, the identity of this individual is uncertain, but no one else seems likely.

also participate in a prayer of praise with the priests and the elders of the rule just before the final pursuit (18.5).

7. *Ritual Purity*. One other Levitical function appears in 4QM1 1 i.9 in which the priests, Levites, and men of the camps review the troops to evaluate their ritual purity so as to disqualify all those unfit for fighting alongside holy angels.

8. *Other Fragments*. There are a few other references to Levites in the fragments from Cave 4, but they are so isolated from surrounding material as to be of very little value. 4QM1 11 ii.5 mentions the Levites in connection with conducting the battle and Baillet boldly fills in the rest of the missing line with 'and the whole of the horn band shall blow a battle blast'.[43] 4QM2 1 i.11 reads, 'and the Levites with the prince of the battle and all the heads of the arrays and their divisions'.[44] Finally, 4QM4 1 i.2-3 reads, 'and the priests and the Levites and the heads of...the priests and therefore the Levites and guards...'[45] What seems evident is the familiar association of the Levites with priests and lay leaders in the course of battle. Beyond this observation, very little can be said for certain.

B. *Evaluation*

The War Scroll, then, elevates the Levites in the leadership of cult and combat. In worship they are to serve continuously alongside the priests, offer prayers and moral exhortations, and enforce laws of ritual purity. In war they are visibly prominent, direct troop movements and activities under priestly leadership.

Current scholarship identifies the type of warfare described in the scroll with the Roman legion of the Republican period but is divided as to whether the anticipated battle was to be real or fictional.[46] The

---

43. DJD, VII, p. 30.
44. DJD, VII, p. 45.
45. DJD, VII, p. 53.
46. The older views associating the style of warfare depicted in the scroll with the Hellenistic phalanx (E.L. Sukenik) or the Roman Imperial army (G.R. Driver) have since faded. Although the envisaged war is highly schematized and seems impractical due to the demands of ritual purity, Sabbath year rests, and battlefield liturgy, the extensive detail regarding weapons, banners, inscriptions, instruments, trumpet calls, combatants, and battle formations together with their close relationship to contemporary Jewish military practices favor the view that the Qumran community

detailed specifics of battle support the former opinion, the highly schematized progress of the war buttress the latter. In either case, because the war is in the future and there is no archaeological evidence for the existence of battle-ready troops at Qumran, the value of the scroll relative to the Levites is in the realm of ideology not real history. This ideology, however, should not be confined to pure speculation for there is every indication in the scroll that the community was bracing itself for an inevitable and impending military confrontation.[47]

The contents of 1QM bear many similarities to 11QTemple, as indicated by Yadin, a master of both works.[48] Beyond these points of agreement lies a more fundamental similarity: both documents are future-oriented and idealistic, revealing more of the community's values than actual cultic and civic practices. As in 11QTemple, the Levites are clearly exalted far above their tribal brothers and work in tandem with the priests to whom they are obedient and ever loyal. Such esteem must have held a degree of correspondence to real conditions, but the evidence does not yield any conclusions on specific details.

3. CD

A. Data

Evaluating the place of the Levites in the Cairo Damascus Document (CD) is complicated by the diversity of opinions regarding its composition, nature, and provenance. Indeed, the forty-seven page introduction to P.R. Davies's monograph on CD is 'intended as no more than a sketch' of scholarship so far.[49] The organizational difference of the community envisioned here and in 1QS support the conclusion that CD addresses the needs of a lay community living in camps while 1QS concerns itself with existence at Qumran.[50]

CD 2.14 begins a section of the work with the exhortation, 'And now,

---

interpreted the war as a coming reality, a holy war for which they must be ready, not a fictitious or devotional account of the perpetual spiritual battle between good and evil.

47. P.R. Davies, *1QM, The War Scroll from Qumran: Its Structure and History* (BibOr 32; Rome: Biblical Institute, 1977), p. 124.

48. Yadin, *Temple Scroll*, I, *passim*; and *War Scroll*.

49. P.R. Davies, *The Damascus Covenant: An Interpretation of the 'Damascus Document'* (JSOTSup, 25; Sheffield: JSOT Press, 1983), p. 3.

50. G. Vermes, *The Dead Sea Scrolls: Qumran in Perspective* (rev. edn; Philadelphia: Fortress Press, 1977), ch. 4.

sons, listen to me'. Murphy-O'Connor extends this unit to 6.1 and calls it a 'Missionary Document' because it seems to address outsiders and delivers a call to choose together with a discussion of punishment if the right choice is not made; for him it is central to the whole document.[51] Whether or not one concurs, it is clear that one aim of the section is to explain the founding of the movement which now stands squarely in God's covenant. Beginning at 3.12, the text explains that the earliest members survived the exile as a remnant from whom God would build an entire community (house) destined for eternal life. This development is cast as a fulfillment of Ezek. 44.15, slightly changed. CD 3.21–4.4 thus reads:

> This is as God has established for them by the hand of Ezekiel the prophet saying, 'The priests and the Levites and the sons of Zadok who kept charge of my sanctuary when the sons of Israel strayed from me, they shall approach me [with] fat and blood'. The priests are the 'captivity of Israel', the ones who went out from the land of Judah; [and the Levites are] the ones who joined them; and the sons of Zadok are the chosen ones of Israel, those called by the name who arise at the end of days.

In actuality, the MT of Ezek. 44.15 reads (literally):

> And the priests the Levites, sons of Zadok, who kept charge of my sanctuary when the sons of Israel strayed from me, they shall draw near to me to serve me and stand before me to offer to me fat and blood.

That the identity of 'those who joined them' is missing may appear strange. Certainly the text requires some kind of emendation to achieve minimal readability, and the phrase 'the Levites' is the only real candidate. The words הם הלוים ('and the Levites are') may have been accidentally omitted just before והנלוים ('and the ones who joined them').[52]

It is not known what text of Ezekiel the author was using, and there are no extant variants which testify to the reading in CD. The verse is certainly abridged from the MT regarding the description of liturgical service rendered, but the sense is similar. Of greater importance is the number of groups involved. The Ezekiel text lacks *waws* separating the priests, Levites and sons of Zadok, leaving an ambiguity which is commonly resolved by positing two groups: the Levitical priests and the sons of Zadok. CD, on the other hand, distinguishes three groups by the

---

51. J. Murphy-O'Connor, 'An Essene Missionary Document? CD II, 14-VI, 1', *RB* 77 (1970), pp. 201-29.
52. Davies, *Damascus Covenant*, p. 95.

use of two *waws* and subsequently interprets the identities of each one relative to the movement. Qimron, however, believes the הכהנים of 4.2 really stands for the phrase הכהנים והלויים.[53] This solution tries to make the best of an awkward sentence but is accompanied by no substantiation or other explanation. Davies summarized the various interpretations that have arisen at this point.[54] Stegemann, Murphy-O'Connor, and Cothenet take the three named groups as referring to the entire community. Betz takes them as representing three levels of status: priests, Levites, and laymen. If so, then it seems odd to have the laymen listed under the rubric 'the sons of Zadok'. O. Schwartz reflects more of the text itself by maintaining that the three represent levels of historical development, the 'priests' being the original members, the 'Levites' the present members, and the 'sons of Zadok' the future community. The point is not only chronological because the emphasis is on the discontinuity of the three. More probable is the view of Dupont-Sommer, Davies and Maier who all stress continuity. The 'priests' are the founders, the 'Levites' those joined later, and the 'sons of Zadok' the eschatological members, namely the present members with whom the addressees are called to join.

The next reference to Levi is in 4.15, a midrash on Isa. 24.17 in which the author describes how Belial has been unleashed on Israel, meaning those outside the sectarian community of course. Where Isaiah says a snare is on the inhabitants of the land, the author says:

> Its interpretation [פשר] is the three nets of Belial of which Levi the son of Jacob spoke, in which he traps Israel and makes them appear to them as three kinds of righteousness. The first is lust, the second wealth, the third uncleanness of the sanctuary (4.14-18).

In this way, the author illuminates the disobedience of those Jews outside his circle. No actual reference to Levi speaking about Belial has been found at Qumran, nor in any other so-called intertestamental literature, and certainly not in the Bible.

CD 10.4-10, which occurs in the greater section known as 'Laws', has to do with the rule (סרך) of the judges of the congregation. Of the ten men selected from the congregation, four must be from the tribe of

---

53. Qimron, 'The Text of CDC', in *The Damascus Document Reconsidered* (ed. Magen Broshi; Jerusalem: The Israel Exploration Society and the Shrine of the Book, 1992), p. 17 n. 2.

54. Davies, *Damascus Covenant*, pp. 91-92.

Levi and Aaron, and six from Israel. The age requirement runs from twenty-five to sixty years and each judge must be instructed in the book of the 'Hagu'[55] and in the teachings of the covenant.

Another rule in which the Levites figure concerns the meeting of the camps (12.23–13.7). Groups shall be formed at the levels of tens, fifties, hundreds, and thousands. Each meeting of ten men is to be presided over by a priest who is, like the judges of 10.4-10, instructed in the book of the 'Hagu'. If, however, there is a shortage of competent priests and a Levite happens to be properly instructed, then *he* may serve in place of the priest. In language reminiscent of Num. 27.21 the Levite regulates the coming and going of the camp. The hierarchical assignment of duties, then, is relative and conditioned by both practicality and competence. The only limitation on the Levite is that he is prevented from issuing judgments concerning blemishes.

The last rule which touches on the Levites is titled 'the meeting of all the camps' (14.3-12). Here the hierarchical nature of the community is clear in the order of mustering:

> All of them shall be mustered by their names. The priests first, the Levites second, and the sons of Israel third, and the proselyte fourth. And they shall be recorded by their names, each after his brother. The priests first, the Levites second, the sons of Israel third and the proselyte fourth (14.3-4).

B. *Evaluation*

As in 11QTemple and to a lesser degree in 1QM, the Levites in CD hold leadership and judicial positions. Their overall status is just below the priesthood. What is unique is the attribution of a saying to Levi and its midrashic exposition along with a creative use of Ezek. 44.15 distinguishing the Levites. The modern interpretations attending this reference have been no less creative and exemplify some of the fundamental difficulties involved in interpreting this document.

4. *1QS*

A. *Data*

All five of the references to Levites in the Rule of the Community occur within the section dealing with entrance into the covenant community

---

55. For the possible explanations of this term see Chaim Rabin, *The Zadokite Documents* (Oxford: Clarendon Press, 1958), p. 50.

(1.16–3.12). The Levites thus have a liturgical function in the Qumran community as in the Temple. The first reference (1.19) describes the joyful rite of entry in which the priests and Levites bless God and the initiates respond with 'Amen, Amen!'.

As part of this entrance rite the priests recount the merciful deeds of God, the Levites recount the iniquities of Israel during the reign of Belial, and the initiates confess their sins together with bestowal of God's everlasting grace (1.21–2.1a).

Following this, the priests bless the men of the lot of God (2.1b-4a) and the Levites curse the men of the lot of Belial (2.4b-9), and the people respond after each utterance with the familiar 'Amen, Amen!' (2.10).

Then the priests and Levites together issue a covenantal curse on the initiate who attempts to enter the community while harboring a stubborn heart (2.11-17). Again the people respond with 'Amen, Amen!'.

On the whole, the covenant entrance ceremony in 1QS bears a similarity to the covenant affirmation ceremony of Deuteronomy 27 and 28 which was prescribed to take place on Mt Ebal after Israel's entrance into the land. The biblical rite provides specific curses for the Levites to recite but the blessings which follow in Deuteronomy 28 are not assigned to priests by name. The antiphonal nature of the liturgy in 1QS emulates the people's 'Amen!' response after each curse (Deut. 27.15-26). The scroll, however, puts a double 'Amen!' in their mouths quite reminiscent of the ceremony in which Ezra read the Book of the Law and the Levites explained it to the attentive assembly (Neh. 8.1-9). Additionally, in the report of Hezekiah's celebration of the Passover, Josiah's renewal of the covenant, and his subsequent celebration of the Passover, the Chronicler specifically notes the presence of priests and Levites in leadership (2 Chron. 30.27; 34.30; 35.11-14).

The final reference to the Levites in 1QS pertains to the ceremony in which the covenant is renewed annually during the reign of Belial (2.19-25a). It may have been that this particular ceremony was one with the entrance rite, thus indicating the annual induction of new members.[56] 1QS does not specify the occasion for this ceremony. The fact that the giving of the Law was celebrated during the Feast of Weeks prompted Leaney to place the Qumran ceremony here,[57] but Wernberg-Møller

56. P. Wernberg-Møller, *The Manual of Discipline: Translated and Annotated with an Introduction* (Leiden: Brill, 1957), p. 55.

57. A.R.C. Leaney, *The Rule of Qumran and its Meaning: Introduction,*

chose the Day of Atonement instead because of the presence of repentance and confession of sins in both the biblical and Qumranic rites.[58] Whatever the day, each member enters into the order according to his status, but always in groups. The priests enter first, followed by the Levites, and then the rest grouped by thousands, hundreds, fifties, and tens (2.19-22a). CD 14.3-6 pictures a similar scene, but with the addition of a fourth group: proselytes. In 1QS the case is slightly different for a regular session of members: the priests sit first, then the *elders*, then the rest (6.8-9). The significance of this change is difficult to assess, especially given the complicated source history of 1QS; it may reflect another structure at this level of organization or simply a variance in nomenclature, the elders consisting of Levites.[59]

One further veiled reference to the Levites may be in 8.1-4, the description of community's council of twelve men and three priests. It is possible to conceive of this council as representative of the twelve tribes and each of the three clans of Levi; an Israel in miniature.[60] The words, 'When these exist in Israel, the council of the community shall be established in truth as an eternal plant' (8.4-5) do have an ideal ring to them.

B. *Evaluation*

The most visible function of the Levites in 1QS concerns the recital of blessings and curses. These are quite accurately paralleled in 1QM 12.1ff.; 13.1-2, 4).[61] Together with the priests, the Levites bless God and curse secretly hypocritical initiates, but on their own they recount the sins of Israel and curse the lot of Belial. Organizationally, there are slight differences between 1QS and CD.

This last point has led Colin Kruse to conclude that CD reflects a later

---

Translation, and Commentary (Philadelphia: Westminster Press, 1966), pp. 104-107, 135.

58. Wernberg-Møller, *Manual of Discipline*, p. 60.

59. Wernberg-Møller, *Manual of Discipline*, p. 104. Schiffman, on the other hand, relies on data from 1QM to conclude that 'elders' and 'Levites' are not identical in this passage (*Sectarian Law in the Dead Sea Scrolls: Courts, Testimony and the Penal Code* [BJS, 33; Chico: Scholars Press, 1983], p. 100 n. 12).

60. M.A. Knibb, *The Qumran Community* (Cambridge Commentary on Writings of the Jewish & Christian World 200 BC to AD 200, 2; Cambridge: Cambridge University Press, 1987), p. 130. Vermes notes that they may merely constitute a quorum (*Qumran in Perspective*, p. 92).

61. Yadin, *War Scroll*, p. 224.

stage of development than does 1QS and so postdates it. His investigation considers the priests and Levites, the *mebaqqer* (the Guardian), and the *rabbim* (the Many), a type of ruling group. The scope of his article is somewhat beyond this one, but it nevertheless has some fundamental weaknesses which require evaluation. Based on the observation that a Levite in CD may perform the teaching role in the absence of a qualified priest and a few other minor points, he concludes that CD is more detailed while 1QS 'tends to speak in more general terms'.[62] On the premise that a community formulates general laws first, 1QS is less developed and earlier. In a similar vein, he assumes that under 'normal' circumstances, organizational power is gradually transferred from the one to the many, concluding that the *rabbim* of CD reflects a more advanced structure. He does not take stock of the redactional studies published on these documents and concedes that the differences may not be related to dating at all, but rather to the fact that the documents were produced by separate communities with differing needs. In my opinion, this one fact is enough to explain all of the organizational differences between CD and 1QS regardless of matters of dating and literary composition.

On a more helpful note, Donaldson's investigation of Levitical messianology in Early Judaism[63] touches on the prominence of Levi at Qumran in texts not considered above. On the strength of the messianic evidence in CD 9.10, 29; 15.4; 18.8, 1QS 9.11, 4QTestim, and to a lesser extent in 1QSa, 1QSb, and 1QM, he concludes that in distinction to the groups that produced Jubilees and the Testaments of the Twelve Patriarchs,

> ...the Qumran community carried on the hope for a Levitical Messiah long after this hope had died within mainstream Judaism and the emerging Pharisaic movement had renewed the traditional hope for a Davidic Messiah.[64]

Thus the community reconciled the relationship of the Messiahs of Aaron and Israel and kept alive their hope for a Messiah from the tribe of Levi. The prominence given to Levi in the life of the community is thus paralleled in its eschatology as well.

---

62. Kruse, 'Community Functionaries', p. 545.
63. Donaldson, 'Levitical Messianology', pp. 193-207.
64. Donaldson, 'Levitical Messianology', p. 206.

5. *1QSa*

1QSa 1.6-25 calls itself 'the rule [סרך] for all of the hosts of the congregation and all of the native Israelites'. It lays down prescriptions for
members according to their age and concludes with rules for simpletons
followed by those for Levites. The relevant section running from 1.22-
25 reads:

> And the sons of Levi shall serve, each in his position, according to the
> authority [mouth] of the sons of Aaron to bring the whole congregation in
> and lead them out, each according to his rule, according to the direction
> [hand] of the heads of the families of the congregation—as commanders
> and judges and officers of all their hosts—according to the authority
> [mouth] of the sons of Zadok the priests and all the heads of the families
> of the congregation.

It is ambiguous whether the Levites shall *serve* as commanders (שרים),
judges (שופטים), and officers (שוטרים)[65] or whether these three terms
delineate the roles of the family heads.[66] The former seems more likely
though this must not be taken to mean that all such officials must be
Levites.[67]

What seems clear is that the Levites serve under priestly and lay
direction managing the movements of the congregation similar to how
Moses instructed Joshua (Num. 27.21). The context is clearly military.

Further on in the rule, prescriptions are laid down regarding those
who shall be called to the council of the community (1.25–2.11). These
include the wise men of the community, tribal commanders with their
judges and officers, commanders of thousands, hundreds, fifties and
tens, and 'the Levites in the division [מחלקת] of his duty' (2.1). Here the
Levites are assembled according to their 'courses', perhaps a stream-
lined reference to a twenty-four-part organizational structure as in the
books of Chronicles.

This short document again shows the Levites exercising leadership
functions under the authority of the priesthood, but provides little new
information. What this tells us of actual historical conditions cannot be

---

65. So Knibb, *Qumran Community*, p. 148.
66. Vermes, *The Dead Sea Scrolls in English* (3rd edn; London: Penguin, 1987),
p. 101.
67. Schiffman, *The Eschatological Community of the Dead Sea Scrolls: A Study
of the Rule of the Congregation* (SBLMS, 38; Atlanta: Scholars Press, 1989), p. 29.

ascertained for the rule is written for the 'last days' (1.1), envisions a future war, and an eschatological meal with the Messiah of Israel in attendance. Its ideology, then, has somewhat in common with the War Scroll and the Temple Scroll in that they are both future oriented as well.

6. *4QTestim*

4QTestimonia (4Q175) is a series of five biblical quotations, the last of which is followed by an interpretation. The fourth one is found in 1.14-20, Moses' blessing on Levi.[68] The text has numerous corrections in the forms of an erasure, crossed-out letters, written-over letters, and supralinear letters and words. It differs from the MT in some dozen places, sometimes reflecting readings in the LXX.

The selection and arrangement of quotations indicates an interest in several messianic figures: (1) a prophet like Moses (Deut. 18.18-19); (2) a star to come out of Jacob and a scepter to rise out of Israel (Num. 24.15-17); (3) the Levites (Deut. 33.8-11); and (4) a man of Satan, or some kind of 'anti-Messiah'. The three messianic figures, then, are prophetic, royal, and priestly, given that the blessing on Levi is taken as referring to an individual from that tribe. These three offices appear elsewhere in the Qumran corpus only in 1QS 9.11 where three figures are expected: [the] prophet and the messiahs [plural] of Aaron and Israel.[69]

4QTestim is yet another, but more brief, example of eschatologically focused documents which favor Levi. Like the others, it testifies to a pervasive fascination with Levi and most likely reflects the high reputation this tribe enjoyed in community life.

7. *5QRègle*

The second fragment of 5QRègle (5Q13) contains a reference to Levi (1.7) and to the sons of Levi in 1.8.[70] These two lines contain only six and four words respectively. In the first case, Levi was appointed to do

68. See J.M. Allegro, 'Further Messianic References in Qumran Literature', *JBL* 75 (1956), pp. 174-87.

69. Donaldson, 'Levitical Messianology', p. 205; and Knibb, *Qumran Community*, p. 264.

70. There is a lacuna with enough room for three letters just before 'Levi', leaving room for 'sons of' (DJD, III, p. 182).

something which remains unclear, and in the second, God chose them 'to go out'.

While the short and fragmentary document is replete with names (sons of God, Enoch, Noah, Abraham, Jacob, Bethel, and Israelites), there is not enough of it left to gain any clear sense of the meaning. That Levi is the only one of the twelve tribal heads mentioned or that he is included with other major figures of the past may or may not be significant; the text is simply far too laconic to be of much help.

8. *Single References*

A. *Data*

1. *1QDM*. Four documents, according to the graphic concordance, contain single references either to the Levites or Levi. 1QDM, known as the Words of Moses (1Q22), purports to be the text of Moses' farewell speech which God commanded him to address to several groups: part to all Israel, some to Eleazar and Joshua, and the first part to the sons of Israel and more specifically to 'the heads of the families [fathers] of the Levites and to all of the priests' (1QDM 1.3).[71] They are charged with the task of proclaiming the words of the Sinaitic Torah. In 2.8-9, although the fragments are broken, it appears that the Israelites are commanded to appoint teachers of some kind[72] to explain the Torah to them. In light of the earlier reference, these individuals are likely Levites and priests. Additional support for this conclusion comes from Neh. 8.7-9 where the Levites assist Ezra the priest by not only reading but explaining the Torah.

2. *3Q7*. 3Q7, entitled An Apocryphal Mention of the Angel of the Presence, was assembled from six small fragments which, all told, comprise only fifty letters (of which thirty-four are certain) and five words, one of which is 'Levi'.[73] The value of this lone reference for this study is small.

---

71. Milik supplies 'heads of' and 'priests' in the lacunae (DJD, I, p. 92). The validity of Thiering's identification of these heads with Kohathites, Gershonites, and Merarites rests on the strength of this conjecture (Thiering, '*Mebaqqer* and *Episkopos*', p. 63).

72. Milik probably supplies 'wise men' because of Deut. 1.13.

73. DJD, III, p. 99.

3. *4QPssJosh*. As briefly stated above, Carol Newsom does not consider this fragment of the Psalms of Joshua to be authored by the Qumran community due to its diction, the use of the Tetragrammaton and the fact that the author of 4QTestim treated it as a received text.[74] It is nevertheless of some interest in that in its listing of the sons of Jacob (or the twelve tribes), the adjective 'beloved' which is applied to Benjamin in Deut. 33.12 applies rather to Levi. His name may likely have been at the head of the list, but a break in the fragment prevents proof of it.

4. *4QOrd*. Finally, 4QOrd (4Q159) 5 i.2 reads, 'the interpretation of...The sons of Levi...in judgment'.[75] The fragment seemingly deals with interpretations of biblical laws as does the rest of the document, but is too broken to yield anything more valuable than one more reference to the Levites in the Dead Sea scrolls.

B. *Evaluation*

These fragments are of little value for illuminating the Levites in the Dead Sea Scrolls. True, one does indicate the Levites assigned a teaching function, but the others are too short and without context to be of much help beyond providing additional references to this person or tribe.

9. *The Psalter*

The irregular order of psalms now in the Massoretic psalter together with the presence of noncanonical psalms in some of the approximately thirty manuscripts of the Qumran psalter have engendered much discussion.[76] J.A. Sanders contends that these phenomena indicate that the content and order of the psalter was in flux until well into the first century CE.[77] Others, such as M.H. Goshen-Gottstein, P.W. Skehan, and Roger Beckwith, argue that the Qumran evidence reflects a liturgical order and need.[78] Beckwith has worked out an elaborate reconstruction of an order which would have met the requirements of twenty-four

---

74. Newsom, 'Psalms of Joshua', p. 59.

75. DJD, V, p. 9.

76. Seven manuscripts are of particular interest: 4QPs^a, 4QPs^e, 11QPsAp^a, 4QPs^f, 4QPs^d, 11QPs^b, and 11QPs^a.

77. Sanders, *The Psalms Scroll of Qumrân Cave 11 (11QPs^a)* (Oxford: Clarendon Press, 1965).

78. Beckwith, 'Eccentric Psalms Scrolls', p. 503.

courses of Levites each serving a week at a time. Additional psalms were needed in the collection because of a shortage in the 150-psalm canon and the irregular sequence was due to the Essene solar calendar and the practice of singing a different one on each regular day, Sabbath and holy day. Scriptural examples (1 Chron. 25; 2 Chron. 23.18; 29.25-30), evidence of twenty-four priestly courses,[79] and the presence of Levites at Qumran, together with their interest in hymnody, form the basis for his inference that Levitical singers existed in the community even though they lacked a Temple, for nothing in scripture confines the singing of Psalms to the sanctuary.[80] The logic of his reconstructed order lends confirming weight to the claim.

Because nothing in the scrolls of the Qumran psalter mentions the Levites, let alone their liturgical functions, it is impossible to be certain as to the existence and organization of Levitical singers there and so these texts may fall outside the strict boundaries of this study. As has been seen, however, the future-oriented War Scroll assigns them musical functions. The Rule of the Community surely reflected actual practice; 1QS 1.18-20 has them along with the priests 'blessing the God of salvation and all of his faithful deeds' while those entering the community rejoin 'Amen, Amen!'. The scene is almost certainly lyrical and may even have utilized portions of the psalter. The reasoning behind Beckwith's article is cogent; in light of the evidence from the LXX supporting a closed canon early on, his conclusions about the firm state of the canon in the first century CE seem closer to reality than Sander's alternative proposals. More to the point, Beckwith's work offers a reasonable basis for extending the knowledge of the actual function of the Levites at Qumran.

Conclusion

Examination of these references to Levi and the Levites in the Dead Sea Scrolls has shown them in striking prominence, most notably in material concerning the future, be it cultic service, combat, or community life and organization. The bounds of their functions extend well beyond the

79. The Book of the Priestly Courses from Cave 4 reveals an organized rota of priests similar to those officiating in Jerusalem and 1QM 2.2 describes priests serving in twenty-six courses instead of the twenty-four of 1 Chron. 12.1-19 (Leaney, *Rule of Qumran*, pp. 92-93).

80. Beckwith, 'Eccentric Psalms Scrolls', p. 506.

statutes of the Bible and the expectation of a Messiah from the tribe of Levi appears to be especially persistent. Commitment to a specific method of scriptural interpretation (homogenization) certainly accounts for a degree of literary prominence in the Temple Scroll, a cause which may overlap with a polemic drive to restore usurped Levitic rights and roles.

Using the scrolls, however, to investigate the real extent of Levitic presence in the Qumran community and the breadth of their responsibilities remains problematic for several reasons. Two of the documents, 11QTemple and 1QM, envisage the future. Nevertheless, that the community was engaging in more than purely theoretical speculation seems obvious enough; their eschatological orientation made the as yet unrealized future very much present and therefore 'real' as far as they were concerned. Even so, the fact that 11QTemple, for example, shows the Levites receiving double portions of sacrifices or acting as judges does not necessarily mean that they actually enjoyed these particular expressions of esteem within the community. Their musical roles in 1QM, though a logical extension of their functions in scripture, actually tell very little about their liturgical duties at Qumran. The third scroll considered, CD, appears to address the needs of lay communities located away from Qumran. Unlike 11QTemple and 1QM, it reflects historical reality and demonstrates the activity of Levites in civil leadership and the administration of law. To what extent these practices found their counterpart at Qumran is uncertain; 1QS is concerned mostly with liturgical matters. 1QSa, on the other hand, speaks of the Levites in civil and military life, but it purports to be a rule written for the last days. 4QTestim is likewise eschatological. All other references to either Levi or the Levites occur in texts which are too short to be of much help. The unique form of the Qumranic psalter, however, lends support to the existence of a well-organized guild of Levitical singers. On the whole then, much of the literary data in the Dead Sea Scrolls relative to the Levites is not directly suitable for investigating the historical particulars of liturgy and community leadership.

Still, the very fact that the Levites surface so often in the literature and that they are afforded such esteem is evidence that this tribe was both highly respected and the subject of extensive theological reflection. This observation fortifies the conclusion that such prominence in eschatological or otherwise future-oriented material paralleled the exalted stature of Levites who were involved at the center of the life of the Qumran community.

INDEX OF REFERENCES

OLD TESTAMENT

Genesis
1 — 154
1.2 — 154
3.1 — 158
3.3-4 — 37
3.16 — 23
6.18 — 43
9.6 — 57
12.19 — 26
14.7 — 26
14.12 — 27
18–19 — 107
20.13 — 24
21.6-7 — 118
29.6 — 43
30.23 — 118
34.19 — 157
41.46 — 45
49.10 — 122

Exodus
3.18 — 43
21.13 — 57
28.30 — 44
28.35 — 52
29.7 — 46
29.32 — 47
34.10 — 157
34.34 — 44
46.9 — 44

Leviticus
16 — 56
4.3 — 49
4.6-17 — 49
4.6 — 48
4.13 — 49
5.7 — 128
8.12 — 46
12.8 — 128
16 — 47-49, 169
16.3 — 128
16.5 — 48
16.6 — 48
16.11 — 48
16.12-15 — 61
16.14-15 — 48
16.15 — 48
16.16 — 48
16.17-24 — 53
16.17 — 48
16.18-21 — 61
16.18-19 — 48
16.24 — 48
18.16 — 144
19 — 37
19.20 — 36
20.21 — 144
20.24 — 27
21.10 — 46
23.42–24.2 — 169
24.10-16 — 52
24.12 — 52
25 — 169

Numbers
2.17 — 167
2.33 — 167
3 — 175
3.23 — 167
3.29 — 167
3.35 — 167
3.38 — 167
8.11 — 154
12 — 54
12.6-8 — 54
12.6-7 — 38
12.7 (LXX) — 38
12.8 — 38
13.19 — 88
24.15-17 — 186
24.17 — 35, 122
27.2 — 45
27.21 — 181, 185
27.22 — 45
29.8 — 49
29.11 — 49
30.17 — 33
31.25-30 — 171
31.30 — 170

Deuteronomy
1.13 — 187
4.29 — 154
4.41 — 158
7.10 — 157
11.7 — 157
12 — 33
12.14 — 42
12.29-31 — 33
13 — 30-35, 41, 53, 54, 56, 58

13.1-2	59	32.15-18	109	22.2	143
13.1	33, 34, 42	32.25-27	109	22.5	143
13.2	31, 35	32.33	89	23.9-13	143
13.2 (MT)	33	32.35	116	23.13-14	143
13.2-6	30	33.8-11	186	23.13	144
13.2-3 (Heb.)	59	33.12	188	23.24-29	143
13.2-3	53	34.1	128	23.25	143
13.3	31, 59	34.3	128	30.24-25	171
13.4 (Heb.)	59				
13.4-5	35, 43	*Joshua*		*2 Samuel*	
13.6	31, 32, 53	6.20	176	1.24	118
13.18	35, 42	8.24	116	2.4	139
14.22-23	128	8.33	41	5.3	139
15.2	53	21.9	154	5.6-9	139
17	41, 42, 45,	22.27	154	5.9	140
	46, 56	23.2	41	5.10	139
17.8-13	46	24.31	157	5.11	140
17.8-9	41			6.12-19	137
17.8	42, 46	*Judges*		6.17	140
17.9	41, 42, 46	1.7	158	7	139
17.10-11	38	2.7	157	7.12-16	137
17.10	43	4.16	116	7.13-16	138
18	32, 54	7.20	176	7.14	138
18.1-5	170	20	58	14	57
18.1-3	170	20.13	58	14.7	57
18.1	170			14.8	57
18.3	170	*Ruth*		14.11	57
18.6-8	171	2.12	109	17.13	112
18.18-19	186			19.3 (Eng.)	44
18.18	34	*1 Samuel*		19.4	44
21.5	170, 172	1.10-15	139	19.8 (Eng.)	43
23.22	157	2.12-17	106, 129	19.9	43
24	37	2.16	129	20.8	43
25.18	155	2.22-25	106	20.19	155
27	182	2.31	111	22.51	139
27.15-26	182	3.20	38	24.21	137
28	182	8.20	52	24.25	137
28.37	107	14.45	37		
28.41	116	15.22	156	*1 Kings*	
28.64	116	16.12-13	139	1.23	45
29.9	41	16.13	139	1.28	45
29.10 (Eng.)	41	17.19-54	139	1.32	45
29.28	50	18.7	139	2.27	141
29.29 (Eng.)	50	18.10-11	139	2.35	141
30.3	107	18.20-29	139	5.6	105
31.6	50	18.27	139	6–7	137
31.29	50	19.12	139	8.1	158
32.11	109	21.1-6	144	8.5	140

8.63	140	24.20-21	108	12.2	155
9.11	158	29.3	140	13.6	156
9.15-19	141	29.4-19	140	15.2	38
12.18	154	29.20-24	140	17.8	109
13.11	36	29.25-30	189	18.50	139
13.25	36	29.31-36	140	19.10	38
17.17-24	162	30.17	171	21.8	156
		30.22	171	23.6	156
2 Kings		30.27	182	24.7-10	65
2	36	33.6	107	26.4	43
2.3	36	34.30	182	31.24	155
2.5	36	35.1-19	140	31.25	154
2.15	36	35.11-14	171, 182	32.6	154
4.18-37	162	35.16	154	52.10	156
5	162	36.15-16	109	78	109
5.1-14	162	36.17-21	109	78.71	160
6.14	111			79.11	44
8.11-13	110	*Ezra*		80.19	153
8.12	112, 116,	3–6	137	85.11	38
	118	9.7 (LXX)	116	87.3	157
14.25	36	10.18-24	107	88.2 (Eng.)	44
20.17	111			88.3	44
20.18	108	*Nehemiah*		89.6	153
23.17	36	8.1-9	182	96.8	44
23.21-23	140	8.7-9	187	146.7-8	153
23.25-26	32	10.35	169	100.2	44
25	137	13.23-29	107	105	109
25.9	108			105.3	154
		Esther		106	109
1 Chronicles		1.2	45, 155	137.9	111
12.1-19	189	1.11	45	146	153, 157,
14.15	158	1.12	45		162
16.10	154	1.13	45	146.6	153
16.29	44	1.14	45	146.7-8	155, 162
16.37	45	1.15	45		
20.20	38	1.19	44	*Proverbs*	
25	189	5.14	43	10.27	129
28.5	155	8.1	44	28.5	154
		9.25	44	28.15	156
2 Chronicles					
7.1-3	140	*Job*		*Ecclesiastes*	
10.18	154	1.14	158	5.3	157
13.7	154	13.16	44		
17.7-9	170	22.4	43	*Isaiah*	
19.8	170	23.3	154	1.9	107
20.17	52			1.21	38
23.18	189	*Psalms*		1.23	107
23.30	156	4.3	66	1.26	38

2.12-16	123		
3.9	107		
3.14	43		
5	161		
5.1-7	125		
5.5	117		
5.23	107		
8.19	107		
10.3	113		
10.34	105, 123		
11.1-2	137		
14.5	156		
16.5	138		
22.20	126		
22.22 (MT)	126		
22.23 (Heb.)	126		
24.17	180		
26	155		
26.2	155		
26.19	159		
26.21	159		
28.1-13	126		
28.1	126		
28.14-15	107		
28.14	156		
28.21	154		
29.3	107, 111, 113		
30.1-5	107		
33.9	123		
35	161, 162		
35.1-2	161		
35.3-6	155, 161		
35.5	161, 162		
37.33	111		
39.7	108		
40	161		
40.1	162		
40.3	161		
40.10	155		
40.11	108, 159		
40.16	123		
40.26	154		
40.31	155		
41.26	37		
42.7	126		
48.18	110		
49.7-11	159		

49.7	155, 159		
49.9	159		
49.10	159		
51.1	154		
54	118		
54.1-10	118		
58.6	163		
60.13	105		
61	159, 162		
61.1	159, 161, 162		
61.1 (LXX)	155, 161		
61.1-2	162, 163		

Jeremiah

4.20	108		
5.19	108		
6.1	108		
6.6	111		
6.8	110		
6.14	110		
6.15 (LXX)	113		
7	119, 120, 122, 123		
7.2-24	119		
7.2	119, 123		
7.3	119		
7.4	119		
7.5-6	119		
7.9	107		
7.11	119, 136, 150		
7.14-15	119		
7.14	119, 136		
7.21	119		
7.25-27	119		
7.29	119		
7.30-32	119		
7.32	108, 111, 118		
7.34	119, 122, 136		
8	120		
8.3	120		
8.23 (LXX)	110		
9.1 (Heb.)	110		
9.16	108		
9.20	118		

9.21-22	107		
10.15	113		
10.22	121		
11.22	107		
12.3	108		
12.7	109, 136		
12.7 (LXX)	109		
12.10-11	121		
12.15	107		
14.17	110		
15.2	108, 116		
15.13	108		
16.4	116		
17.3	108		
17.6	36		
18.18	127		
19.8	121		
19.9	107		
20.1-2	108		
21.7	107		
21.8-9	107		
21.8	115		
22.5	109, 136		
23.3	108		
23.5	138		
23.10	107		
23.14	107		
24.16	36		
25.18	107		
25.34	107		
26	36		
26.6	95, 107		
26.9	136		
26.10 (LXX)	116		
26.11	36		
26.16	36		
26.18	95		
27.1-11	108		
27.7	117		
27.9	107		
28	54		
28.1	36		
28.6 (LXX)	115		
28.8-9	54		
28.16	31		
29.13	154		
29.18	107		
29.32	32		

30.9	138	17.22	138	10.14	111, 118
31.10	108	17.24	119		
32.37	107	18.9	37	*Amos*	
33.15	138	20.41-42	108	4.11	107
33.17	138	21.10	108	5.12	107
33.21	138	21.22	111	7.12	36
34.1	98	22.4-16	112	9.11	138
34.1 (Heb.)	113	22.6-12	112	9.11	138
35	86	22.15	108		
35.6	87, 89	23.41	65	*Micah*	
35.7	89, 90	26.11	117	2.12	107
35.8	87, 89	26.12	112	3.12	95
35.9	89	30.3	117	5.2	138
35.11	90	34.11-12	154	7	121
38.6	108	34.23-24	138	7.5-6	121, 122
41.1 (LXX)	113	34.23	159	7.6	121
46.10	116	34.37	108		
50.8	115	37.24-25	138	*Nahum*	
51.6	115	38.15	43	2.12	99
51.10	157	40.27	122	3.10	111
51.45	115	42.1-14	168		
51.46	156	44.15	179, 181	*Habakkuk*	
51.53	127	45.2	122	1.6	121
52.4-5	111	46.9-10	53	1.14-17	121
52.13	108	48.16	122	2.4	38
52.17	121	48.17	122	2.9-10	134
		48.20	122	2.17	99
Lamentations					
4.13	109	*Daniel*		*Zephaniah*	
		2.40	155	1.15-16	116
Ezekiel		4.31	26		
4.2	111	8.5-7	121	*Zechariah*	
5.2	107	8.24	153	3.8	138
6.6	121	9	96	3.12-13	138
6.9	107	11.38	155	11.1	105, 123,
6.11	107	11.39	156		132
6.14	121	12.11	113	12.3	116
7.15-16	115			12.10	117
7.21	108	*Hosea*		14.5	115
9.4	115	2.9-10	106		
12.19-20	121	3.4-5	138	*Malachi*	
14	54, 55	5.6	154	1.7	107
14.1-11	54	9.7	115	1.12	107
14.9-10	55	9.17	107	3.11	107
16	107	10.8	118, 120	4.5-6	162

APOCRYPHA

1 Esdras   28.18   116   3.45   117
1.1-22   140   34.2   39   4.36-51   140
                     36.20-21   39   4.52-59   140
Tobit   42.18   52   4.54   140
1.10   116   42.19   51   7.13   155
14.5   117, 139 44.20   39   14.41   38
                     46.13-15   39   2 Macc. 9.2   111
Wisdom of Solomon 48.20-25   51
3.7   113   49.9   39   *2 Maccabees*
                                             14.6   155
Ecclesiasticus   *1 Maccabees*
3.22   52   2.42   155

NEW TESTAMENT

Matthew   24.45-51   124, 136   11.19   143
1.2-16   141   11.27-33   137
2.1-18   138   *Mark*   12.1-9   124, 126,
2.1-2   122   2.15-17   143   136
3.3   161   2.15   143   12.2-8   109
3.7   136   2.23-26   142, 143   12.12   137
5.23-24   120   2.25   142   12.13-17   145
5.31-32   144   2.27-28   142   12.13   145, 146
9.13   120   3.1-6   145   12.35-37   142
10.35-36   122   3.5   146   12.38-40   120, 136
11.2-6   160   3.6   145   12.41-44   120, 136
11.2-3   144   4.11-12   146   13   93
11.4-6   144, 148 6.1-6   163   13.1-2   100
11.5-6   160   6.13   148   13.2   92-94, 101,
11.5   120, 162 6.14-16   145   110, 112,
12.7   120   6.15   162   120
16.1   145   6.17-29   144   13.12   121
16.6   145   6.17   144   13.14-20   113
16.14   162   6.18   144   13.14   113-15
16.19   123   6.52   146   14.43-50   137
17.11-14   162   8.11   145   14.58   92, 93, 120
17.24-27   128, 136 8.15   145   15.17   149
19.3-9   144   8.17-19   146   15.26   139
21.9   142   8.28   162   15.29   93
22.7   118   9.13   162   15.38   102
23.27   120   10.42-44   148
23.37-39   108   10.47   142   *Luke*
23.37-38   136   11.15-17   119   1.25   118
23.38   109, 120 11.17   119, 120,   1.32-33   137
24.30   117   136   3.2   131, 133

3.7	136	14.13	120	*John*	
3.15-17	144	14.15-24	118	1.23	161
3.16	144	16.1-8	124	7.42	142
3.19-20	144	17.11-19	163	18.13	131, 132
3.19	144	19.11-27	146	18.24	131
3.20	144	19.12	147	19.37	117
3.23-38	141	19.13	147		
4.16-30	118, 163	19.14	147	*Acts*	
4.18	161	19.15-19	147	2.24-36	142
5.16	143	19.27	148	2.30	137
7.11-19	163	19.38	149	4.6	131
7.18-23	160	19.41-44	100, 110,	12.21	149
7.18-19	144		112, 113,	13.30-37	142
7.21-23	144		117		
7.22-23	148, 160,	19.42-44	114, 120	*Romans*	
	163	19.43	113, 118	1.3	141
7.22	160-63	19.44	118	11.25	117
7.24	143	21.6	112		
7.34	143	21.20-24	101, 113,	*2 Corinthians*	
9.6	148		114, 117,	6.18	137
9.7-9	145, 162		120		
9.9	145	21.21	114, 115	*Hebrews*	
9.19	162	21.22	113, 118	1.5	137
11.50-51	108	21.23	118	11.37	108
12.42-46	136	23.2	146		
12.52-53	122	23.7-8	145	*Jude*	
13.11-16	163	23.8	145, 148	11.22	107
13.31-33	143	23.9	148		
13.31	143	23.11	149	*Revelation*	
13.33	144	23.14-16	149	1.7	117
13.34-35	100, 108,	23.27-31	101, 117	3.7	123
	136	23.29	120	21.16	122
13.34	110	23.30	120	22.16	122
13.35	108	23.31	117		

PSEUDEPIGRAPHA

1 Enoch		90.29	139	32.2-4	124
89.50	97	91	98		
89.54	97	91.11-13	97	*4 Ezra*	
89.56-67	126	91.11	97	3.23-24	141
89.56	97	91.12-13	97	11.37	138
89.72-73	97	91.13	97	12.31-32	138
89.73	97, 98			13.52	138
90.9	98	*2 Baruch*			
90.12-17	98	1.4	124	*Lives of the Prophets*	
90.28-29	97	10.18	123	1.1	108
90.28	97	29.3	124	2.1	108

3.1-2	108	*Sibylline Oracles*		14.5	106
5.1	36	3.665	98	14.6	107
6.1	36	4.119-27	103	14.8	107
6.2	108	4.128-29	103	15.1	107
7.2	108	4.155-18	103	15.3	96
8.1	36	5.398-402	98	16	96, 107
10.10-11	101			16.1-5	95
10.11	102, 120	*Testament of Benjamin*		16.1	107
11.1	36	9.2	139	16.2	107
12.11	102, 121			16.4-5	107
13.1	36	*Testament of Judah*		16.5	107
		23	96, 107		
Martyrdom of Isaiah		23.1-5	96	*Testament of Moses*	
5.1-14	108	23.1	107	5	134
		23.2	107	5.6	134
Psalms of Solomon		23.3-4	107	6–7	134
17.4	138	23.5	108	6	134
17.6	138			6.2-6	134
17.21	138	*Testament of Levi*		6.2	137
17.22	117	10.3	95, 96, 106	6.7	134
18.5	153	14	96	7	134, 135
		14.1–15.3	95		

QUMRAN LITERATURE

1Q20		2	20	21.30	26
	22	2.1	22, 23	21.12-3	26
		2.15	22	22.3	27
1Q22		2.25	23	22.34	27
	55, 169, 187	11.12	26		
		12.17	26	*1QDM*	
1Q29		19	20		187
	51, 56	19.15	23	1.3	187
5-7, 2	51	19.17	24	2.8-9	187
		19.19	23, 24		
1Q30		19.23	24	*1QH*	
i 1-2	157	19.25	25		13
		19–22	20	1.31	40
1Q33		20.6	26	3.25	90
	18	20.7	25	4.8	90
1Q34ᵇ		20.18	25	4.15-18	32
3 21.8	38	20.26	25, 26	4.40	40
		20.32	26	5.5	90
1Q51		21.1	26	8.4	90
	18	21.3	26	16.18	64
		21.14	25		
1QapGen		21.33	27	*1QHab*	
	13	21.34	27		13

1QIs^a		19.5-8	173	2.10	182
16.14	65			2.11-18	80, 81
		1QpHab		2.11-17	182
1QM			59, 74	2.11	69
	13, 18, 88,	1.13	133	2.12-14	68
	172, 173,	8.1-3	38	2.19-3.12	70, 75
	178, 184,	8.8-12	133	2.19-25	182
	190	8.9	133	2.19-23	70
1.2-3	90	8.12	133	2.19-22	183
1.2	173	9.2-7	99	2.24-3.12	70
2-9	176	9.4-5	133	2.24	70
2.2	173, 189	9.5	133	2.25-3.12	80, 81
2.7	173	9.9-11	99	2.25	70
3.13-4.17	173	9.9	133	3.13-4.26	70
3.13-16	173	9.12-10.1	134	3.13-4.14	82
4.1	175	10.1	133	3.13-4.26	81
4.6-8	175	11.4	133	3.13-15	70, 78, 82
4.6	39	12.3-5	99	3.13	69, 70
5.1	175	12.8-9	133	3.15-4.1	70
5.11	66	12.10	133	3.15-18	70
7.9-9.9	175			3.18	69
7.14-15	175	*1QS*		4.2-14	70
7.16	175		13, 18, 67-	4.2	69
8.9-10	176		69, 71, 74,	4.15-26	70
8.13	176		76, 79, 80,	4.15-23	82
8.15	176		88, 89, 164,	4.15-18	70
9-14	176		171, 181-	4.15	82
9.8	46		84, 190	4.23-26	70, 82
11.6	35	1-4	81-84	5-7	71, 76, 79,
11.7	173	1-3	74		83
12	176	1	84	5-6	85
12.1	183	1.1-17	75	5	68, 74, 79,
12.10	65	1.1-15	70, 81		84
12.13	173	1.1	69	5.1-6.23	75, 81
13.1-2	176, 183	1.16-3.12	70, 182	5.1-6.8	71
13.3	40	1.16-2.25	70, 81, 83	5.1-7	71, 75
13.4	183	1.16-17	32, 78	5.1-6	71
13.7-13	173	1.18-2.18	70	5.1-3	78
14-20	176	1.18-20	189	5.1-2	71, 79, 84
15.4	176	1.19	182	5.1	68-70
16.3-9	176	1.21-2.1	182	5.2-7	71
16.6	65	1.21	69	5.2-3	72, 76, 77,
16.7-8	176	1.22-23	83		79, 84
17.7-8	173	2.1-4	182	5.6-7	79
17.10-17	176	2.4-10	80	5.6	77, 84
17.13	176	2.4-9	182	5.7-20	71
18.5	177	2.4-7	68	5.7-13	81
19.1	65	2.4	69	5.7-10	51, 71, 78

5.7	69, 81
5.8	51
5.9	72
5.10-20	71, 81
5.10-11	80
5.10	71, 80
5.11-12	51
5.11	81
5.13–6.8	81, 83
5.13-20	75, 81
5.13-15	80, 81, 83, 84
5.13	69, 77
5.15-20	81
5.15	77
5.20–6.8	71, 81
5.20-24	71, 81
5.20	81
5.25–6.1	71, 81
6–7	74
6.1-8	71
6.1-7	75
6.3	81
6.3,06	64
6.6	50, 51, 81
6.8-23	71, 81
6.8-13	71
6.8	69, 71, 77, 80
6.10	69
6.13-23	71, 75, 81
6.24–7.25	71, 72, 75
6.24	69, 71, 72, 74
7–8	68
7.16-17	79
7.25	69
8–10	77, 83
8–9	74, 77, 79, 83-85
8	84
8.1–10.8	76
8.1–9.26	72, 84
8.1–9.11	71, 72
8.1–9.6	75
8.1-16	72, 76
8.1-10	74, 78
8.1-4	72, 183

8.1	72
8.3-4	79
8.4-8	72
8.4-5	183
8.4	72, 76
8.6-7	79
8.6	79, 84
8.8-12	72, 73
8.8	73
8.10-13	68
8.10-12	73, 75, 77
8.10	72, 73, 77, 79
8.11-12	50
8.11	50, 76
8.12-16	72, 78
8.12-14	75
8.12	72, 76
8.13-14	68, 72, 90
8.13	76, 79, 84
8.15–9.11	68, 74, 76
8.15-16	79
8.15	68, 77
8.16–9.2	72, 75, 77, 83
8.16-19	72, 76-78
8.16-17	78
8.16	72
8.17–9.2	76
8.17	78
8.19	72
8.20–9.2	72, 76, 78
8.20	69, 72, 73, 78, 79
8.23	78
8.25-27	68
9.3–10.8	76
9.3-11	72, 76-79
9.3	72, 73
9.4-5	79
9.4	77
9.5	72, 73, 76
9.7	72, 76, 77, 84
	81
9.8-9	
9.10	73, 76
9.11	58, 68, 72, 77, 184, 186

9.12–11.22	73
9.12–10.8	76
9.12-26	72, 77-79
9.12-21	73
9.12	68, 69, 73
9.14-15	78
9.16-17	76
9.19-20	75, 76
9.19	69, 76
9.20	90
9.21–11.22	73
9.21-26	73
9.21	69, 73
10–11	83, 84
10.1-8	73
10.4	81
10.6	81
10.9–11.22	73, 82, 83
10.9–11.22	81
11.9	83
11.12-15	82
11.15	69
1QSa	
	13, 18, 77, 88, 171, 184, 190
1.1	186
1.6-25	185
1.22-25	185
1.25–2.11	185
2.1	185
1QSb	
	13, 18, 184
2Q25	
9	18
2Q28	
	18
3Q7	
	187
4Q156	
	61

Reference	Pages	Reference	Pages	Reference	Pages
4Q158		1 i 6-7	32, 35, 37, 42, 56, 60 30, 38	*4Q400* 1 I 6	65
VI l. 6-10	58	1 i 6	28, 29, 35, 37, 53, 56, 58-60	*4Q402* 1, 2	43
4Q159	18, 128, 188	1 i 7	28, 29, 35, 37, 40, 41, 43, 45, 53, 56, 58, 59	*4Q404* 5.6	39
4Q166 2.3-5	32, 33	1 i 8-9	42, 46	*4Q405* 19.4	39
4Q175	186	1 i 8	28, 29, 36, 40, 42, 43, 58	20 ii 21-22 20 ii 21-22.5	65 39
l. 5-8	58	1 i 9	28, 29, 40, 42, 43, 46, 53, 56	*4Q408* 2	50
4Q180-181	18	1 ii	56	*4Q491*	174
4Q255-264	18	1 ii 1-3	47	11.15	66
4Q287	153	1 ii 1-2 1 ii 1 1 ii 2	47 29 29	*4Q492*	174
4Q375	31-33, 35-38, 40, 41, 43, 45-49, 51-59	1 ii 3-4 1 ii 3	48 29, 47	*4Q493*	174
1 i	56	1 ii 4	29, 47, 48	*4Q494*	174
1 i 1-5	41	1 ii 5-6	47		
1 i 1-4	30, 33	1 ii 5	29, 47	*4Q497*	18
1 i 1-3	33	1 ii 6	29, 47, 48		
1 i 1-2	35	1 ii 7	29, 43, 47-50, 56	*4Q513*	18
1 i 1	28, 29, 32-35, 42, 55	1 ii 8-9	41, 52		
1 i 2-3	35, 43	1 ii 8	43, 47, 49, 50, 52, 53, 56	*4Q514*	18
1 i 2	32-34, 42, 55	1 ii 9	29, 47, 49, 52, 53		
1 i 2	28, 29	*4Q376*	55, 56	*4Q521*	150, 152, 154, 157, 159, 160, 162
1 i 3-4	35	1 i	55		
1 i 3	28, 29, 32, 33, 35, 42, 43	1 ii 2-3	55		
1 i 4-9	30	1 ii 2	55, 56		
1 i 4-5	31, 33	1 ii 3	55		
1 i 4	28, 29, 31-33, 35	*4Q379*	165	1 ii 1-14	152
1 i 5-7	40			1 ii 1-2	153, 156, 160
1 i 5	28, 29, 31,			1 ii 1	152

1 ii 2	152, 153	1 i 17	176	*4QPs^f*	
1 ii 3	152, 154,	11 ii 5	177		188
	160	13 i 6	176		
1 ii 4-9	160			*4QPssJosh*	
1 ii 4	152, 154,	*4QM2*			188
	155		174		
1 ii 5-8	157	1 i 11	177	*4QS^{a-j}*	
1 ii 5	152-54				68
1 ii 6	152-54	*4QM3*	174	*4QS^a*	
1 ii 7	152, 153,	13 i 9	176		67
	155				
1 ii 8	152, 153,	*4QM4*		*4QS^b*	
	162		174		
1 ii 9	152, 153,	1 i 2-3	177		68, 79
	155, 156				
1 ii 10	152, 153,	*4QOrd*		*4QS^d*	
	156, 157		188		68, 72, 73,
1 ii 11-13	156	5 i 2	188		78, 79
1 ii 11	152, 153,				
	157-60	*4QpHos*		*4QS^e*	
1 ii 12-13	160		32, 59		68, 72, 76,
1 ii 12	152, 153,				79
	157-59, 162	*4QpNah*			
1 ii 13	152, 153,	1.1-3	99	*4QS^g*	
	155, 159		80		68, 79
1 ii 14	152, 153	1.11	133		
				4QTestim	
4QD		*4QpPs37*			77, 184,
	18, 157	2.1	90		186, 188,
					190
4QEn^a		*4QPatrBless*		1.14-20	186
1I1	26	1–5	122		
		1–2	137, 138	*4QTgJob*	
4QEn^g					61
	97, 98	*4QpsDan A*			
		1.7-9	137	*4QTgLev*	
4QFlor		2.1-4	137		61
1.1-13	137				
1.4	90	*4QPs^a*		*5Q11*	
1.6	100		188		18, 68
1.11-12	138				
1.11	51	*4QPs^d*		*5Q13*	
			188		18, 186
4QM1-6					
	18	*4QPs^e*		*5QD*	
			188		18
4QM1					
	174				

5QRegle		25.12-16	49	2.14	178
	186	26.3-13	49	3.7	90
1.7	186	27	49	3.19	38
1.8	186	27.3-4	49	3.21–4.4	179
		28–29	169	4.2	180
6QD		29.8-10	99	4.6	90
	18	39.12	167	4.14-18	180
		39.15	167	4.15	180
11QMelchizedek		39.16	167	5.2-3	50
	159	40.14	167	5.4	184
		40.15	167	6.1-2	32
11QPs[a]		44.3–45.2	167	6.1	179
	188	44.14	167	6.5	90
24.6	64	54.5-7	33, 34	6.7	51
24.13	65	54.8-18	31	6.21	90
24.14	66	56.1-11	46	7.18	51
		56.3-4	38	7.19-20	35
11QPs[b]		56.9	45	8.9-10	89
	188	57.11-13	170	9.10	184
		58.13	170	9.21-22	38
11QPsAp[a]		58.18-19	46	9.22-23	38, 89
	188	60.6-9	170	9.29	184
		60.12-14	171	10.4-10	180, 181
11QTem		61.8-9	169	10.5	175
	164-66,	63.3	172	12.23–13.7	181
	171, 172,	63.4	170	13.10	89
	178, 190			14.3-12	181
13–29	169	*11QTgJob*		14.3-6	183
21.1	169		61	14.3-4	181
21.4	169			14.4	90
22.4	171	*CD*		14.6	90
22.10	170		18, 74, 88,	18.8	184
22.12	169		164, 178,	19.10	157
23–25	168, 169		179, 183,	20.30-33	76
23.9–24.11	168		184		

TARGUMIM

Targum Onqelos		49.10	122	*Numbers*	
Genesis				24.17	122
49.10	122	*Numbers*			
		24.17	122	Fragmentary Targum	
Numbers				*Genesis*	
24.17	122	Targum Neofiti		49.10	122
		Genesis			
Targum Pseudo-Jonathan		49.10	122	*Numbers*	
Genesis				24.17	122
45.15	133				

Targum Jonathan

1 Samuel

2	124, 129
2.1-10	124
2.2	124
2.3	124
2.4	124
2.5	124
2.6-10	124
2.10	124
2.17	107, 124, 125
2.29	107, 124, 125
2.32	124, 125
2.35	125

Psalms

20.6	66

Isaiah

5.1-7	125
5.2	125
5.5	125
5.7	125, 126
5.10	128
5.23	127
17.11	127
20.20-24	127
20.25	127
22–24	127
22.20	126
24.5	127
24.6	127
25.2	126
28.3	126
28.5-6	126
28.7-8	126
28.10-13	126
28.10	126
29.1	126
42.7	126
51.19	133
53.5	126

Jeremiah

6.13	127
7.9	127
8.10	127
14.18	127
23.11	127
23.33	127

Ezekiel

24.6	133

Habakkuk

2.17	105

Zechariah

6.13	125

RABBINIC LITERATURE

Mishnah

Baba Batra

10.6	45

Horayot

3.1	46
3.2	46

Keritot

1.7	128, 131

Menahot

6.3	46

Roš haš-Šanah

1.5	45

Šeqalim

1.4	128
4.3-4	128
4.4	130, 132

Sotah

9.9	121
9.12	121
9.13	121
9.15	121

Ta'anit

4.5	91

Yebamot

12.5	45

Babylonian Talmud

Baba Meṣi'a

88	128

Gittin

56	105, 106

Pesahim

57	107, 124, 129-31

Šabbat

104	141

Sanhedrin

106	91, 141

Sotah

11	91

Sukkah

27.2	36

Ta'anit

28–29	133
29	132

Yebamot

61	133

Yoma

18	133
39	105

Palestinian Talmud

Ma'aser Šeni

5 15	131

Pe'ah
1.6   128
2.16   131

Sotah
6.3   105

Tosefta
Me'ilah
1.16   126

Menahot
13.18-19   130
13.21   131, 137
13.22   132, 133

Sukkah
1.9   36
3.15   126

Yoma
1.5   130
1.6   129
1.7   132

1.8   132

Zebahim
11.16-17   130, 131

Midrashim
'Abot R. Nathan
A, 4   106, 132
B, 7   132

Mekilta Amalek
2 (Exod.
17.14-16)   128
2 (Exod.
17.14)   105

Mekilta R. Ishmael
Exod. 18.27 91
Exod. 18.27 91

Pesiqta Rabbati
47.4   129, 132,
                133

Sifre Numbers
78   91

Sifre Zutta Numbers
10.29   91

Sifre Deuteronomy
105
  (on 14.22)   128, 131
357
  (on 34.1)   128

Lamentations Rabbah
1.5 §31   105, 106

Leviticus Rabbah
19.6
  (on 15.25)   132
21.9
  (on 16.3)   129

PHILO

De Vita Contemplativa
73-74   89

Hypothetica
11   88

14   88

On The Special Laws
1.55   54

Quod Omnis Probus
76   89, 90

JOSEPHUS

Against Apion
1.37-39   40
2.8 §108   123

Antiquities of the Jews
2.15.4 §327   109
8.7.3 §185   149
8.7.3 §186   149
10.5.1 §79   121, 123
10.11.7 §276 121
10.35   40
13.14.2
 §379-83   99

14.10.6
 §202-203   130
14.15.10
 §450   145
14.15.11
 §455   139
15.3.1 §39-41
15.9.3
 §320-22   141
15.9.3 §320   131
15.10.5 §373   139
15.11.1
 §385-87   139

15.11.1 §396 139
15.11.6 §422 140
15.11.6 §423 140
15.11.7 §425 140
17.9.3 §219 147
17.9.3 §220 147
17.9.3 §223 147
17.9.3-11.4
 §219-320   147
17.9.4 §227 147
17.9.5 §237 147
17.9.5 §239 147
17.11.1 §300 147

17.11.1 §302	147	§282-85	139	6.4.2	
17.11.4 §320	147	1.17.1		§232-35	112
17.13.1 §339	148	§340-41	139	6.4.5	
18.1.4 §16	136	1.17.4		§250-53	112
18.2.1 §26	131	§331-32	139	6.4.5 §250	103
18.2.2 §34	131	1.17.4 §331	139	6.4.6–5.2	
18.5.2		1.17.8 §342–		§254-87	112
§116-19	144	1.18.3 §357	139	War 6.5.2	
18.5.4 §136	145	1.18.3 §354	140	§281-82	112
18.7.2		1.21.1		6.5.3	
§245-56	149	§401-402	140	§300-309	120
19.5.2		1.21.1 §401	137, 139	6.5.3 §301	104, 123
§118-19	144	1.21.2-10		6.5.3	
19.6.2 §297	131	§403-21	141	§302-304	104
19.6.4 §313	131	1.21.3		6.5.3 §306	104
19.8.2 §344	149	§429-30	139	6.5.3 §309	104
20.6.2 §131	131	1.21.6 §319	145	6.5.3. §301	120
20.7.6 §168	148	2.1.1 §01-2	149	6.5.4 §311	103, 122
20.8.8		2.2.1-6.3		6.5.4	
§179-81	131	§14-100	147	§312-13	122
20.8.8 §181	131, 133	2.8.2	88	6.7.2 §363	112
20.9.1		2.8.4	90	6.8.3	
§197-200	133	2.8.13	88	§389-91	102
20.9.1 §198	131	2.13.4 §259	148	6.8.5 §407	112
20.9.2		3.8.3		6.9.3 §420	96
§206-207	133	§351-52	103	63.5.3 §305	104
20.9.2 §207	131	3.8.9		7.1.1 § 1-4	93
20.9.3 §208	131	§400-402	102	7.1.3 §21	96
20.9.4 §213	133	3.8.9 §401	122	7.2.1 §24	96
20.9.7 §219	140	5.4.1 §137	139	7.5.5 §138	96
		5.5.6 §222	132	7.5.7	
The Jewish War		5.51 §185	139	§158-62	102
1.4.5 §93-95	99	6.2.1 §109	103, 121	7.5.7 §158	103
1.5.2 §123	137	6.2.1 §110	112		
1.7.6 §152	140	6.2.1 §93	112	*Life of Josephus*	
1.8.9 §181	137	6.2.9		38-39 §193-96	133
1.12.3 §241	139	§165-67	112		
1.14.4		6.4.1 §228	112		

OTHER ANCIENT REFERENCES

Contra Celsus		Epiphanius		*Hist. Eccl.*	
1.32.33	141	*Panarion*		3.5.3	114
		29.7.8	114, 115	3.7.3-6	114
Dio Cassius				4.6.3	114
Roman History		*Treatise on Weights*			
66.1	102	*and Measures*			
66.15	103	15	114		

Jerome
Adv. Iovinianum
2.14   89

Nicholas of Damascus
Historia Universalis
              141

Nilus of Ancyra
De Monastica
Exercitatione
vol. 79, ch. 3,
  col. 721-2   88

Pliny
Naturalis Historia
5.15/373   90

Pseudo-Clementine
Recognitions
1.37   114
1.39   114

Theophania
22 (on Mt.
  25.14-15)   147

Suetonius
Vespasian
4   122
5   102

Tacitus
Histories
1.10   102
2.10   102
2.89   149
5.13   122

INDEX OF AUTHORS

Abegg, M. 14
Allegro, J.L. 33
Allegro, J.M. 186
Allison, D.C. 154, 82
Anderson, H. 94, 142, 143
Angerstorfer, A. 63
Auffret, P. 64
Avigad, N. 20-26

Baillet, J.T. 68
Bauckham, R. 136
Baumgarten, J.M. 16, 18
Becker, J. 75
Beckwith, R.T. 165, 188, 189, 165
Ben Yehuda, V. 65
Ben-Hayyim, Z. 62, 66
Betz, O. 16, 137, 139, 143, 149, 180
Beyer, K. 21-27, 63
Black, M. 86, 87
Bockmuehl, M.N.A. 94, 105, 121, 123, 134, 136
Braude, W.G. 129
Braun, H. 93
Briggs, C.A. 65
Brin, G. 28, 33, 34, 36, 41, 46, 54, 55, 57, 58
Broshi, M. 21
Brown, F. 65
Bruce, F.F. 94, 146
Bultmann, R. 92, 110, 117, 142, 146
Burgmann, H. 165, 172

Chandler, R. 15
Charles, R.H. 39, 97, 134
Charlesworth, J.H. 15, 16, 18, 66, 68, 74, 80, 91, 151, 164, 166, 172
Chilton, B. 125-27

Collins, J.J. 98, 103
Colson, F.H. 54
Conzelmann, H. 142
Cothenet, E. 180
Cranfield, C.E.B. 94, 142
Creed, J.M. 115, 148
Cross, F.M. 18, 67, 68, 167

Dalman, G. 141
Danby, H. 130
Davies, P.R. 86, 87, 178-80
Davis, M.T. 18
Del Medico, H.E. 68, 69
Delcor, M. 83
Denis, A.-M. 75
Diez Macho, A. 62
Dillard, R.B. 164
Dimant, D. 67, 70-73, 84
Dodd, C.H. 110, 113
Donaldson, T.L. 165, 184, 186, 165
Driver, G.R. 177
Driver, S.R. 33, 65
Duhaime, J. 18
Dupont-Sommer, A. 13, 67, 70-73, 75, 78, 99, 100, 134, 138, 180

Eisenman, R.H. 151, 14
Evans, C.A. 134-36
Feldman, L.H. 133

Fitzmyer, J.A. 20-26, 62, 63, 108-10, 113, 116-19, 141, 143, 144, 148, 149
Flusser, D. 40
Forestell, J.T. 63
Freedman, H. 130, 131
Freyne, S. 128

Frick, F. 87
Funk, R.W. 147

Gagg, R.P. 143
Gaston, L. 94, 97, 100, 110
Geiger, A. 66
Gesenius, W. 65
Ginzberg, L. 109
Gnilka, J. 93, 142
Goguel, M. 93
Goldin, J. 106, 132
Goldman, A.I. 15
Greenfield, J.C. 20, 24, 141
Grimm, W. 143, 144
Guelich, R.A. 145
Guilbert, P. 67, 69-74, 84

Haenchen, E. 93, 142, 146
Hammer, R. 128
Hanson, J.S. 136
Hare, D.R.A. 101, 102
Harrington, D.J. 124, 125
Hartman, L. 93
Hayward, R. 63, 127
Heinemann, J. 40
Helfmeyer, 87
Hengel, M. 94
Hirsch, E. 142
Hoehner, H.W. 144, 145, 148, 149
Hölscher, G. 92
Hooker, M.D. 136
Horbury, W. 128
Horsley, R.A. 94, 120, 128, 136, 146
Howard, G. 162
Hurvitz, A. 51
Hurviz, A. 64

Isaac, E. 97

James, M.R. 91
Jeremias, J. 136, 141
Johnson, M.D. 124
Jongeling, B. 22-26, 66
Jung, L. 105

Kasher, M.M. 63
Kee, H.C. 96, 106
Klausner, J. 93

Klein, S. 87
Klijn, A.F.J. 123, 124
Klostermann, E. 93
Knibb, M.A. 67, 70-73, 79, 81, 84,
    183, 185, 186
Knights, C.H. 91
Koester, C. 114, 115
Kohler, K. 90, 91
Kruse, C.G. 164, 183, 184
Kümmel, W.G. 93, 144
Kutscher, E.Y. 23, 65

Labuschagne, C.J. 22-24
Lambrecht, J. 92, 93
Lampe, G.W.H. 94
Le Déaut, R. 62
Leaney, A.R.C. 67, 70-73, 75, 76, 182,
    189
Leivestad, R. 94
Levey, 126
Licht, J. 62, 70, 84
Lichtenberger, H. 13
Lohmeyer, E. 93, 142, 143
Lohse, E. 13, 16
Lüdemann, G. 114

Magne, J. 64
Maier, J. 75, 99, 100, 180
Mann, C.S. 94
Manson, W. 93
Marshall, I.H. 108, 110, 112, 113, 117,
    141, 142, 144
Martínez, F. García 62, 13, 14
Marxen, W. 92
McNamara, M.J. 63, 62
McNeil, B. 91
Meyer, B.F. 94
Milgrom, J. 18, 164-66, 168-73
Milik, J.T. 187, 23, 61, 62, 67, 68, 72,
    74, 80, 83
Moraldi, L. 13
Moule, C.F.D. 94
Muñoz Leon, D. 62
Murphy-O'Connor, J. 84, 67, 70, 72,
    75-83, 179, 180

Neusner, J. 105, 129-32
Newsom, C. 39, 43, 165, 188

O'Connor, M. 156, 158
Ofer, Y. 18
Osten-Sacken, P. von der 71, 82

Perrin, N. 93
Pesch, R. 92, 93, 142
Philonenko, M. 13
Pouilly, J. 77, 78, 80, 81, 83, 84
Priest, J. 134, 137
Puech, E. 22, 24, 62, 67, 77, 78, 80, 81, 83, 151

Qimron, E. 15, 18, 21, 25, 65, 166, 180

Rabin, C. 181
Reed, S.A. 151
Riemann, P.A. 87
Riesner, R. 16
Rietz, H.W.L. 18
Roberts, J.J.M. 18
Robinson, J.M. 151, 14
Rohrbaugh, R. 146, 147
Rowley, H.H. 145

Saldarini, A.J. 124, 125
Sanders, E.P. 94, 100, 119, 120, 135
Sanders, J.A. 16, 64-66, 118, 188
Schalit, A. 138, 141
Schiffman, L.H. 185, 18, 51, 62, 80
Schniewind, J. 93
Schoeps, H.-J. 89-91
Schubert, K. 94
Schürer, E. 63, 89
Schwartz, D.R. 16, 18
Schwartz, O. 180
Schweizer, E. 94, 149
Shanks, H. 16
Simon, M. 105
Slotki, J.J. 129
Sokoloff, 22
Stanton, G.N. 94, 142
Stegemann, 180

Strawn, B.A. 18
Strugnell, J. 28, 30, 32, 35, 37, 38, 48, 50, 53, 55, 56
Stuckenbruck, L.T. 18
Sukenik, E.L. 177
Sutcliffe, E.F. 75, 76, 89

Tal, A. 23, 24, 26
Taylor, V. 93, 142, 145, 146
Thackery, H. St. J. 103, 104
Thiering, B.E. 100, 164, 168, 187, 165
Tiede, D. 110
Torrey, C.C. 101, 120
Treves, M. 70
Tyson, J.B. 143

Ubigli, L. Rosso 14

Van Rooy, H.F. 64
VanderKam, J. 50
Vaux, R. de 68, 76
Vermes, G. 13, 62, 70, 71, 79, 80, 89, 105, 178, 183, 185
Voltz, P. 97

Wacholder, B.Z. 100, 141
Waltke, B.K. 158
Weinert, F.D. 109
Weis, R. 24
Wernberg-Møller, P. 70, 72, 182, 183
Wilford, J. Noble 15
Wilson, E. 15
Wise, M.O. 168, 169
Witherington, B. 94, 146
Wood, D.E. 15
Woude, A.S. van der 22-24

Yadin, Y. 20-26, 167-71, 175, 176, 178, 183

Zuckerman, B. 21

THE BIBLICAL SEMINAR

1   ANTHROPOLOGY AND THE OLD TESTAMENT
    J.W. Rogerson
2   THE ISRAELITE WOMAN:
    SOCIAL ROLE AND LITERARY TYPE IN BIBLICAL NARRATIVE
    A. Brenner
3   KINGSHIP AND THE PSALMS
    J.H. Eaton
4   COLOSSIANS AS PSUEDEPIGRAPHA
    M. Kiley
5   ANCIENT ISRAEL:
    A NEW HISTORY OF ISRAELITE SOCIETY
    N.P. Lemche
6   PROBLEMS AND PROSPECTS OF OLD TESTAMENT THEOLOGY
    J. Høgenharven
7   JUDAISM IN ANTIQUITY:
    POLITICAL DEVELOPMENT AND RELIGIOUS CURRENTS
    FROM ALEXAMDER TO HADRIAN
    B. Otzen
8   GOD IN STRENGTH:
    JESUS; ANNOUNCEMENT OF THE KINGDOM
    B.D. Chilton
9   ESSAYS ON OLD TESTAMENT HISTORY AND RELIGION
    A. Alt
10 RUTH:
    A NEW TRANSLATION WITH A PHILOLOGICAL COMMENTARY
    AND A FORMALIST-FOLKLORIST INTERPRETATION (SECOND EDITION)
    J.M. Sasson
11 TRADITION AND THEOLOGY IN THE OLD TESTAMENT
    D.A. Knight
12 NARRATIVE ART IN GENESIS
    J.P. Fokkelman
13 NARRATIVE SPACE AND MYTHIC MEANING IN MARK
    E.S. Malbon
14 THE PSALMS IN ISRAEL'S WORSHIP
    S. Mowinckel
16 THE ORPHAN GOSPEL
    D.W. Chapman
17 THE NEW TESTAMENT IN FICTION AND FILM:
    ON REVERSING THE HERMENEUTICAL FLOW
    L. Kreitzer
18 COPING WITH TRANSIENCE:
    ECCLESIATES ON BREVITY IN LIFE
    D.C. Fredericks

19   INVITATION TO THE NEW TESTAMENT
     W.D. Davies
20   THE MANTLE OF ELIJAH:
     THE REDATION CRITICISM OF THE PROPHETICAL BOOKS
     T. Collins
22   A TRANSLATOR'S FREEDOM:
     MODERN ENGLISH BIBLES AND THEIR LANGUAGE
     C.A. Hargreaves
23   FROM HER CRADLE TO HER GRAVE:
     THE ROLE OF RELIGION IN THE LIFE OF THE ISRAELITE AND THE
     BABYLONIAN WOMAN
     K. Van Der Toorn
24   THE OLD TESTAMENT IN FICTION AND FILM:
     ON REVERSING THE HERMENEUTICAL FLOW
     L.J. Kreitzer
25   THE GOSPEL AND THE LAND:
     EARLY CHRISTIANITY AND TERRITORIAL DOCTRINE
     W.D. Davies
26   JESUS THE LIBERATOR:
     NAZARETH LIBERATION THEOLOGY
     M. Prior
27   LIBERATING PAUL:
     THE JUSTICE OF GOD AND THE POLITICS ON THE APOSTLE
     N. Elliott
28   THE ILLEGITIMACY OF JESUS:
     A FEMINIST THEOLOGICAL INTERPRETATION OF THE INFANCY
     NARRATIVES
     Jane Schaberg
29   THE CITY IN ANCIENT ISRAEL
     Volkmar Fritz
30   THE ANCIENT LIBRARY OF QUMRAN (THIRD EDITION)
     F.M. Cross
31   THE SYNOPTIC GOSPELS:
     A SHEFFIELD READER
     Edited by Craig A. Evans and Stanley E. Porter
32   THE JOHANNINE WRITINGS:
     A SHEFFIELD READER
     Edited by Stanley E. Porter and Craig A. Evans
33   THE HISTORICAL JESUS:
     A SHEFFIELD READER
     Edited by Craig A. Evans and Stanley E. Porter
34   THE PAULINE WRITINGS:
     A SHEFFIELD READER
     Edited by Stanley E. Porter and Craig A. Evans

35   TEXT AND EXPERIENCE:
      TOWARD A CULTURAL EXEGESIS OF THE BIBLE
      D. Smith-Christopher
36   QUMRAN QUESTIONS
      Edited by J.H. Charlesworth

2006.01.27   33.95 (6.98)